W9-CRJ-076

The Maid Narratives

The Maid Narratives

BLACK DOMESTICS AND WHITE FAMILIES IN THE JIM CROW SOUTH

Katherine van Wormer, David W. Jackson III, and Charletta Sudduth

LOUISIANA STATE UNIVERSITY PRESS
BATON ROUGE

Published by Louisiana State University Press
Copyright © 2012 by Louisiana State University Press
All rights reserved
Manufactured in the United States of America
First printing

DESIGNER: Mandy McDonald Scallan
TYPEFACES: Whitman, MrsEaves, and Nutcracker
PRINTER AND BINDER: McNaughton & Gunn, Inc.

Library of Congress Cataloging-in-Publication Data
Van Wormer, Katherine, 1944–
The maid narratives : Black domestics and white families in the Jim Crow South / Katherine van Wormer, David W. Jackson III, Charletta Sudduth.
p. cm.
Includes bibliographical references and index.
ISBN 978-0-8071-4968-3 (cloth : alk. paper) — ISBN 978-0-8071-4969-0 (pdf) — ISBN 978-0-8071-4970-6 (epub) — ISBN 978-0-8071-4971-3 (mobi)
1. African American household employees—Southern States—History—20th century. 2. Women household employees—Southern States—History—20th century. 3. Southern States—Race relations—History—20th century. 4. Southern States—Social conditions—20th century. 5. Southern States—Social life and customs—20th century. I. Jackson, David W., 1972– II. Sudduth, Charletta, 1968– III. Title.
HD6072.2.U52S989 2012
331.4'8164089960730 75—dc23

2012010390

The paper in this book meets the guidelines for permanence and durability of the Committee on Production Guidelines for Book Longevity of the Council on Library Resources. ♾

To Teen (Celestine Holmes) and Elizabeth Griffin, who played such active roles in my early life—I dedicate this book to you in memory. I didn't thank you then, and now it's too late. But maybe for some readers of this book there is still time to get in touch with those people whose lives touched yours—whether it was as servant, teacher, or mentor.

—KATHERINE VAN WORMER

To my grandmother Beverly Jackson and my great-aunts, who worked as maids in Iowa; and to my ancestors, who lived in the South under many of the conditions described in this book.

—DAVID W. JACKSON III

To my great-grandmother Helen Sisk; my grandmother Annie Davis-Sisk; my great-aunt Pearline Sisk-Jones; and my mother, Annie Pearl Sisk-Stevenson. Through their tireless efforts as daughters, sisters, mothers, cooks, and maids, I have come to know all things are possible if you believe in God.

—CHARLETTA SUDDUTH

Contents

Part III. THE WHITE FAMILY NARRATIVES

Illustrations

Acknowledgments

We wish to thank Rand Dotson, senior acquisitions editor of LSU Press, who recognized the historic significance of these interviews from the start and who worked with us to broaden the scope of the book. We are also grateful to Susan Murray for her thoughtful and meticulous copyediting of the final manuscript. Acknowledgments additionally go to the social work graduate students Erica Wegner and Rachel Fleishman, who transcribed dozens of lengthy interviews. Finally, I wish to thank my husband, Robert van Wormer, for his help in transcribing interviews and with the photography.

—KvW

I am grateful to Katherine van Wormer and Charletta Sudduth for recognizing what we could accomplish by working together on this book. I also want to thank my family for believing in the project and sharing their stories with me. I gratefully acknowledge the encouragement of my colleagues Winston Grady-Willis and Jacqueline McLeod in the Department of African and African-American Studies at Metropolitan State College of Denver. I must give a very special thanks to my mentors Pita Agbese and Fredrick Woodard for sustaining me during my years as a graduate student and for continuing to offer their support during this project. Finally, I owe much gratitude to the students of the Des Moines Area Community College, who were tremendously helpful in identifying people in their families and the community who had stories that needed to be told.

—DJ

I would like to thank Katherine van Wormer for believing in me and asking me to be a part of this project. I am also grateful to have worked with David Jackson on this project as he is a remarkable historian.

—CS

Prologue: *Notes from the Authors*

KATHERINE VAN WORMER

I've written other books, but they were textbooks. This is the one I've been waiting to write; this is my dream book. As a white southerner who grew up cared for by some wonderful black women, I have a longing to tell their stories. The problem is, I don't know their stories, and these women are now dead and gone. But I have found those stories in another way, in the voices of other women who lived as they lived and worked as they worked and who shared part of their lives with white families. This is history now, and much of it is a collective history.

The story of segregation is my story, too, only viewed through a different lens. I rode in the front of the streetcar; they rode in the back. The memories are haunting; sometimes they come to me out of the blue and out of context. Here is my mother saying to me, a child of the 1950s, "Don't ever move up north. Those poor Yankee women have no help; they have to do all the housework themselves." Here is my grandfather in the early 1960s telling me, "Separate is equal. You should see the fine colored school that has been built." And then there was my father, almost ready to join the White Citizens' Council. And here is the turning point, in the form of a small paperback that my mother and I bought off the stand at the K&B drugstore. This was *Black Like Me*, by John Howard Griffin (1960). Soon my mother was on talk radio telling listeners about this white reporter who darkened his skin with the aid of medication and dye so as to appear to be a black man. My mother told of the treatment he faced in New Orleans, shining shoes, and of his much worse experiences traveling through rural Mississippi. "Read this book," she told the listeners, "*Black Like Me*." Our lives were not the same from then on because our viewpoints about our way of life had changed.

We did not, however, talk to the women who had worked for us about the racism they endured or about their personal lives. We moved away from the area, and the past was past. So here I am, decades later, poring over the old scrapbooks and writing to my cousins for copies of their photographs of Teen (Celestine) and Elizabeth. I want to embark on a journey back in time, and I want to go with native guides who know the way. This has been my plan since the 1990s, when my research on oppression and resilience turned my thoughts to the community of African American women who live in the town next door. These are women of the Great Migration; they had settled in Waterloo, Iowa, years before. And their roots are in the cotton fields of rural Mississippi. Many among them would have worked as cooks, maids, and nannies to the white landowners. One day, I thought, I will get, must get, their stories. My library is full of the slave narratives, but where are the maid narratives? Don't these women of a later generation, these descendants of slaves who lived under a later version of white supremacy, have stories and recollections of value as well? And as the obituary columns in Iowa and elsewhere remind us, this whole generation of migrants from the South is dying off.

And now we come to the present. In the end, it was to take almost a decade before my dream was reified. That was when I had the opportunity to collaborate with two African American scholars who lived in the local area and knew the history of the Great Migration from their own family backgrounds. Together we conceived of this project. The starting point was locating and interviewing storytellers from the local community who had engaged in domestic service in Mississippi and recording the narratives. Much later, someone who heard about our project suggested we interview white southern women who once employed African American maids or who had grown up with maids in their homes to hear their perspectives. I took up this task and began to ask questions of people I had never dared to ask before. And I got some remarkable answers.

DAVID W. JACKSON III

I was born in Des Moines, Iowa, and raised in Cedar Rapids. My major areas of interest, personally and professionally, are African and African American studies. For my Ph.D. dissertation from the University of Iowa I chose to study yard art collections among African Americans living in Iowa. The dissertation was titled "The Walking Nkisis: African-American Material Culture in Iowa: A Case Study of Yard Art in Waterloo, Iowa."

Recently, I produced an oral video history project, *African-American Voices of the Cedar Valley.* The twenty DVDs that comprise this series contain interviews with notable African Americans in the Waterloo–Cedar Falls area. The interviews were broadcast on several television stations in Iowa during Black

Beverly Jackson, 1978
From the family collection of David Jackson.

Norma Jean Knox, David Jackson's great-aunt, with her husband, Walter Knox, Des Moines, Iowa, 1949.
From the family collection of David Jackson.

History Month of 2006, 2007, and 2008. The second phase of the project involves the development of a culture-specific curriculum for grades nine through twelve.

Building upon my previous work, I joined colleagues to conduct research on resiliency and optimism from an African American senior citizens' perspective. These surveys provided data to indicate that African Americans residing in the northern states reported significantly less stress than those who lived in the South. Our findings identify resiliency and optimism as stress buffers for older African Americans.

I come to the writing of this book with a keen personal interest that stems from the stories I heard as a child from my grandmother and great-aunts about the times they spent employed as day workers. Generations of women in my family worked as domestics in the South and in Des Moines and the surrounding area. My grandmother Beverly Ann Jackson, who called herself a day worker, worked for three white families in West Des Moines. She recalls riding the bus to the suburbs there, "where the rich white folks" lived. She discussed how she vacuumed, dusted, and swept floors. She did not like cleaning other people's homes because she feared that she would accidentally break something and find herself working for free to pay for that object. My great-grandmother and several of my great-aunts also worked as day workers and maids. So this is my legacy. The narratives in this book provide insight into the lives of African American women who worked for white families, narratives that are now a part of the history of African American experience.

CHARLETTA SUDDUTH

Hope is a dream as the soul awakes. It was not in a classroom but in a church basement that I was taught about the struggles of my people as they marched, sat-in, sang, and demanded equality in all segments of American society. I remember sobbing quietly, listening to the older church members applauding, cheering, and crying. I left that basement changed. Lesson learned: It is up to communities to teach their own, or better yet, each one should teach one. Parents should never forget that they are their child's first teachers.

I believe my soul was ready to receive the message on that afternoon due to the foundation my mother had established through the numerous stories she had shared with me about growing up in Mississippi as a black girl, a domestic, a cotton picker, and a backseat bus rider. I remember watching, at Mama's request, the television series *The Autobiography of Ms. Jane Pittman,* the fictional account of a 110-year-old black woman's memories of slavery, civil rights, and the quest for equality. Pittman's story concludes with the depiction of the day she drank from a water fountain marked "whites only" outside the county courthouse in the town square surrounded by law enforcement and other townspeople, both white and black. Usually after each night of this series and for some days later, Mama would take many trips down memory lane, sometimes with me figuratively kicking and screaming, as she recounted what life had been like for her in the South. I am glad she did, as I now believe it is up to my generation to pass on our ancestral stories, just like my mama did, to make sure our children know where we have come from so they can appreciate where we are now and where we need to go.

I was born in 1968 to a middle-class African American couple. Before I entered kindergarten in 1973, I attended Parker Academy, a preschool run by Dr. Henry Parker, a black professor at the local university. My mom said that Dr. Parker's focus for the school was to prove that black children could learn and achieve if given experiences that were the same as or better than white children's. I faintly remember his strict code of discipline, his high expectations, and social studies and Spanish being part of the curriculum.

I attended kindergarten at a predominantly African American neighborhood school. Our house was three blocks from school. I remember the short walks to school and attending school with students who looked like me.

As a fourth-grader in 1976, when busing was introduced in Waterloo as a way of integrating the schools, I began riding the bus from my home in the ghetto to Orange Elementary, a forty-five-minute, one-way bus ride. There I encountered Ms. Hamm, a teacher of Filipino descent, my first brown-skinned teacher. She was different and proud to be different: she wore high-heeled shoes; wore her hair in a frazzled bun; and ate mold off rotten oranges for its antibiotic properties. More astonishing than that, she picked me, one of only several black students in the building, to play the lead role in the school play.

Three years later, our pastor invited everyone who could, especially the youth, to meet him down at the church to watch a documentary on the civil rights movement. This was the meeting, mentioned above, that changed my life. I remember being in the basement, the fresh smell of popcorn, and the large reels of film. There I learned of the story of Emmett Till; the fight to desegregate schools following the landmark Supreme Court decision *Brown v. Board of Education;* and the Jim Crow laws of the South. And it was there that I heard Martin Luther King Jr.'s "Letter from a Birmingham Jail," and watched fire hoses being turned on my people as they were beaten down and treated like dogs in their fight for equality.

My mother's stories, as I said, had prepared the ground for my response to this meeting. I had listened to her tell of trying to purchase a bus ticket to leave town and go home. She would arrive at the bus station early so as to avoid any problems. As she approached the ticket counter, a white ticket agent would say, "Nigger Gal, you have to wait." Although no one else was in line, my mother would step back, wait for a while, and again approach the ticket counter, only to be told, "Nigger, didn't I say wait?" This would go on until the bus arrived at the station, filled with all the white passengers, and began to depart. Then the ticket agent would yell to my mother, "What you waiting for? Do you want a ticket, Gal? You better get up here." My mom would frantically purchase the ticket as she heard the bus door slamming and the bus pulling off. She would have to run a little ways before the bus driver would stop the bus and say, "Gal, you got a ticket?" She would say, "Yes, sir," and get on, hand him her ticket, and head to the back, exhausted. This is one of many stories my mama told me about life in those times.

My mother was adamant that I get my schooling. She always had more than one job, so I wanted to help with the housework. But she did not want me to clean at the expense of my schoolwork and would often say, "Get your schoolwork out." In 2011, I received my doctoral degree, and my mother was there to see the hooding ceremony. The degree was as much for her as it was for me: her labor had not been in vain. From descendants of slaves, my grandfather was a sharecropper, my mother a maid, and now here I am—an educated black woman. Mama, your stories worked: they freed me and made me strong.

This project—recording the stories of older women from the Great Migration—is meaningful to me because it allows me to capture stories of African American women who have endured trials, suffering, joys, and triumphs to further advance themselves, their children, and their families. Although these are the stories of African American women, I believe that the shared bond in the plight of oppression speaks to all women. The narratives of these admirable women have been a great source of strength and encouragement to me.

Part 1

The Background

(1)

Introduction

The past is a foreign country, they do things differently there.

—LESLIE HARTLEY, *The Go-Between*

THIS BOOK IS INTENDED to take its readers on a journey back in time to a place that, to many, will be a foreign country. We will travel there with the help of our storytellers—African American migrant women and southern whites—who have been there and who have been generous enough to share their experiences. The destination is not the Old South—a term that refers to the slave South—but the South in the era of segregation, a period roughly from the 1920s through the mid-1960s, in which sharecropping and a kind of quasi-feudalism replaced a social system based on slavery and slave labor.

Our first guides on this voyage to the past will be the African American women whose lives there revolved around domestic service, women who worked as maids, cooks, and "nurses" for white families. To what extent these guides look back in anger or with a sense of nostalgia will be explored as we go on. Their stories will also raise the question of whether the narrators are heroes who prevailed over hardship or victims of their time and circumstances. Juxtaposed with their narration is testimony from our second group of guides, women and one man who also grew up in a culture that is no more, persons who had the privilege of race and class, a privilege they must now go to great lengths to explain, or to explain away. Norms that were taken for granted at the time and institutionalized into law are hard to fathom in the light of the present day. As one white narrator said, "That's just the way things were done; we didn't really stop to think about it."

In the accounts of the black women who worked in the white households, whose personal stories are largely absent from the historical literature, as well as in the narratives of their white employers, we hope to capture the essence of a period. Although hundreds of books have dealt with the living conditions and work during this period, what is missing from the archives, as the social historian Lisa Krissoff Boehm (2009) suggests, is documentation regarding the women of the Second Great Migration. "Domestic work," she writes, "sits outside of the purview of American historical collections because it has never been championed as an important aspect of American labor" (21).

Today, the reality of the times is preserved in old photographs, in accounts by anthropologists from northern universities and southern historians, in southern literature, and in the living memories of those who experienced it. In these interviews, we hope to get at the truth—or truths—as only the personal story can. As we hear from the character Minnie in Kathryn Stockett's 2009 novel *The Help:* "It's something about that word *truth.* It feels cool, like water washing over my sticky-hot body. Cooling a heat that's been burning me up all my life. . . . I've been trying to tell white women the truth about working for them since I was fourteen years old" (129).

Unlike Minnie, who decides to risk her job to tell her story, our narrators are older and retired; they have nothing to lose. They are women of the Great Migration, who left Mississippi, most often with their menfolk, who had been recruited for work opportunities in the North, in this case, Iowa. Not all came with their menfolk: some came by themselves at the encouragement of sisters and cousins. Some came for a short visit to a relative, liked what they saw (despite the weather), and stayed on. But they did not forget the families, the communities, and the life they left behind. Like Minnie, they want to tell their stories and preserve their memories for posterity.

In recording these memories, we hope to aid in the transmission of this knowledge, first about the daily reality of working in the kitchens of southern white folks, and, second, through gathering facts about survival under the restraints of what John Dollard (1937) famously termed a caste system. These narratives detail life in the segregated South, often called the "Solid South" for its one-party politics dominated by white males. They describe a time when people of color had no rights, when black girls were virtually born into domestic servitude, and when the descendants of slaves were literally at the mercy of white people, who controlled the power structure. We want to show how these women who worked in white homes survived and overcame, and how they finally reached the decision to leave and to build new lives in a place far from their homes of origin. Only in getting these personal recollections down on paper can we hope to bring this history alive for later generations. We present these narratives with a sense of urgency that corresponds to our awareness of the advanced age of many of the storytellers.

We wondered if the white women, too, had stories to share about the black women their families employed. Although we made many requests for interviews with southern whites who lived in families that employed black maids, only a handful agreed to venture to a place referred to by one interviewee as "the dark past." "It is time to move forward," several individuals said, implying that it is better not to dig up the relics of the past. More often than not, individuals whom Katherine van Wormer knew well from childhood failed to acknowledge her request for an interview. Some old friends said they would think about it and were not heard from again. Others, though, did agree to accompany us to this place in the past that is now almost as foreign to them as to the black women who moved away. These respondents expressed a keen interest in the project; they, too, have truths they want to share—truths about conditions beyond their control, about their sheltered and privileged upbringing, and about their joys and regrets. Their contributions inform both in what they say and in what they do not.

The project took on a new life with the release of the film version of the best-selling novel *The Help*. White women who discovered in a LISTSERV announcement that we were collecting narratives and conducting interviews rushed forward to get their stories told. The response was especially strong from women who were born in the 1950s and who grew up during the civil rights era, when segregation was coming to an end, the time period of the film. The movie, filmed in Greenwood, Mississippi, probably brought to the surface long-forgotten memories, encouraging reflection on aspects of the past that strongly contrast with the reality of the present. In response to the recent willingness of white women to get involved in the project, we were able to add to part III more narratives by white women who grew up with a maid in the home and more from a younger generation of respondents.

PRESERVING STORIES FROM THE PAST

On receiving her honorary doctorate from Howard University, Oprah Winfrey (2007) spoke of opportunities for today's students and of the dreams of her grandmother in 1950s Mississippi: "My grandmother was a maid, and she worked for white folks her whole life, and her idea of having a big dream was to have white folks that at least were kind to her and treated her with dignity and a little respect. She used to say, 'I want you to grow up and get yourself some good white folks.' And I regret that she didn't live past 1963 to see that I did grow up and get some really good white folks working for me."

The world that Oprah Winfrey's grandmother inhabited in segregated Mississippi was a different world from the one her granddaughter enjoys today. We know about Oprah's world and how one talented woman achieved her potential. It is her grandmother's world, however, that is the subject of this book. The history of this period is almost as fascinating as the individual accounts themselves. Chapter 2 presents the social historical context for our stories, delineating the extent of the challenges our storytellers faced. Slavery may have been a "peculiar institution," but the institution that followed, in many ways, was more peculiar still. The economic structure built on sharecropping was accompanied by an ethos known as paternalism, in which the white landowners were to take care of their black workers as long as they "knew their place"; physical intimacy between black and white women in the household was not matched by social intimacy. To present the historical context and the paradox of paternalism, we draw on three classic works from the period—John Dollard's classic *Caste and Class in a Southern Town* (1937), Hortense Powdermaker's *After Freedom: A Cultural Study of the Deep South* (1939), and Kim L. Rogers's *Life and Death in the Delta: African American Narratives of Violence, Resilience, and Social Change* (2006).

Because some of the most powerful character portraits of household servants are found in semi-autobiographical fiction (for example, the character of Calpurnia in Harper Lee's *To Kill a Mockingbird*) and in biographies and autobiographies (for example, Judith Sensibar, *Faulkner and Love: The Women Who Shaped His Art*; Lillian Smith, *Killers of the Dream;* and Sallie Bingham, *Passion and Prejudice: A Family Memoir*), we draw on this literature throughout the text. To capture truths found in fictional accounts, we go to the novels of African American writers such as Ann Petry, Kristin Hunter, and Toni Morrison, all of whom deal with domestic workers who have migrated from the South. Additionally, quotes from the writings of Langston Hughes, bell hooks, and Maya Angelou highlight the discussion.

Chapter 3 describes the history of the migration from the Deep South to the Midwest and can be considered as a prologue to the transcriptions that follow. The interviews of part II constitute the heart of this book, in which we hear from the women of the Great Migration in their own words. Their stories contrast sharply with those of the whites interviewed, even though their lives were intertwined in so many ways. Themes from the interviews—education, the personal impact of key historical events, the norms of racial etiquette, resilience in the face of oppression, and the role of the black church in community life—are discussed in chapter 5. Not surprisingly, there is also much common ground in the reminiscences of blacks and whites. All participants in the study agreed that black people—who were then referred to politely as "colored" people—were ruthlessly held back from education and economic opportunity. In rural Mississippi, the home of the majority of our interviewees, the harsh segregation laws and racial mores unique to the South lingered long after segregation was dead elsewhere.

Chapters 6 and 7 present the voices of white women who grew up in Louisiana, Mississippi, and other southern states. A theme of cognitive dissonance emerges as the women seek to reconcile their earlier compliance with laws and norms with the modern-day perspective of this social system as downright evil.

The seventeen interviews with African American women that appear in part II (thirteen given in depth in chapter 4, and four shorter interviews in chapter 5) were selected from a total of twenty-three transcripts as the most outstanding, emotionally moving, and informative. Eleven of the women whose stories are presented here were interviewed by David W. Jackson III; Charletta Sudduth interviewed five; and one respondent chose to submit her narrative in writing. We are grateful to these women who gladly came forward to share a part of their lives and who asked of us only that we listen, not only to their recollections of the big historic events of the time, but also to their descriptions of the everyday details of how they lived, what they ate, what they wore, and how hard they had to work. They came forth, as several stated, in the hope of recording their stories for posterity.

BACKGROUND AND METHODOLOGY

What is it like for the oldest generation of African American women to harbor memories of a society built on social customs so strange they can scarcely be imagined today? How do children raised with little education become competent adults? How is it possible to remember a past of constant personal oppression and deprivation and not be consumed with rage and bitterness?

We three authors of this book have our own personal reasons for wishing to find answers to these questions. Katherine van Wormer grew up in uptown New Orleans in the 1950s as a privileged white person in a neighborhood in which virtually every family had a black maid. David W. Jackson III, a scholar of African American studies and oral histories, grew up in Des Moines, Iowa, and has a historian's interest in preserving the oral histories of older African Americans who migrated from the South. Charletta Sudduth grew up in Waterloo, Iowa, in an African American community, raised by a mother who had previously worked in domestic service in rural Mississippi. Her research area is early childhood education.

Drawing on Oral History

Oral history, through gathering the recollections of ordinary people who often lived through extraordinary circumstances, provides a unique reservoir of knowledge about everyday life in the past. Not just the facts contained in the stories but also the feelings that emerge in the telling reveal a lot about the deep emotions attached to race relations today, especially concerning the South. Information obtained from oral histories can help identify a collective understanding of race relations in both the past and the present (Bindas 2010). This last point holds a special significance for the present effort. Our book covers two time periods in the migrant women's lives—the period that is frozen in the memory of childhood, and the more recent time frame, including where the storytellers are today. Isabel Wilkerson, in her recent book on people of the Great Migration to Chicago, writes of how the past is preserved in one's mind: "They had gone off to a new world but were still tied to the other. Over time, the language of the geographic origin began to change; the ancestral home no longer the distant Africa of unknown forebears but the immediate South of uncles and grandparents, where the culture they carried inside them was pure and familiar" (366). Like Wilkerson, we make use of two reference points—the Jim Crow South of the 1930s to 1960s and the modern-day Midwest. In the taped interviews of the African Americans, we observed what seemed to be different emotions in play depending on the time period described: the storytellers' voices changed in pitch when they recounted the memories of childhood—memories that resonate in their lives, as in all our lives—and assumed a more matter-of-fact tone when describing their adult accomplishments and lives.

The richness of expression contained in the oral memoirs can aid readers to better understand why people acted as they did or why they often seemed to fail to confront or resist the daily cruelties of the era. Specific episodes described—for example, taking humiliating orders from white employers to scrub the floor on hand and knees or to address a white teenager as "Miss" or "Mister"—convey the personal, feeling dimension of racism. At the same time, description of instances in which the domestic servant took on great responsibility in the white household—helping to raise children, providing lavish meals, offering sage advice to family members—tells us much about the resourcefulness of the storytellers and of the pride they took in their work. The wealth of such detailed historical information and the richness of self-expression enable the interviewer (and the reader of the transcripts) to appreciate the high level of competence of the individual storyteller while seeing beyond the original story to a larger collective piece about injustice and oppression and hope for a brighter future.

Oral history, as Bindas (2010) indicates, is especially relevant to African American history. Besides allowing for a more nuanced collective memory than do facts obtained by more conventional methods, it is also, as the social historian Lisa Krissoff Boehm (2009) suggests, "the methodology of choice for capturing pieces of the American past that have not been adequately preserved in the traditional archive sources" (21).

For our research on older African American and white women, we chose to use a narrative gerontological approach to oral history. This format evolved during the twentieth century as a scientific means to explore the lives of older adults, and to learn how they overcame life challenges (Greene et al. 2009). As the storytellers reminisce about the realities of their day, they provide knowledge that is both personal and political. The narrative interview technique allows researchers to capture the multifaceted dimensions of life during critical moments across the person's life span and to discover, with the storyteller, themes of self-reliance as well as emotional responses, such as despair and joy. In recording stories of oppression, the researcher can take note of shifts in voice tone, outbursts of laughter, expressions of grief and sorrow, silences, and can analyze the choice of words used and the meaning behind the words. Narrative gerontology combined with resilience theory helps us understand how the storytellers "muddled through" and found meaning in their experiences of pain and suffering.

Through the narrative interview technique, both the interviewer and the interviewee can simultaneously see the personal in the political and the political in the personal. The recollection of political and social events of long ago can be considered a community narrative, one that links us to collective historical events (Greene et al. 2009).

Learning from the Personal Narrative

In his introduction to the archive collection of slave narratives gathered in the 1930s by the New Deal's Federal Writers' Project, Norman Yetman quotes John Little, a former slave, on attempts to convey the reality of slavery: "'T'isn't he who has stood and looked on, that can tell you what slavery is—'tis he who has endured" (1). The view that slavery can best be described by those who endured it is the view that has guided our gathering of these narratives.

The Library of Congress, in whose archives the slave narratives are held, is now gathering war memories as part of the Veterans History Project. Several universities are gathering the oral histories related to Hurricane Katrina; others are documenting the histories of Holocaust survivors. Oral history, or verbatim testimony about one's experiences, has increasingly come into its own as a way to chronicle the past (Kingsbury 2007).

Unlike the narrative told by a young person, the life story told by a person toward the end of life is based on a much greater range of experience; events that might have been emphasized closer to the time of their occurrence are often relegated to a lesser role when viewed later, in the context of a long life. Or conversely, events that might have been glossed over at the time or taken for granted, such as participating in the civil rights movement, might later be recognized as pivotal historically and also for the individual personally.

Narrative texts, as the gerontologists Randall and Kenyon (2004) suggest, embrace beginnings, middles, and ends; how we interpret the past depends in large part on our sense of the present. Thus if life has turned out to be fulfilling, aspects of the past might take on a special meaning in terms of helping one to achieve one's goals. As storytellers review their lives in old age, new awarenesses emerge concerning, for example, one's identity as a person and as a member of a social or ethnic group, a grasping of the spiritual dimension of life, and one's contributions to the next and future generations. Randall and Kenyon term these insights the wisdom in narrative gerontology.

In his introduction to the WPA slave narratives, Yetman (2001) lists several widely cited limitations in the use of these personal accounts for historical research. Most of Yetman's objections concern the lack of interviewer skill and training and interviewer bias toward extracting positive descriptions of life under slavery. Desperate to receive government help in a time of abject poverty, the former slaves might have censored their responses in the hope of pleasing the government representative. Yetman points to a second influence of the near famine conditions experienced by southern blacks during the Depression years; their state of neglect in the midst of dire poverty might have encouraged a view of past events and living standards as better than they actually were. But the major question concerning the accuracy and reliability of the narratives concerns the fact that the interviewees were not only old but sharing memories that went back sixty or seventy years. Who knows how people's minds might have distorted events and impressions after such a long time?

"Revision occurs," notes Tucker (1988), "because the past that really was and the past that is remembered are always separate" (4). This tendency Tucker found to be especially pronounced among the whites she interviewed. These whites had grown up under the laws and customs of segregation, probably accepted them, but then were looking back from the present with a sense of defensiveness. While protesting that the whites did a lot for black women, they simultaneously voiced feelings of guilt and sorrow. "These white women," Tucker writes, "had reinterpreted their memories in light of an awareness of social and political change that had sometimes been accompanied by education and self-analysis" (4). We can take this tendency into account as we interpret the results of our interviews with women who grew up with maids in their families and/or who employed them later. Another issue is that presumably women who were not good to their servants could be expected to shy away from consenting to an interview about times they would just as soon forget. On the other hand, white women who feel good about their treatment of their servants would more readily volunteer to share their memories.

Regarding shared memories, we can turn to psychological studies on memory reliability. The psychologists Carol Tavris and Elliot Aronson (2007) assert that over time we tend to shape memories consistent with our self-image. We might remember, for example, that we got better grades in school than we actually did, or that we made certain decisions for reasons that are contradicted in preserved records from the period. When it comes to traumatic memories about brutal treatment, however, the recollections tend to stay intact. Citing Holocaust research, Tavris and Aronson state that survivors have been shown to recall details with almost perfect accuracy. This fact was revealed when documents from forty years before were compared with survivors' current recollections. Repression of such events, according to these researchers, is exceedingly rare.

Indeed, there are certain advantages to interviewing older adults about events that took place in their youth. When he collected World War II narratives from combat war veterans for his documentary *The War*, for example, Ken Burns concluded that he had gotten to the informants at the perfect time in their lives to record their highly disturbing memories. In their mid- to late eighties, the survivors were eager to at last reveal the truth about events they had long covered up. Had Burns waited any longer, these former soldiers would have been dead. When asked by a reporter, "What does the film say about memory?" Burns (2007) replied: "War is the great lie of civilization: it is a collective forgetting. When people bear witness to it, they help resurrect it. Memory becomes the agent of our transformation, and we have an obligation to it. Like the still photograph, for me, remains the primary building block of visual communication, individual memory becomes the building block of our collective consciousness" (51).

In our collection of interviews with whites and blacks who were at the same place in history but on opposite sides of the story, we anticipated that older women would be much more willing to share of memories of oppression. This assumption is consistent with research from gerontology on the readiness of people late in life to share personal details from the past, many of which they may never have revealed before. Another advantage to interviewing older people is that they have a greater expanse of history from which to draw. And there is something else as well. These African American women had been removed from their southern origins, except for occasional trips down South, for decades. We have never seen this mentioned in the social science literature, but we believe that, when individuals have moved away from the land and culture of their origin, their images and memories of the past may be, to some extent, frozen in time. We say "to some extent" in recognition of the fact that memory is selective and modified through repetition. But it is our supposition that migrants' memories of the social customs and landscapes of their original homes are not modified as much as they would have been if they had experienced the alterations in social customs and development of landscapes there over the years. The Mississippi of the 1930s, 1940s, and 1950s, after all, is not the Mississippi of today. We think we have an advantage, therefore, in our choice of interview subjects: those who took part in the Great Migration from the South to the North describe a life and livelihood that are still real to them, relatively uncontaminated by the forces of time.

This sentiment is best expressed by bell hooks (2009), who has recently returned to her roots in Kentucky after living most of her adult life in New York: "Memories offer us a world where there is no death, where we are sustained by rituals of regard and recollection" (5). For hooks, "the differences that geographical location imprinted on my psyche and habits of being became more evident away from home" (13).

Obtaining the Stories

In the belief that interviewers from the same racial/ethnic background as the informants have the best chance to establish rapport with them and to obtain a narrative that is uninhibited and rich in detail, we chose to have the African American researchers initiate contact and conduct the interviews. After gaining approval to conduct the research from the University of Northern Iowa Institutional Review Board (IRB), we contacted older African American women from the community who were known to the research team to have engaged in domestic service work in the Deep South. Because we live near a meatpacking area in Iowa to which thousands of African Americans migrated in the 1930s through the 1960s from rural Mississippi, a sample of appropriate respondents was easy to obtain. The study was guided by a series of open-ended questions concerning experiences growing up during a certain time and place, standards of living, early education, descriptions of the households in which they worked, initiation into domestic service, the rules that applied to them as servants and as black persons, working conditions, and relationships with the woman of the house and with other members of the family.

The project got off to a rapid start when six older African Americans from Waterloo, Iowa, agreed to be interviewed—five women who had worked as maids in the South and one man whose mother had once worked as a maid in Mississippi and had lived to be more than one hundred years old. Interviews were conducted at an ethnic senior center and at the individuals' homes. The interviews, which were audiotaped, ranged from forty to ninety minutes. The purpose of the interviews—to gather oral histories about life and work conditions for women in the South during the days of segregation—was explained at the start of the interviews. There were no specific questions on resilience, nor were the informants asked specifically how they coped or survived. This approach is consistent with research that shows that information that is volunteered is believed to be more objective than information and insights that are actively solicited (DeMichele 2009). Accordingly, so as not to slant the results in a certain direction, we asked most of our questions in response to details provided in the narrative and to clarify facts that emerged in the story. The audiotaped narratives were then transcribed for analysis.

Data analysis of the interviews of the African Americans involved gauging the magnitude of mistreatment and discrimination experienced and categorizing the coping mechanisms and expressions of fear and bitterness, the evidence of resilience in the face of deprivation, and the expressed attitudes toward whites. Content analysis of the transcripts was conducted to explore not only the influence of early childhood and work experience but also the interviewees' perceptions of the same. The same mode of critical analysis was applied to the interviews and written material of the white respondents, but the focus there was on the level of discomfort shown, if any, in the recollections and on the selectivity of the shared memories.

A Word on Terminology

In the 1950s and earlier, domestic workers were called "the help," maids, and cooks (in New Orleans, where cooking was an art form, some of the servants called themselves "Creole cooks"). In those days, the women themselves often simply said, "I work for Mrs. Jones," or "I used to work for Mrs. Johnson" as the type of work they did was obvious. For the title of the book, we chose to use the contemporary term that best conveys the present-day meaning. "Maid narratives" also nicely parallels the term "slave narratives" of the century before.

We do not refer collectively to the white contributors to this project as women because two of them are men. Hence the title of part III is simply "The White Family Narratives." The use of the term "family" is not intended to imply that the servants were members of the white families but rather that the speakers and writers in this section grew up with maids who worked for their families.

THE PARADOXES OF PATERNALISM

The story of black and white race relations in the early- to mid-twentieth-century South is of course two stories, one told by members of the ruling classes and one told by their servants. Viewed from another angle, it is the same story perceived differently, depending on the perspective of the narrator. In novels such as William Faulkner's *The Sound and the Fury* (1929), in which the tale of a decadent white southern family is told by several family members and an omniscient observer, and Kathryn Stockett's *The Help* (2009), the same situation conjures up very different reactions on different sides of the fence.

Among the older African American women recounting their experiences of servitude in the premodern South and the older white southern women who were willing to share their memories, race was not a comfortable issue. And it remains an uncomfortable issue as we reflect on it today. The culture of the premodern South was characterized by paradox. Among the paradoxes that emerged as salient in our interviews:

~ Separate but equal was not separate and certainly was not equal.

~ The maid who invariably was seen by whites as part of the white family was in no sense truly a member of their family.

~ While the South insisted on rigid separation of the races, black domestic workers were on intimate terms with whites by the very nature of their work.

~ Small white children sometimes felt closer to their black caretakers than they did to their mother, a love that often was not acknowledged by others.

~ While the domestic servants gave such dutiful care to the white children in the family, their own children were often necessarily neglected.

~ White segregationists who opposed racial equality were often extremely fond of their black help and good to them on the personal level.

~ Black women servants were sometimes treated like children by the "lady of the house," but during tough times the white women looked to them for strength and comfort.

~ White women and black women were both politically and economically powerless within the patriarchal system that was ruled by white men of a certain class.

~ Both blacks and whites suffered under the cruelties of segregation, although in different ways.

As we go forward, our hope is to enrich the history of the time of sharecropping and segregation by recording stories of survival and resilience and endurance that can be an inspiration for future generations.

(2)
History and Context

The past is never dead. It's not even past.
—WILLIAM FAULKNER, *Requiem for a Nun*

IN THE 1930S, as part of Roosevelt's New Deal, the Works Progress Administration (WPA) hired writers under the auspices of the Federal Writers' Project to collect slave narratives as a way of preserving important historical testimony for posterity. This major undertaking culminated in the gathering of 2,500 interviews of former slaves. It was urgent work, as the generation of people who had survived slavery was then dying off.

Today, historians and others often focus on slavery and its legacy while overlooking another generation of oppressed but resilient people who endured a social system that has now passed. The stories of these people have been suppressed for some time, perhaps because of a lack of interest on the part of the next generation, perhaps out of a desire to bury embarrassing facts about the past by the class of whites who grew up with servants in their household.

In this chapter, we explore the social life and the ethos of the period from the 1920s through the early 1960s that is variously termed the "age of cotton," the "days of segregation," "once upon a time when we were colored" (Taulbert 1995), and "the Jim Crow South." In the tradition of the historian Howard Zinn, who argues that the best way to learn about the history of a time is to go to the people (Zinn 2002; Zinn and Arnove 2009), we provide the historical context for the stories of individuals who occupied the bottom rungs of society, with a focus on the facts from history that resonated with them and might have been of little note for their employers. Their personal stories will bring to life the daily struggles and living conditions of this period in ways that traditional historical records alone cannot.

In this chapter, we draw on more conventional sources, including the work of historians, psychologists, novelists, and other commentators, in order to provide a context for these women's voices. The table below presents many of the key events referred to in the narratives of the women who form the subject of this book.

Key Historical Events

1861–1865 U.S. Civil War fought, initially with the goal of saving the Union, but later under the banner of emancipation.

1865 Thirteenth Amendment to the Constitution abolishes slavery in every U.S. state.

1865 Many former slaves stay on the land and work as sharecroppers; the sharecropping system remains in place until the workers are replaced by machinery.

1865–1877 Reconstruction. Blacks enroll in schools, and black elected officials hold public office in large number.

1877 Federal oversight of the former Confederate states ends; a new racial system is put in place; black voters disenfranchised.

1881 Washerwomen's strike sets the stage for future collective organizing of domestic workers.

1896 *Plessy v. Ferguson.* This U.S. Supreme Court decision rejects Homer Plessy's right to refuse to change his seat on a New Orleans train, effectively legalizing segregation and the "separate but equal" argument.

1909 The National Association for the Advancement of Colored People (NAACP) is founded, an important step in the long fight for racial and political equality.

1917 The *Chicago Defender,* the most widely circulated black newspaper in the United States, wages an aggressive campaign urging African Americans to migrate northward.

1900–1930 The Great Migration. Millions of blacks leave the failing southern economy for well-paying industrial jobs in the North.

1924 The Ku Klux Klan claims 4.5 million members.

1929 The Great Depression begins; in 1933, the worst year of the Depression, twenty lynchings are officially recorded.

1933 President Roosevelt introduces the New Deal, which helps black farmers buy land and supports education and training of young blacks; the Works Project Administration collects narratives of former slaves.

1940–1970 Second wave of the Great Migration. Five million blacks flock to cities in the North and West.

1946 NAACP membership surges to 400,000, with the fastest rate of growth in the South.

1954 *Brown v. Board of Education.* The U.S. Supreme Court knocks down the "separate but equal" argument in this ruling against segregation in the public schools.

1955 Savage murder of fourteen-year-old Emmett Till, who was visiting relatives in Mississippi and accused of whistling at a white woman.

1955 Rosa Parks refuses to give up her seat on a Montgomery bus, sparking a citywide bus boycott. Domestic workers played a key role in this successful protest.

1956 U.S. Supreme Court rules that Alabama's bus segregation laws are illegal.

1961–1964 Height of the civil rights movement under the leadership of Martin Luther King.

1962 Following riots on the campus, the African American student James Meredith enrolls in his first class at the University of Mississippi.

1964 U.S. Civil Rights Act passes, putting an end to segregation and sounding the death knell of Jim Crow.

1974 Domestic workers covered under Fair Labor Standards Act and given protection of the government in their right to minimum wage.

LEARNING FROM THE SLAVE NARRATIVES

One can get some sense of what it was like to live and work as a slave and also about the early days of freedom by reading the slave narratives. The stories are available on the New Deal Network at http://newdeal.feri.org/asn/asn00.htm. Listen, for example, to the words of Matilda Hatchett, estimated to be between ninety-eight and one hundred years old:

> Yes Lawd! I have been here so long I ain't forgot nothin'. I can remember things way back. I can remember things happening when I was four years old. Things that happen now I can't remember so well. But I can remember things that happened way back yonder.
>
> I learnt to read a little after peace was declared. A ole lady, Aunt Sarah Hunly, learnt us how to spell and then after that we went to school. I went to school three weeks. I never went to school much.

> Didn't git no chance to learn nothin' in slavery. Sometimes the children would teach the darkies 'round the house their ABC's. I've heard of folks teachin' their slaves to read the Bible. They didn't teach us to read nothin'. I've heard of it, but I've never seen it, that some folks would cut off the first finger of a nigger that could write.

These remarkable recollections from "slavery times," as the storytellers referred to them, were gathered over several years as part of the WPA's effort to record the history of slavery from the point of view of former slaves. *The Slave's Narrative*, an anthology edited by Charles T. Davis and Henry Louis Gates Jr. (1985), provides a thorough methodological and historical analysis of the WPA interviews of former slaves. The interviewers were instructed to be careful not to influence the informants, and to cover the general subjects of work conditions, food, clothing, religious worship, and resistance (Escott 1985).

The contribution of this endeavor cannot be overestimated: the wealth of the information provided and the revelation of little-known facts about daily life in bondage have advanced our appreciation of how slavery was experienced by the slaves themselves. Although a number of former slaves wrote autobiographies, these highly educated writers—who had often escaped or migrated to the North—were not entirely representative of the slave population. The WPA interviews, on the other hand, provide a record from a population more characteristic of former slaves as a whole. The interviews conducted by black interviewers obtained especially valuable information as informants talked freely about such matters as miscegenation, hatred of whites, courtship, punishments meted out, the separation of families, and resistance (Blassingame 1985). As the renowned southern historian C. Vann Woodward (1966) concludes, the WPA narratives contain "one of the deepest reservoirs of ex-slave testimony on two of the most profound historical experiences of the race" (55). Those two experiences were slavery and freedom. And although all the scholars included in the Davis and Gates anthology acknowledge the historical value of the data collected in the slave narratives, they offer the following criticisms of the methodology:

~ Because the overwhelming majority of the interviewers were white, local, and segregationist, one can assume that the former slaves were less than completely candid in responses to questions (Woodward 1985).

~ An inhibiting factor to getting the full story of slavery was that many of those interviewed were sharecroppers dependent on the goodwill of white people, including some of the interviewers who were from the local area (Escott 1985).

~ Analysis of the interviews reveals that many of the interviewers asked leading questions to elicit positive accounts of the treatment received by the slaves (Woodward 1985).

~ The fact that a large majority (88 percent) of the interviewers were male limited the nature of the content provided (Woodward 1985).

~ Only a few of the interviewers used a recording device, and most took notes that were not direct transcriptions of the interviews (Escott 1985).

~ Because so many years had passed since the abolition of slavery, many of those interviewed were very old, and many others had only been small children under slavery (Escott 1985).

Despite these criticisms, the slave narratives are highly informative in a way that no other method of data collection can match. An outstanding source for delving directly into the world of slavery is the narrative collection *Lay My Burden Down: A Folk History of Slavery* (1945). Organized and presented by Ben Botkin, a folklore scholar and an editor who worked with the Writers' Project, this anthology is drawn from the recorded narratives that were gathered during the last decade when men and women born under the yoke of slavery were alive to talk about it. Botkin believed that this project represented a new kind of history—a history constructed from the bottom up. He viewed folklore as an important source for the writing of history of every group, but especially for those whose perspectives are omitted from the history books, which rely on public records. A reliance on public records results in a history devoid of soul and passion. "From the memories and the lips of former slaves," Botkin writes, "have come the answers which only they can give to questions which Americans still ask: What does it mean to be a slave? What does it mean to be free? And, even more, how does it *feel*?" (ix).

As gripping as any novel, the stories cover the periods from slavery through Reconstruction and are presented in excerpts related to five major themes: Mother Wit (tales of tricking the master); Long Remembrance; From Can to Can't; A War among the White Folks; and All I Know about Freedom. Although many of the former slaves interviewed in the 1930s were living in abject poverty worse than what they had known in slavery, they clearly prized their freedom. Taken together, these narratives teach us of the feelings evoked by both the cruelty and the kindness of the masters and overseers. More specifically, we learn of the fact that "part white children sold for more than black children; they used them for house girls" (55); of the stability of many marriages but of one woman who became the "wife to all seven Negro slaves" (76); of slaves owned by Indians; of a woman who was beaten almost to death for eating a biscuit she found; of a man who had been sold away as a child and who later discovered he had accidentally married his mother; of promises by a white preacher that "You may get to the kitchens of heaven if you obey your master, if you don't steal, if you tell no stories" (25).

In the post–Civil War world, we learn of the shock people experienced on being told they were free; of how fraud and violence were used for social control of the freed blacks; and of how some were not told they were free but were kept on as slaves until word spread. In reading the original words of the storytellers, we discover the terms they use for themselves, terms such as house servant, darky, nigger, Negro, colored folks, Mammy (for mother), and pickaninny baby. They frequently refer to the slave owners as Old Master, Marse, and Old Mistress. Here is one example from the testimonial of Millie Evans of North Carolina:

> Now, child, I can't 'member everything I done in them days, but we didn't have to worry 'bout nothing. Old Mistress was the one to worry. 'Twasn't then like it is now, no 'twasn't. We had such a good time, and everybody cried when the Yankees cried out: "Free." T'other niggers say they had a hard time 'fore they was free, but 'twas then like 'tis now. If you had a hard time, we done it ourselves. (65)

And, as we hear from Jenny Proctor of Alabama:

I's hear tell of them good slave days, but I ain't never seen no good times then . . . . None of us was 'lowed to see a book or try to learn. They say we git smarter than they was if we learn anything, but we slips around and gits hold of that Webster's old blue-back speller and we hides it till 'way in the night and then we lights a little pine torch and studies that spelling book. We learn it too. I can read some now and write a little too. (89, 91)

Today, an interest in the period of history known as the Great Depression has revived under conditions of a global economic collapse, threatened bank failures, and mass unemployment. The focus of the popular literature, however, has been on people from those days who had a lot to lose in a failing economy—the landowners, the bankers, the planters—not the people who already struggled at the margins, and certainly not on people who slaved in the fields as sharecroppers or who worked as maids.

FROM SLAVERY TO SHARECROPPING

Racism is often most readily apparent in the economic arrangements of a society—who gets what in terms of opportunity for success, well-paying jobs, and social welfare programming. In *Color-Blind*, Tim Wise (2010), a popular white, antiracist speaker on college campuses, reveals how institutionalized racism is engrained in American social policies as it has been since the days of slavery. He debunks the liberal dogma that we can separate the forces of racism from the forces of classism and claim that color-blind policies will overcome racial inequality through treating everyone the same. To bolster his argument, he points to labor history from the first decade of the twentieth century through the New Deal, when union bosses colluded with politicians to block the access of people of color to the skilled trades, effectively relegating blacks to the lowest-wage jobs available. This very poverty of black families, especially in the South, meant that all family members from the oldest to the youngest had to work in the fields or by other means for their survival.

Obtaining an education was therefore often out of the question. In the South, spending per capita for black schools was only about one-third of the amount spent for white schools, and some counties had no black high schools at all. Institutionalized racism was less apparent in progressive laws to end poverty. Without high school education, for example, few African Americans could utilize the GI benefits granted to soldiers returning from World War II. Southern states were accorded the right to determine the standards of eligibility for GI benefits in the same way that they could set the standards for eligibility to vote. Literacy requirements were strictly enforced for one race but not for the other. And until Social Security policies were changed in the 1950s, African Americans were rarely even provided with this safety net for their old age since exclusions were implemented relating to domestic workers and agricultural labor. Access was denied to black would-be home owners as well through the discriminatory practices of the Federal Housing Administration home-loan program, which guaranteed mortgages written by banks to working-class families. In all these ways, whites were enabled to get ahead; many accumulated wealth that could be passed down through generations. But their rise—their enrichment—as Wise indicates, came at the expense of individuals and communities of color.

Since our focus is the era of segregation, a special note on its history is in order. A common misconception is that the Jim Crow laws were enacted in the states of the former Confederacy immediately upon the end of slavery or that these laws were passed as soon as the period of Reconstruction was over. In fact, according to C. Vann Woodward (1966) in his classic study of segregation *The Strange Career of Jim Crow,* the barriers did not come up—for example, the signs "White Only" and "Colored" or "No Colored Except Maids in Uniform"—until around 1900. Prior to that, few African Americans moved to the North, and thanks to Reconstruction, many owned farmland of their own. Some stayed on the land and worked for the same white families who had once owned them.

Then, around the turn of the century, the political atmosphere changed. In conjunction with an economic change—resulting from the boll weevil's assault on the cotton plant and the increasing mechanization of the crop's cultivation—that drove black farm laborers into the towns, a backlash against the blacks ensued. New racist laws were passed to keep the races separate in public places. With little reason for black people to remain in the South, the Great Migration got under way. By 1970, 6 million had made the move from the rural South to the urban North (Berlin 2010).

SOUTHERN PATERNALISM

The term "paternalism" derives from the Latin *pater,* which means pertaining to the father; it denotes a role of caretaking by one who takes responsibility for another who is vulnerable in some way. Although paternalism toward blacks, like sharecropping, arose out of slavery, unlike sharecropping it was an ethos rather than an economic arrangement. In the paternalistic view, slaves were often seen by the white slave owners as lovable, somewhat primitive, childlike beings who needed a firm hand to guide them in work and in life. The good blacks were grateful, obedient, and knew their place; and good white people would treat black people with kindness and reward them for their work with spontaneous gift giving that could never be taken for granted (see Handley 2007). But even this description is too simple; Woodward (1966) suggests that noblesse oblige, an aristocratic philosophy in which the wealthier classes recognized some obligation to care for the poor, also played a part. Among the landowning class of southerners, the belief in white supremacy, concern for the well-being of members of the black race, and prejudice against poor and uneducated whites went hand in hand. Fear of close contact with black people in the later nineteenth century was commonly identified in contemporary writings cited by Woodward as a characteristically lower-class white attitude.

Visitors from the North expecting to find expressions of race hatred among southerners were often astonished by something they could not quite put their fingers on—behavior that was demeaning and loving at the same time. When John Dollard, a northern psychologist, ventured to the town of Indianola, Mississippi (which he called Southerntown), in the 1930s to study the personalities and child-rearing patterns of "Negroes," he was so struck by how closely black and white lives were intertwined that his research took an 180-degree turn, shifting from the psychological to sociological realm. As Dollard himself later explained, "[The] study of the social context of the lives of Negroes has crowded out the original objective of the research" (2).

Dollard's groundbreaking *Caste and Class in a Southern Town* (1937) is among the classic works on Mississippi segregation. We have chosen it as a starting point because Dollard's research was conducted in the same general region of the cotton-growing South in which the majority of our interviewees grew up. For the oldest of our storytellers, the period of time they describe coincides roughly with that covered by Dollard's research—the Great Depression. As a complete outsider to the region, Dollard could ask questions that insiders dared not, while his status as outsider provided a perspective unavailable to most local residents, to whom their rituals and social norms would have seemed a natural part of southern life.

Dollard describes Southerntown as "a whole region bound to the American cotton economy" (1), depicting it as being dominated by a strict social etiquette, an inviolable racial code that was understood by all. According to this unwritten code, Dollard writes, white was separated from white on the

Workers with a connection to the Stuart family on the way to church. *From the family collection of Katherine van Wormer.*

basis of class, and black from white on the basis of caste: "Caste has replaced slavery as a means of maintaining the essence of the old slavery order in the South. . . . A union of members of both castes may not have a legitimate child. All such children are members of the lower caste. . . . Caste in Southerntown is also a categorical barrier to sexual congress between upper-caste women and lower-caste men. It does not result in such a barrier between upper-caste men and lower-caste women" (62). As we will see, this was the ultimate taboo of yesterday's South—any sexual involvement between black men and white women. Endemic to southern paternalism were the strict social controls placed on the behavior of white women and black men.

Other landmark studies of rural Mississippi, such as *After Freedom*, by the anthropologist Hortense Powdermaker (1939), also describe a southern paternalism that was at once protective and punitive. Powdermaker's focus is on the master-servant relationship that prevailed during the time of her writing. The whites were then absolutely dependent on blacks to do the manual labor. Such labor, according to Powdermaker, was avoided by middle- and upper-class whites who, as she suggests, saw the Negro as "childlike, irresponsible, and dependent by nature" and "destined to be a servant" (39). Significantly, one white informant is quoted as saying: "I'd much rather have a Negro servant than a poor white. . . . [T]he Negro's disposition is so much more pleasant" (39). The speaker is clearly used to being in a superior position in relation to others and has little understanding of the race and class privilege evidenced in her words. Through the 1950s at least, such Jim Crow paternalism was a characteristic of southern social life. A form of racism, the attitudes of the day were demeaning to those seen as social inferiors but often loved as people who were described as "like family." Physical separation of the races was not the goal here; the drawing of social boundaries defined by race was.

The sociologist Mary Jackman (1994) terms this pattern of contact between races "a velvet-glove strategy of sweet persuasion" (2). Seen as a legacy of slavery, paternalism involved the coercion of subordinates through relationships presented as being grounded in love. The members of the dominant group saw themselves as benevolent caretakers who provided for the needs of their workers. Love, affection, and praise were offered to subordinates on the strict condition that they complied with the unequal terms of the relationship.

The intricacies of interracial relationships in the rural South permeate the literature of the Nobel Prize–winning author William Faulkner, a native son of Mississippi. Faulkner's groundbreaking portrait of a southern white family in *The Sound and the Fury* (1929) is a story of moral decline and generational conflict. A recurring theme of the novel is that white people—whether they are of gentry stock or what the character Dilsey calls the "trash white folks" (362)—inhabit a society that is haunted by its past. "The Negro cook, Dilsey" (416), the black caretaker of the dysfunctional white Compson family, embodies strength. The dependence of white families on their dutiful black servants is a recurrent theme in Faulkner's work based on his own astute observations and personal background. For a more objective account of everyday life in the segregated South, we turn to the scholarship of modern historians.

INSIGHTS FROM PRESENT-DAY HISTORIANS

Except when comparing statistical data over time, social scientists today rarely offer the type of whole-society studies they once did. Social historians, however, continue to analyze social patterns and trends over time with attention to historical records. Present-day historians and sociologists have the advantage of perspective, the ability to look back with hindsight over a broader sweep of time in order to examine patterns of social life. If too much time passes, however, the witnesses will be gone and, with them, their remembrances of the nuances of daily life. Examples of more recent articles analyzing the social norms within domestic service are, in chronological order: Howell Raines's *New York Times* essay "Grady's Gift" (1991); Michele Tully's "Lifting Our Voices: African American Culture Responses to Trauma and Loss" (1999); Katherine Stovel's "Local Sequential Patterns: The Structure of Lynching in the Deep South, 1882–1930" (2001); and Fiona Handley's "Memorializing Race in the Deep South: The 'Good Darkie' Statue" (2007).

The following books are invaluable modern historical resources: *Telling Memories among Southern Women: Domestic Workers and Their Employers in the Segregated South,* by Susan Tucker (1988); *Southern Women: Black and White in the Old South,* by Sally McMillen, (1992); *Growing Up Jim Crow,* by Jennifer Ritterhouse (2006); *Life and Death in the Delta,* by Kim Lacy Rogers (2006), *Labor of Love, Labor of Sorrow: Black Women, Work and the Family, from Slavery to the Present,* by Jacqueline Jones, 2nd ed. (2007); and *Clinging to Mammy: The Faithful Slave in Twentieth-Century America,* by Micki McElya (2007). Devoted exclusively to the people of the Great Migration from South to North are: *Living In, Living Out: African American Domestics and the Great Migration,* by Elizabeth Clark-Lewis (1996); *Making a Way of No Way: African American Women and the Second Great Migration,* by Lisa K. Boehm (2009); *The Making of African America: The Four Great Migrations,* by Ira Berlin (2010); and *The Warmth of Other Suns: The Epic Story of America's Great Migration,* by Isabel Wilkerson, 2011).

Michele Tully (1999) describes the paternalistic form of race relations that existed in the South as an experience of captivity that "creates a relationship of coercive control where the captor seeks to achieve not only power over the victim but also to extract affirmation, gratitude, and even love" (26). Fiona Handley (2007) puts this system in historical context. Consistent with the facts revealed by C. Vann Woodward (1966), Handley indicates that Jim Crow laws did not directly follow emancipation but that legal equality existed for several decades under northern-ruled Reconstruction following the Civil War. When the South reverted to self-rule, and in conjunction with a severe economic depression that took place around the turn of the twentieth century, Jim Crow laws mandating strict segregation of the races were put in place. We know from sociological research that such scapegoating of minority groups under situations of dire stress is common (van Wormer and Besthorn 2011). In the Deep South, the lynching of black men who violated the social and sexual norms instilled fear throughout the population and operated as a major form of social control (see Angelou 1969; Stovel 2001; and Woodruff 2003). Official records show that more than 1,200 blacks were lynched between 1882 and 1930 in the Deep South, and of course the precise number of these vile acts will never be known. This explosion of violence, according to Katherine Stovel, profoundly shaped the southern social landscape for much of the early twentieth century.

Regardless of the laws, the way of life and the unwritten rules that had developed under slavery for the slaveholding whites continued, according to Handley, in the postbellum period. The attitudes were passed down from generation to generation, often mother to child. In the segregated South of the early twentieth century, the rules of racial etiquette guided every aspect of individual behavior, from how blacks and whites stood, sat, ate, drank, walked, and talked to how they addressed each other and even made eye contact. Raised from childhood by black "nurses," white children commonly grew up playing with black boys and girls who they knew were destined to become their servants in adult life. In her study of childhood socialization, the historian Jennifer Ritterhouse describes how the social norms pertaining to racial etiquette were learned by children mainly through observation, but also by making mistakes and being scolded for it. White children in the Deep South developed a strong race consciousness early on while at the same time realizing that race was not something talked about in polite adult company or in the presence of a servant. A common theme in jokes among white kids pertained to embarrassing situations in which a white child ended up in the "colored" section by mistake or drank out of a water fountain designated "colored only."

One of the outstanding descriptions in the literature of the pains of segregation from a white perspective is provided by the journalist Howell Raines (1991) in his *New York Times* biographical essay "Grady's Gift." This essay, for which Raines was awarded the 1992 Pulitzer Prize for feature writing, begins with Raines's family reunion with his childhood maid.

> I know that outsiders tend to think segregation existed in a uniform way throughout the Solid South. But it didn't. Segregation was rigid in some places, relaxed in others; leavened with humanity in some places, enforced with unremitting brutality in others. And segregation found its most violent and regimented expression in Birmingham—segregation maintained through the nighttime maraudings of white thugs, segregation sanctioned by absentee landlords from the United States Steel Corporation, segregation enforced by a pervasively corrupt police department. (1)

In *Living In, Living Out*, Elizabeth Clark-Lewis brings together the personal experiences of eighty-one women who worked for wealthy white families. This work of oral history portrays the lives of African American women who migrated from the rural South to work as domestic servants in Washington, D.C., in the early decades of the twentieth century. The women narrators describe how they encountered—but never accepted—the master-servant relationship, and recount their struggles to change their status from "live-in" servants to daily paid workers who "lived out."

With candor and passion, the women interviewed tell of leaving their families and adjusting to city life "up North," of being placed as live-in servants, and of the frustrations and indignities they endured as domestics. By networking on the job, at churches, and at penny savers clubs, they found ways to transform their unending servitude into an employer-employee relationship—gaining a new independence that could be experienced only by living outside of their employers' homes. Clark-Lewis points out that their perseverance and courage not only improved their own lot but also transformed work life for succeeding generations of African American women. A series of in-depth vignettes about the later years of these women bears poignant witness to their efforts to carve out lives of fulfillment and dignity.

As did Dollard (1937) in his earlier participant observational study and Faulkner in his works of fiction, Ira Berlin (2010) and Lisa Boehm (2009) graphically depict the abject poverty of the region in the 1930s. And like the earlier writers, they fill in important details about how the black sharecroppers lived—their hot and crowded shacks that were former slave cabins, the higher infant mortality, the lack of indoor plumbing, the ingenuity required by mothers to provide clothing of which their children would not feel ashamed. Looming over the whole period were the lopsided economic arrangements that kept the sharecroppers in perpetual indebtedness to their landowners.

Informed by these landmark sources of literature, we turn now to two of the forms of structural violence used as means of social control in the South—lynching and sharecropping.

Lynching

White men could violate black women and girls with impunity (Rogers 2006). The law professor Adrien Wing, herself a descendant of Confederate general P. G. T. Beauregard and one of his slave-mistresses, draws a gripping parallel between the ethnic cleansing and forced impregnation that took place in Bosnia, and the history of rape and miscegenation in the American South (Wing and Merchan 1993). Common ground is found, Adrien Wing and Sylke Merchan state, in several key attributes related to what they term "spirit injury," or "the slow death of the psyche, of the soul, and of the identity of the individual" (2). Among these key attributes are the emasculation of the men due to their helplessness to protect their wives and daughters; the birth of racially or ethnically mixed offspring; and silence concerning their rape as the women internalize their experience of oppression. It was not uncommon for young males in the white household to sexually experiment with young black women. "Many southern boys," as Dollard (1957) notes, "began their sexual experience with Negro girls, usually around the ages of 15 or 16" (139). These things were widely known but rarely commented on in polite company.

Vigilante justice was a key means racists employed to strengthen the divisions between the white and the black worlds (Boehm 2009). This system, which inflicted terror on one segment of the population, sometimes targeting whole communities, guaranteed white farmers and landowners a steady and docile supply of cheap labor, a labor force kept subdued by low wages and a lack of legal protections. Black residents lived in fear of mob violence against their people. From a sociological standpoint, the intended audience of this sort of mob violence is not the dominant class in a society but, rather, the group or social category of the victim (Smångs 2011). The underlying purpose is to preserve the status quo. In the case of southern whites, it can be understood as a reaction to real or perceived threats from blacks to their dominant position and privileged access to scarce resources, above all economic or material ones. There is another, more sinister, aspect to the lynching as well, which has to do with access to women of both races (see chapter 4).

The fear experienced in segregation-era rural Mississippi was so intense that it would remain alive for years in those who experienced it, as Kim Rogers (2006) discovered in her interviews with black civil rights workers from the area. Under a system of injustice they dared not confront, their sense of powerlessness had been absolute. Any kind of political assertion was out of the question as the representatives of law enforcement were among the worst violators of people's rights. In the rural South, therefore, segregation was kept in place by terror. And people who could not vote and dared not organize were ripe for economic exploitation.

Sharecropping

To understand the attraction of domestic service for the black woman, one has to know the conditions of the alternative—sharecropping—and to place sharecropping in context, one has to go back to the plantation system, which depended on the heavy agricultural labor of slaves.

While the black women worked both in the fields with their menfolk as sharecroppers and in the homes of white families, the men mainly sharecropped. The cotton season extended from March to November, with the crops planted in the early spring. From April until June, the cotton was chopped and thinned to remove any weeds that had grown up with the plant. Nearly all black people in the community, children included, picked the cotton that blossomed in September. The work was as backbreaking as it had been under slavery.

Economically, the exploitation of the slave for his or her labor continued under freedom in an altered form—indebtedness. Widespread cheating practiced by many planters left their sharecroppers and tenants indebted for years at a time. For the landless poor in rural Mississippi, survival depended on the family economy—on the labor of every family member, who had to work from sunup to sundown. In the Black Belt South (a phrase that referred to the rich, black soil in the Mississippi Delta), the economic conditions of segregation were highly destructive of life and livelihood. Death rates were high for both children and adults, with the average life expectancy around fifty-six for males and fifty-eight for females born in 1939, which was an increase of ten years from 1900 (Rogers).

Within this context of relative powerlessness, individuals who had close relationships to white people of influence had certain advantages, as Susan Tucker (1988) indicates. Aligning themselves with whites of the professional class, black women often earned the respect of members of the white community and formed alliances that could render them and their families a certain degree of protection. Black domestic workers, as Tucker further indicates, moved freely between the white and black communities. Dressed in a maid's uniform, they had a mobility denied to others of their race. Domestic workers often fell into the role of go-betweens, as interpreters of black life to white people and of white life to black people.

In *Voices of a People's History,* Howard Zinn and Anthony Arnove (2009) provide us with a quote that well illustrates this point. From Neb Cobb, a Depression-era leader of the Alabama Sharecroppers' Union, we hear:

> If a Negro was a servant for white people, then they'd carry him to church with 'em, accept him to come in and take a seat on the back row and listen to the white people. . . . [I]f they was maids for white people, well thought of, they'd take 'em out to their home churches, dupe 'em up in a way. . . .
>
> And when the white folks would come in the colored churches, good God, the niggers would get busy givin' 'em first class seats. (325)

This is not to say that African American women gravitated to domestic service in order to get to know the right people, but rather that the making of important contacts was an indirect consequence of the type of work they chose. Probably they entered domestic service because the work was physically less demanding, with some aspects of it—the cooking and child care—carrying rewards of its own. The drawback, of course, was the daily humiliation attached to being a servant.

MATERNALISM: MISTRESS AND MAID

Although most writers characterize the white southern treatment of blacks in past generations—the combination of love, protection, duty, and exploitation—as a form of paternalism, the sociologist Judith Rollins suggests that the term "maternalism" is far more relevant to the description of the mistress-servant relationship. In *Between Women: Domestics and Their Employers* (1985), Rollins's participant-observation investigation of domestic service work, Rollins takes us beyond the decidedly masculine concept of paternalism. The character of the mistress-servant relationship, Rollins argues, is distinctly female. In contrast to paternalism, which stems from the tradition of patriarchal authority, maternalism "is a concept related to women's supportive intrafamilial roles of nurturing, loving, and attending to affective needs" (179). There is also the factor of exploitation.

Rollins describes the work arrangement as a unique form of exploitation, one in which the contacts are highly personal and based on a relationship of forced dependency. In many ways, the dependency was mutual, but for different reasons. The white woman depended on her maid to perform necessary household tasks, to cook for the family, and mind the children. The servant depended on her employer for the income and sometimes for help of a practical nature. The relationship was highly uneven and therefore could not be described, objectively speaking, as friendship, despite the emotional bonds that often formed. The exploitation, Rollins maintains, in fact, was exacerbated because of the very close personal nature of the employer-employee relationship.

Relationship inequality was confirmed in two ways; the first was through the required social etiquette. Servants were expected to show their employers deference, for example, by using the terms "yes ma'am" and "no ma'am," and addressing the employer as "Miss" or "Mrs." (usually "Miz"); servants, on the other hand, were addressed by their first names. Black women, regardless of class, were never referred to as "ladies," a fact that was true down to at least the late 1960s; this term was reserved for white women deemed worthy of respect (Ritterhouse 2006; Tucker 1988). Black women were always referred to as "women" and "girls" even when they were of a mature age (Rollins 1985). Under slavery, house servants were addressed as "aunt" and "uncle" or with a standardized form such as "Mammy." As late as the 1930s, white employers were sometimes still using this form of address, especially in the country.

Maternalism is a term similarly used by Pierrette Hondagneu-Sotelo (2001) in *Doméstica*, a study of working conditions among immigrant domestic workers in Los Angeles. Hondagneu-Sotelo defines maternalism as "a unilateral positioning of the employer as a benefactor who receives personal thanks, recognition, and validation of self from the domestic worker" (172). This one-sided relationship generally is between an older woman and a younger one. Their relationship goes far beyond the bounds of business, and their communication goes far beyond mere conversation. Hondagneu-Sotelo describes the case of an employer who got to know her housekeeper's whole family and who took care of the housekeeper in various ways. She watched out for her housekeeper's health by prohibiting the use of certain chemical products; she even took her maid to her own doctor so that the maid could avoid having an unnecessary hysterectomy. This kind of relationship is described by the author as very rewarding to the maternalistic homemaker employer: not only will she get better job performance and loyalty from her worker, but she can also derive pleasure from her voyeuristic involvement in the intimate details of the worker's life and from seeing herself as altruistic and kind.

In *Telling Memories among Southern Women*, which is based on oral histories of domestic workers and their white employers, Susan Tucker (1988) quotes a white woman who says: "And in our family, we had four generations of help from the same colored family: Uncle Isaac, Aunt Mary, Abigail, Lucretia—they were all from the same family" (223). The context makes clear that that this form of address was used with the older house servants. Still, one member of the next generation down "became Mammy" (224). Consistent with this custom, the Pullman porters who worked on the trains during this same era were addressed generically as "George" (Tye 2004). Even more extreme, in South Africa, in Cock's sample, black women were generally called "Sissy." Only a small minority of the whites interviewed knew their domestic workers' full names.

In her analysis of the mistress-maid relationship in the Philippines, Janet Arnado (2003) views the maternalism she found there as a part of "an inequitable class-gender structure in which middle-class women, subordinated by their gender, delegate the unglamorous domestic work to poor women for low wages" (154). Arnado identifies an emphasis on benevolence and charity as the controlling aspect of maternalism. The pretense that the servant is part of the family, even to the extent of having the maid call her employer "Auntie," makes it very difficult for the hired help to assert her independence.

White people undoubtedly associated the use of the terms "aunt," "uncle," and "Mammy" with feelings of trust and affection. The historian Micki McElya (2007), in her historical analysis of the role of Mammy in white southern mythology, reveals how a mythical image of the ever-faithful slave achieved great popularity among southern whites around the turn of the century. Throughout the early twentieth century, Aunt Jemima (in her original portrayal as a slave) represented this image of the caring mammy who beamed at shoppers from the front of the box of pancake mix. McElya draws on this representation of a doting enslaved cook to show the appeal of this happy-slave fantasy. Generations of consumers of Aunt Jemima pancake mix in effect were buying a picture of a lush world of plantation grandeur. McElya also examines newspaper accounts of stage productions that reveal the lengths to which southern whites went to promote false memories of a romanticized plantation life. They advocated for the construction of a monument in Washington, D.C., to honor the faithful Mammy, and they produced and attended minstrel shows in which white actresses blackened their faces and mastered black dialect to portray lovable black mammies. These stage productions were wildly popular all over the South and favorably reviewed in regional newspapers of the day. If we are to understand the nature of race relations in the United States, McElya argues, "we must confront the terrible depths of desire for a black mammy" (14). This "clinging to mammy" was in effect a clinging to old ways, ways that never were. The faithful slave narrative, interestingly, was mostly espoused by women, such as the southern elite members of the United Daughters of the Confederacy.

An interesting twist on the maternalism that Rollins describes is that the ultimate maternal figure was the black mammy herself; she represented the earth mother. And yet society treated her as someone who had to be mothered, although not always in the nurturing sense of the word. Rollins also discusses the "infantilization" of the maid, the treating her as if she were a child or at least childlike. Like children, black servants were often scolded. They were expected to be obedient without question and to suppress any defiant reactions to orders given (Dollard 1957). And they were often patronized: Behaviors deemed irrational or irresponsible were often expected and tolerated to an extent beyond what would be accepted from persons regarded as mature adults (see Dollard 1957; Rollins 1985; and Tucker 1988). Control of the domestic worker's use of house space was problematic to many segregation-era servants just as it had been to the house servants under the institution of slavery, as McMillen (1992) suggests.

Domestic workers had to hide behind a mask any resentment they may have felt at the required public deference and subservience. The expected social etiquette required black workers to conceal their intelligence as well, reinforcing their employer's sense of white superiority. Northern observer John Dollard saw right through the performance of the black residents of Southerntown. "The deference, subservience, and dependence of the lower-class Negro," he said, "are often a social mask, which he wears because he must" (440). Black women who worked in southern homes were often referred to as "uppity," but they could get away with a certain amount of sass.

From the white perspective, black adults, unlike other adults, were expected to reconcile themselves to owning only a small portion of whatever was of value—land, property, businesses—because they were not seen as quite grown up, and also because these assets were desired by others. The mask that many black people wore reflected their position of powerlessness in the white world. In their own communities, the mask came off. While she was growing up, Tucker (1988) discovered that blacks acted differently outside of their employers' homes when she went home with her maid. As she describes the scene: "There, she had her own language; we heard this in her changed voice. And there—but this we only barely glimpsed—she took off her mask, a mask that all black domestics, to some degree or other, wore in white homes" (72).

It seems odd, on the surface, that most employers preferred their workers to be ignorant. In this way, however, the employer could control them better, and there were fewer options for them in other lines of work. And remember that in the antebellum period, slaves were largely forbidden to learn to read and write. When Judith Rollins (1985), for example, was trying to get hired for domestic work as part of her participant-observation study, she once accidentally spoke in her highly educated voice. The lady of the house was reluctant to hire her until she played dumb. Then, when she was being instructed in how to use the vacuum cleaner, the employer talked down to her and oversimplified the instructions. In South Africa likewise the preference was for the uneducated maid. Jacklyn Cock (1989), who interviewed South African employers, provides this choice quote: "She's the first girl I've had that's gone to school. . . . She insists on doing things her own way. The completely raw ones are better" (113). This preference for not-too-well-educated workers is stated directly in a number of the interviews of white employers conducted by Tucker (1988). This is revealed also indirectly in the preference for Mexican workers in the Southwest, even if their English skills are limited.

In seeming contradiction to the treatment of the servant as a social and intellectual inferior, there are numerous reports in the literature of the use of the domestic worker as a confidante. McElya (2007) views this intimacy that the whites craved as part of the longing for a faithful mammy to provide unconditional love. In any case, the proximity of the household maids to the joys and sorrows of the members of the family placed the servant in the center of all sorts of dramatic goings-on in the household, so to share one's emotional response to these situations would have followed naturally. Moreover, as McMillen indicates, while many of the house servants even under slavery enjoyed this sense of closeness to their mistress, others feigned an intimacy they did not feel (104). Then, as later, whether or not to offer personal advice to one's employer posed a dilemma for the subordinate.

Keep in mind, as Rollins tells us, that the female employer, like other women, was in a secondary, gendered position. This was even truer in the days before the modern women's movement got under way. For the white woman who was subservient to her husband, the likely breadwinner, having a servant helped boost her status and her self-esteem. The role that the domestic worker played in the household, then, in some ways echoed the role of the housewife vis-à-vis her husband.

ROLES OF THE SOUTHERN WHITE WOMEN WHO HAD MAIDS

In her 1980s participant-observation research, Rollins was struck by the fact that the white women invariably were submissive to their husbands, deferring to them in matters of important decision making. The men worked outside the home, while housework was seen as women's work. Tucker (1988) notes the same phenomenon—a white patriarchal social structure in which white women had as their domain running the household, supervising the meal preparation, and taking charge of the hiring and firing of household staff.

The maternalism of which Rollins speaks derives from the mistress-maid configuration itself and was not restricted to any geographical region. Still, in the South, the stratification pattern was the most rigidly defined. Women of both races, in other words, lived under the dominance of southern white men. For southern women of the pre-1930s segregation era, gender roles were sharply differentiated. This was the time of the southern belle mystique, immortalized in such films as *Gone with the Wind*. The image of womanhood presented was based on romanticized notions straight out of the historical romances of Sir Walter Scott. (So popular were Scott's writings in the U.S. South, in fact, that Mark Twain later claimed that Scott had such a strong hand in shaping the southern character that he was, in great measure, responsible for the Civil War.) Plantation society of the Old South is described by Carol Manning (2002) as "an aristocracy modeled on the feudal system of lords, knights, and ladies with attending servants" (95). Refined ladies who lived on plantations were to be treated by southern gentlemen as if they were helpless damsels in distress. The ladies derived power by being attached to a man of substance. Role models knew how to use their dainty attractiveness and coquettish charms with men to get what they wanted; they often played dumb in the face of male authority (see Jabour 2007; Strepp 2003; and the memoirs of Sallie Bingham 1991 and Pat Conroy 2010). Not only did the black woman in her role of servant wear a mask, but so did the white woman in courtship, when entertaining, and in feminine manipulations to get her way.

Young women of marriageable age were paraded out at cotillion balls in the hope that they would meet eligible young men who could support them in the style to which they were accustomed. These lavish events, even prior to the Civil War, in which a young lady made her first appearance or debut into society sometimes included hundreds of guests (Jabour 2007).

In New Orleans such events—the Mardi Gras balls—continue to this day with the same pageantry they had over a century ago. Rebecca Snedeker (2006), an award-winning documentary filmmaker, provides a rare inside account of the rituals pertaining to the debutante balls, a secret world that few people ever see. Aptly titled *By Invitation Only*, Snedeker's film follows the preparation of a socially prominent young woman in training to be queen of one of the oldest and most prestigious balls. Although the ball remains unnamed in the film, it is probably Comus or Proteus. "These [exclusive Mardi Gras balls] are the ones the men in my family belong to," notes Snedeker. "My mother was a queen and her mother and her mother, and so on." Snedeker didn't have to be told that there would be no place in the celebration for her African American boyfriend. The legacy of these highly exclusive Mardi Gras balls goes back to the days of slavery. To learn of the exotic New Orleans tradition of the Quadroon Balls, in which beautiful quadroons (women who were one-fourth black) and octoroons (one-eighth black) were presented to prominent white men, see Eileen Southern (1997), *The Music of Black Americans: A History*.

Gender roles in old southern society, as in these coming-out balls, were distinctly marked. The class of women who were required to keep up a pretense of leisure required a staff of servants to do the heavy household chores and to provide care for the small children. The South, according to Tucker (1988), whose book uniquely contains numerous interviews with older white southern women on their experiences with their servants, was known as "white housewives' utopia" (52). Southern women further down the social ladder could emulate their social betters by having a maid, as pay levels were relatively, indeed shamelessly, low. Paradoxically, some of the servants were better off financially than the women who hired them (McElya 2007), especially during the Depression, when so many people were poor. The black women, at least, were making some money along with their husbands perhaps, while the white woman did not earn anything, and her husband was paying for the maid and parties and other social events. Black women, in short, played an important role in helping white women maintain a certain lifestyle or appear to do so; their function was social as well as practical.

The Social Control of White Women and Black Men

The historian Anya Jabour (2007) takes us back to slave days through the eyes of the girls and young women from the planter families. Based on analysis of the letters and diaries of more than three hundred young women, *Scarlett's Sisters: Young Women in the Old South* reveals how the South's old social order was maintained through the grooming of girls to play the roles of southern ladies. Although slavery or the possession of slaves is not the focus of this book, Jabour analyzes how gender and racial hierarchies were interlocked. "Virginity before marriage and fidelity within it—female sexual innocence," she writes, "was especially important for wealthy slaveholders, who sometimes defended the institution of slavery by arguing that the sexual availability of enslaved black women ensured the sexual purity of elite white women" (140). Elite white women thus were closely monitored in their comings and goings, while young black women were extremely vulnerable to sexual abuse. These customs would not change for more than one hundred years.

Writing in her personal memoir of southern white upper-class life in the 1940s and 1950s, Sallie Bingham (1991) articulates the complexity of the situation in terms of the sexual fears that lay beneath the surface of traditional southern society, namely, fear of sexual liaisons between white women and black men. The sexual oppression of upper-class white women and the oppression of blacks—both forms of violence—grew from the same root. In the white male-dominated society, the sexuality of black men was ruthlessly monitored, while black women had little protection from the advances of white men. The protection of white women, then, was a part of the whole configuration of southern violence. Protecting white women from the sexuality of black men was the whole rationale for vigilante mobs (Ritterhouse 2006). White women, for their part, were slow to condemn the system or to become liberated themselves. Well-to-do women had vested interests in maintaining the status quo, given that their own standard of living depended on the cheap labor of black people (Tucker 1988).

Toting and Gift Giving

Unlike the situation in the North, where the "day worker" worked for a fixed cash wage and generally performed only the tasks in her job description, the southern maid was at the beck and call of her employer, as the commonly used term "help" implied. In the Deep South, the maternalism, as described by Rollins, was much more pronounced.

Southern maternalism was demonstrated in one-way gift giving of discarded objects, a preference for servants who were not too well educated, viewing the employee as childlike, and an expectation of gratitude and deferential behavior.

In her study of Chicana servants, Mary Romero (1992) views such gift giving as "a form of benevolent maternalism used to buy and bond the domestic" (109). Unlike gift giving in other work settings, the gifts from employers to domestic servants are a substitute for decent wages and other benefits.

Toting is described by numerous writers of the period (Harley, Wilson, and Logan 2002; Rollins 1992; Tucker 1988) as a widespread custom in which servants were paid in kind instead of with a living wage. This custom is actually a vestige from slavery, when house servants could take leftover food back to their families. In this informal arrangement associated with southern culture, servants could expect to carry (or "tote") home food, produce from the garden, and even cast-off household goods including furniture.

Such informal arrangements reinforced the power imbalance in the mistress-servant relationship as the servant's reimbursement for service depended totally on the kindness, generosity, and whims of the mistress. One reason this practice was so widespread, Tucker suggests, is because whites could not raise the servants' pay to a decent standard without antagonizing their white friends, who would then feel pressured to raise their servants' pay. So they supplemented the wages with little extras.

Gift giving also related to gender—it was a woman-to-woman phenomenon. The man of the house generally was responsible for paying the maid her wages, but the typical woman, as a housewife with no earning power of her own, could provide her household servant with items that she might want that were no longer needed by the white family. In any case, as Tucker found in her interviews with former black servants, women on the receiving end often deeply resented the patronizing nature of this gift giving. Dependency, as Tucker explains, excludes gratitude. Some felt obligated to accept items they did not want and to pretend to be grateful.

Paradoxically, there was one gift bestowed by the maid upon the employer—the gift of listening. In all situations, as Tucker explains, listening was the gift by the black woman to the white; listening was her specialty. Black women generally saw themselves as stronger emotionally than the white women for whom they worked. Many of the white employers expressed the same sentiment; they didn't know how they could have gotten through certain crises if it hadn't been for their maid. "She was always like my mother," one such respondent said. "That's why I called her Mama Lou" (140). Said another, "I always think of the maid as being the family therapist" (135).

In "Grady's Gift," his moving, Pulitzer Prize–winning essay, Howell Raines (1991) writes of his relationship with a young woman who, thwarted in her educational plans because of Birmingham's segregation laws, came to work for his family. "It would be many years before I realized that somehow, whether by accident or by plan, in a way so subtle, so gentle, so loving that it was like the budding and falling of the leaves on the pecan trees in the yard of that happy house in that cruel city in that violent time, Grady had given me the most precious gift that could be received by a pampered white boy growing up in that time and place. It was the gift of a free and unhateful heart" (5). Grady gave him something else as well: an awareness of injustice and a will to not let it go unchallenged.

DOMESTIC SERVICE WORK FROM THE 1930S TO THE EARLY 1960S

Between Women Domestics and Their Employers, by Judith Rollins (1985), provides a social history of domestic service in the United States and worldwide. Compared to other nations, such as South Africa, for example, domestic service in the United States was more diversified, with different racial and ethnic groups occupying the role of servants at different points in time. Also unique to the United States, according to Rollins, was the evidence of a certain feeling of discomfort concerning the master-servant relationship, a discomfort that stemmed from a contradiction between having a class of servants and American democratic ideals. Still, this did not deter people from having servants or even slaves.

Rollins differentiates four distinct phases of servitude. During the first phase, or the colonial period, domestic chores were performed by indentured white people, transported convicts, and Africans. The next period, from 1776 to 1850, was characterized by the use of black slave labor in the South and of immigrant help in the North. From 1850 until World War I, a kind of feudalistic paternalism prevailed in states of the former Confederacy. This pattern, referred to by Isabel Wilkerson (2010) as a "feudal caste system" (9), persisted from the slave days into freedom and beyond. The fourth phase is the modern era of segregation from World War I until the Civil Rights Act was passed in 1964.

In the 1920s, servants customarily lived in the homes of their employers (McElya 2007). During the following decades, however, due to the resistance of black women who had roots in their own communities and their own families to care for, this pattern began to change. And, as more domestic workers transitioned away from employment as live-in help and into the role of day workers, they began to see themselves more as people who performed a certain job than as servants (Clark-Lewis 1996). As day workers, these women had more freedom to tend to their own needs, and they could quit more easily if they weren't treated right.

Well into the 1940s, almost 60 percent of employed black women in the United States continued to be engaged in domestic labor. This figure declined to 18 percent by 1970 (Rollins 1985). And twenty years later, only 2.2 percent worked as domestic servants, while a full 60 percent held white-collar jobs (Thernstrom and Thernstrom 1998). During one brief period during World War II, blacks earned real wages working for the war industry as so many of the men had been shipped overseas. In fact, six hundred thousand black women answered the government's call to work in the war factories (Harley, Wilson, and Logan 2002). During that time, therefore, many white southern women would have been forced to do their own cleaning, cooking, ironing, and so forth.

Across the centuries, domestic service has been considered a low-status occupation and one composed of people, mostly women, regarded as social and racial inferiors. Such work was intergenerational; many of the women Rollins interviewed had mothers in the same line of work. Older domestics attributed their drift into this work to their race and to the lack of alternatives. The degree to which they expressed job satisfaction depended on the relationship that developed between them and household members, a finding echoed by Sally McMillen (1992) in reference to house servants in the days of slavery. Generally, all these women preferred to work for women employers as a means of protection from an unmarried man's sexual advances.

In her occupational history *Labor of Love, Labor of Sorrow,* Jacqueline Jones (2010) provides a factual context for our discussion. Her conclusions concerning the state of domestic service in the United States were derived from a study of information collected by the Freedmen's Bureau and census data for more recent times. Just before the Civil War, Jones tells us, enslaved women formed the bulk of the agricultural labor force. Upon emancipation, former slaves were able to labor for their own families, but the nature of their work resembled that of the work they performed during slavery. The hours were incredibly long and the labor—whether in the fields or in the homes of white people—was intensive. Wherever they worked, exploitation was rampant. The lack of protection for the workers left them vulnerable to being cheated out of wages, and having to endure unsanitary or unsafe working conditions. Unlike sharecropping, work in the homes of white families was largely solitary and could be terrifically lonely.

All the researchers Jones consulted on this subject were impressed with the fortitude shown by the black women under very trying circumstances. The contribution of each family member was crucial to the family's survival, and survive they did. As is typical of the rural community, there was a great deal of sharing of bounty and other resources. The collective work ethos meant that family was helping family; this collective ethos extended to the whole community and provided an avenue for personal identity other than that of maid (Harley, Wilson, and Logan 2002).

Coping Mechanisms

So how did these black women forced to serve white families, often at the expense of their own families, cope? They coped, according to the literature, by comparing themselves favorably with their white counterparts (Tucker), mainly on moral grounds. Strategies of coping inevitably included mocking their employers and their idiosyncratic ways behind their backs. Jacklyn Cock (1989) refers to such "rituals of rebellion" by her South African interviewees.

Domestic servants gained a form of power over their employers in that they knew many of the employers' family secrets. Rollins refers to this as their intimate knowledge of the Other. Another means of coping was for those who worked in homes of the socially prominent to identify themselves with the high status of their employer. In all these ways, the household help maintained their self-respect under conditions that otherwise were insulting and demeaning.

The agency of southern black women, even under slavery, was revealed, as Judith Rollins indicates, in ways they found to earn extra money for their families. Thus, when their domestic chores were done, they sold excess produce from their own gardens, served as midwives, quilted, and weaved cloth. Mature women sometimes branched out on their own, taking in laundry at their own homes, for example. Taking in laundry, in fact, was one of the most common occupations for older, married black women in the rural South

(Harley, Wilson, and Logan 2002). Being self-employed as "washerwomen" gave the black women a degree of independence they did not have when they worked at the pleasure of other people. In the absence of modern appliances, laundering was very tough work. Cleaning clothes over a washtub, bleaching, starching, and pressing them with heavy irons was grueling work that could take all day.

A washerwoman's strike—organized to coincide with the first world's fair in the South—took place in Atlanta and other southern cities in 1881. The laundry workers, barely out of slavery, displayed leadership in their fight for a uniform wage rate for their labor. This example of direct action provided the basis for future strikes and helped southern black women recognize the power of collective action in demanding higher wages and better working conditions (T. Hunter 1997). Organizations such as the Cooks' Union were important resources for enhancing the survival of wage-earning black women, including domestic workers (T. Hunter 1997). Anecdotal reports from 1930s New Orleans tell of effective organizing by domestic servants who before that time had been forced to serve the white families their Sunday dinner. Following this collective stand, Sunday was always guaranteed as a day off for the maids.

Historically, the prime example of modern collective agency shown by black domestics took place in Montgomery, Alabama, in 1955. When a group of these women, following the lead of Rosa Parks, refused to ride segregated buses to work at great personal sacrifice, they were in effect shrugging off the image of the faithful slave, the loving black mammy (McElra 2007). Through their organization and endurance—many had to walk miles every day to work in the white side of town—this year-long boycott catapulted Martin Luther King to national leadership and marked the beginning of blacks' struggle for civil rights in the United States. The role that domestic workers played in launching the civil rights movement should not be overlooked. Their nonviolent resistance and determination raised the consciousness of a nation and marked an important turning point in the political life of the nation. Their triumph over injustice is magnificently captured in the 1990 film *The Long Walk Home,* starring Sissy Spacek and Whoopi Goldberg. An earlier Hollywood production, *Giant,* featuring Elizabeth Taylor and Rock Hudson and released in 1956, was an eye-opener to many viewers concerning the wretched conditions facing Mexican American servants and others in west Texas.

Many domestic servants fought for racial equality as active members of the

NAACP, but they kept their membership secret so as not to put their jobs at the risk since many in the white community strongly opposed this organization. From the 1930s, the NAACP had worked to have domestic workers included in the Social Security Act, a goal that was finally achieved in 1952. Fannie Fullerwood, who worked as a domestic for a white family, was serving as president of the St. Augustine, Florida, NAACP in 1963, when President Lyndon Johnson visited the city. The St. Augustine branch of the NAACP was then engaged in a battle to end segregation in the city ("St. Augustine's" 2010), and they hoped to get support from the federal government, a goal that was not achieved until the following year with the passage of the Civil Rights Act.

THE LATINA DOMESTIC EXPERIENCE

As recently as 1930, 45 percent of all Mexican women employed in the United States worked as domestics. In studies conducted in western Texas and New Mexico, Romero (1992) reports, domestic work was by far the predominant occupation for young Chicana women. In the late 1960s, a huge number of visas were granted to live-in domestic servants from Mexico. Romero's findings, based on her interviews with Chicana domestics, reveal a remarkable similarity in almost every respect to those provided in the research on African American domestic workers.

Mary Romero drew on her own past as a servant in her research on Chicana women in metropolitan Denver, Colorado. As a young adolescent, Romero herself had worked as a maid. "I was subjected," she wrote, "to constant supervision and condescending observations about 'what a good little girl I was, helping my mother clean house'" (5). But after doing some very heavy work, she felt more like a full-blown maid than a little girl helping her mother. Her return to domestic service years later as a graduate student conducting research confirmed her earlier observations that members of the households with maids were sloppy and spoiled. In her sociological study of the attitudes of Chicana domestic workers and their employers in the Denver area, Romero found that the Chicana women chose this line of work because it paid better than the comparable low-skilled work available and was more flexible in terms of work schedules.

"Emotional labor" is the term Romero uses to describe the psychological aspect of this work and of the mistress-maid relationship. She finds, like

Rollins and Tucker, that the workers were required not only to do the cleaning, but also to fulfill the psychological needs of members of the family. "They are expected," she said, "to perform the emotional labor of 'mothering' both the women employers and their families" (106). This statement refers to situations where the employee was older than the employer. Traditionally, the older woman was expected to advise the younger ones on matters pertaining to household and family crises. They were expected, over time, to provide love for the children and to mother other household members as well. Companionship was a form of emotional labor expected and highly desired by elderly employers living alone.

The unique aspects of domestic service—the lopsided gift giving, the stigma of the work, the insider viewpoint concerning all the goings-on in a particular white family, the poor working conditions, the neglect of the servant as a whole person with her own family and community, etc.—are, as Romero (1992) indicates, universals that seem to inevitably occur with this line of work.

Doméstica, by Pierrette Hondagneu-Sotelo (2001), takes us behind the scenes into the world of transnational domestic work in Los Angeles. In her surveys of 153 Latina domestic workers, the author finds that the majority had obtained their jobs through referrals but that many of the live-in domestics were more likely to rely on a domestic employment agency. Hondagneu-Sotelo uses the term "nanny/housekeeper" to describe the dual occupational roles required of many. The nanny/housekeepers, as evidenced in the interviews, often complained that the children in the homes where they worked were emotionally neglected but spoiled with material possessions. Others, however, prided themselves on getting these children to mind and behave. And sometimes the relationships between child and servant grew so close that the parents got jealous.

Whereas most of the live-in workers were single, the married women sought jobs as day workers. Some of the women interviewed were grateful for the treatment that was given to them; most, however, had complaints and especially toward foreign employers. Many of the employers, in fact, are immigrants themselves who bring to the United States cultural expectations they learned in their native countries. Women who work for them are at risk of being overworked and underpaid.

In her interviews with white employers, often professional women, Hondagneu-Sotelo found them often too embarrassed or ashamed to discuss their employment arrangements. Of the interviewees who were willing to talk, few had hired African Americans. Their preference was for Latina immigrant women, whom they saw as more hardworking and reliable.

DOMESTIC SERVICE IN OTHER COUNTRIES

To discover if there are universals about the nature of domestic servitude that emerge in different places in difference times, we can explore international literature on the sociology of this kind of work.

Research from South Africa

To learn the facts on servitude in South Africa, we can look to the research of Jacklyn Cock (1989), who conducted a sociological investigation for her book *Maids and Madams: Domestic Workers under Apartheid.* Keep in mind that the laws regarding separation of the races in South Africa were far more severe than those in the rural South. Other than that, the interviews of domestic workers and their employees indicate that the working expectations and the maid-mistress relationship were strikingly similar across continents. In most cases, the employer considered the black woman as one of the family, while in no case did the employee voice the same opinion. Domestic servants complained that their employers seemed to view them only in their occupational roles. They are given privileges but no rights, and are not expected to voice opinions or express their feelings. The role they play is in large part a performance, with the correct performance often involving a degree of obsequiousness. The gift giving itself is intended to seal their loyalty at the same time that it reinforces the hierarchical nature of the relationship. This expression of maternalism consigns the worker to a dependent and subordinate position in the household. Significantly, only 10 percent of the employers in the sample knew their domestic workers' full names. The blacks did at times seek help from the white families, usually related to legal issues. As elsewhere, much of the nature of the work involves intimate contact with the employer, and yet the social relationship is highly formalized.

One difference here is that Cock does not report an intense emotional relationship between the lady of the house and her servant; instead, the interaction is formal and limited to communication concerning the housekeeping tasks. Cock attributes the reserve shown by the employers in her sample to the fact that they were English-speaking; Afrikaans-speaking (of Dutch ancestry) employers are considered less formal and warmer in their dealings with servants.

In 2011, according to information on a South African marketing website, an estimated 1 million people worked as domestics (SouthAfrica.info, 2011). In many cities, almost every home has "domestic quarters" in the yard or garden. In response to a history of rampant exploitation and abuse by employers, the government has taken significant steps to improve their situation: a minimum wage has been set, specific working conditions have been established, and training programs for the workers have been instituted.

The Traditional British Nanny and Servants in the Household

The most comprehensive research on the profession of the British nanny is provided by the journalist Jonathan Gathorne-Hardy (1973) in his *The Unnatural History of the Nanny*. What is interesting for our purposes is the book's description of the social roles played in homes of great wealth by nannies, governesses, and servants. Drawing on an extensive review of novels, biographies, and autobiographies, Gathorne-Hardy juxtaposes literary passages that include descriptions of children and their nannies with excerpts from interviews with women who worked as nannies and with people who grew up with nannies. Thirty-four interviews were conducted altogether.

The nanny's role was to take care of small children and to socialize them to follow the norms of upper-class society. The nanny is not to be confused with a governess, who was a highly educated woman and teacher of older children. Described as occupying a place in the household that was midway between the parents and the servants, nannies tended to be working-class, but they clearly identified with the values—and sometimes the snobbery—of the class they served.

In his discussion of the British nanny, Gathorne-Hardy also provides a historic portrait of the roles of domestic servants. In Britain, the nanny institution evolved uniquely over time and was firmly established by the eighteenth century. A whole domestic servant class grew up, and by 1939, when British wealth reached its highest point, there were around three hundred thousand women working as nannies and a servant class of more than 1 million. World War II, however, in the words of the author, "finished them off" (184) as a force of social significance. As in the United States, former domestic servants moved into more lucrative jobs in the war industry.

Up until the time of the social upheaval brought about by the war, the servant's place in life was accepted by themselves and their "betters" to be waiting, serving, and performing all the unpleasant physical functions in a household. Having a staff of servants in a wealthy household opened the door to the nanny occupying a special place. In contrast to the role of domestic servant, the nanny was a single woman who lived in the home and did not have to engage in housework tasks or cooking. Often, as described in *The Unnatural History of the Nanny,* the cook showed great resentment in being ordered by the nanny to cook entirely special meals for the nursery. Because many of the nannies received special education in their occupation at a nursery training college, they felt very superior to the servants, and many squabbles ensued between nanny and servant.

With domestic servants taking care of the housework chores, the nanny could devote her nurturing efforts entirely to the small children. In contrast to the situation in the American South, therefore, British children's attachments were not to their servants but to the nanny in whose care they were placed. And since in the very wealthy families—as shown in *Upstairs, Downstairs,* the BBC's popular TV series that ran in the early 1970s, and the more recent Downton Abbey—a whole staff of servants was the rule, these women tended to bond with each other rather than with members of the family for whom they worked. Strikingly, in contrast to the servant whose role it was to follow orders, the nanny seems to have been autonomous and to have had almost complete authority over the children. Their role was often that of mother, as Gathorne-Hardy describes: "Once having entered the family as mother, nannies took on, as far as the children went, many other prerogatives. The children were always "their" children: "She was my third child" (131).

Because many of these caretakers, in Gathorne-Hardy's account, were devoted to children and even exhibited some childlike characteristics, their charges often returned their love and went to them for advice later in life. The mothers in the families described in the book were typically very distant, sometimes idolized by the children. Just as the kitchen was the habitat of the maid, the nursery was the "kingdom" of the nanny. An interesting similarity between the British nanny and the live-in American maid is that the term "nurse" is commonly applied to them both, a word that originally was, according to the *Oxford English Dictionary*, "wet-nurse." Another similarity is that, like the uniformed domestic worker, the nanny "wore Nanny clothes" (137). Still, and more importantly, parallels exist in the statements of adults who grew up in the care of nannies who helped shield them from tensions and other difficulties within the family, and some southern white adults among our interviewees who similarly stated that their black maids gave them a sense of stability in a chaotic or hostile environment (see chapter 7).

Domestic Workers Globally

In her discussion of domestic workers who migrate from poor countries to rich societies—for example, Europe, Canada, and the oil-rich nations of the Middle East—Hondagneu-Sotelo (2001) indicates that even many women who are highly educated in their own countries are willing to do domestic work in foreign lands. Canada and Hong Kong formally recruit such workers, who must sometimes endure a status that Hondagneu-Sotelo likens to "indentured servitude" (20) as live-ins for a designated period of time before they can move into other lines of work. In Hong Kong, the rules are especially strict pertaining to the behavior of the worker, who usually comes from the Philippines.

Global Woman, edited by Barbara Ehrenreich and Arlie Hochschild (2003), also describes the plight of the Filipina woman in Hong Kong. Forced to sign a contract that states the domestic worker can be shipped home at any time for violating the rules, these women are subjected to much psychological abuse. Regulations stipulate matters pertaining to hair styles, makeup, submission to pregnancy tests, and work timetables. *Global Woman* details the strict working conditions that women of the Third World face in Greece, Taiwan, Japan, Qatar, and the United States, where they are often abused and exploited. Many times such migrant live-in domestics are required to work around the clock and not allowed to leave the home. Similar to the recent situation in the American South, there are no legal safeguards for the workers, whose lot is strongly dependent on the kindness and ethics of the employer.

We will now briefly return to the history of the southern domestic workers to describe their paths onward to a new life with new possibilities.

(3) The Women of the Great Migration

And the Lord said unto Moses, Depart, and go up hence, thou and the people which thou hast brought up out of the land of Egypt, unto the land which I sware unto Abraham, to Isaac, and to Jacob, saying, Unto thy seed will I give it.

—EXODUS 33:1–2

AS EARLY AS 1917, the *Chicago Defender*, the nation's most significant black newspaper, began a drive to lure southern blacks to leave behind Jim Crow and dire poverty for a life of promise in the North. The *Defender*, in fact, became the primary cheerleader for northward migration. During World War I, as so many men were recruited to war, the departure of workers created a vacuum that blacks from the South could fill. Southern whites fought against this migration, sometimes attacking blacks traveling north on trains, and in some places outlawing the distribution of the *Defender* (Lemann 1992).

The United States experienced another vast labor shortage when the nation entered World War II. Given the drawbacks of domestic servitude, it is not surprising that during wartime so many of these women flocked into high-paying jobs related to the war industry. But as soon as the men returned from the war, the women were sent packing. Once again their occupational choices were limited. But by then both agricultural and domestic employment had undergone major changes related to the new technologies, for example, mechanical cotton pickers and combines for the farm and washing machines and refrigerators for the home (Jones 2010). The northward migration, which had started around the turn of the century, was spurred onward as employment opportunities continued to open up in the cities of the industrial North. By the time it was over—and it lasted until the 1970s, when the southern white codes came down—some 6 million black southerners had left the South, forever changing the cultural landscape of American society. In *The Warmth of Other Suns: The Epic Story of America's Great Migration* (2010) Isabel Wilkerson calls this exodus the most "underreported story of the twentieth century" (9).

Wilkerson's story of the Great Migration is an epic in itself. She talked to 1,200 people before choosing just three as representative of the whole. Her quest was to determine not whether life was better today for the migrants in the urban North but how they had summoned the courage to leave in the first place, what drove them onward. Of the 1,200 she interviewed, not one of them, she said, mentioned the boll weevil or the conditions for growing cotton. Instead, they talked about Jim Crow, and about lynching and the constant mistreatment from which there was no escape. They were escaping one form of violence.

Elizabeth Clark-Lewis uniquely suggests that some of the migrant women were escaping from another form of violence as well—violence within their own families. Her thesis is that as word spread of favorable job opportunities in the North, women who wished to escape from acts of violence committed by parents, stepparents, husbands, and boyfriends would have found a means to migrate. We did not find this to be the case, however, with any of the women who came forward to share their life stories. All the women we interviewed spoke of close family ties, had fond memories of their home communities, and gave other reasons for making the move, usually related to joining loved ones and/or in search of better opportunities.

As the men moved to work in meatpacking, railroad shops, and other industries, their women moved with them. Southern black women, as Micki McElya (2007) suggests, were in big demand as servants since their countrified ways appealed to their urban employers, who found them tractable and easy to please. In hiring a maid, white employers sought workers who spoke with southern accents and colloquialisms. In so doing, McElya argues, they were "listening for the mammy's soft, loving croon described so often in plantation fiction" (214). They were probably also seeking workers who had been socialized to show what was seen as a proper degree of humility and respect for the employer.

As European immigration rates declined and new opportunities for the women created a shortage of domestic servants, southern blacks replaced immigrant housekeepers in the urban cities in large numbers. By 1950, according to Jacqueline Jones (2010), almost one-third of African Americans in the United States were residing in the North and the West.

Although the North figured prominently in the migrants' dreams and hopes, it was not the promised land that many expected. Women migrants, according to Lisa Boehm (2009), "would go on to face the feelings of displacement, economic uncertainty, and persistent discrimination in their new northern homes" (43). Beverly Bunch-Lyons (2002), similarly, found that simply crossing the Ohio River did not mean racial divisions were no more, and former servants moved into service jobs in the public sector such as cleaning hotels or working in the kitchens of restaurants. One striking fact that our interviews reveal is that in Iowa, only blacks with lighter complexions could get the better-paying jobs in the department stores and other establishments. While black men could secure factory work, most of the black women were relegated to various forms of domestic labor.

Homesickness for the southern landscape and climate was inevitable. In *Living In, Living Out* (1996), Clark-Lewis documents the hardships that southern African American women faced as domestic workers in Washington, D.C. Over time, however, new networks developed, churches grew, and the southern migrants located remunerative work. Church life helped bridge the gap between southern and northern living patterns.

Some of the most negative images of northern life for the second generation of migrants from the South can be found in the black novels set in that period. Ann Petry's *The Street* (1946) tells the story of a single mother struggling against racial and class obstacles in a Harlem ghetto. In the book, the narrator likens the Harlem streets to northern "lynch mobs" (323), describing as "drudges" the older black women who work as domestic servants and who walk on the sides of their shoes because their feet hurt so much.

The Nobel Prize–winning novelist Toni Morrison (1970), whose grandparents moved from Alabama to Ohio as a part of the Great Migration, and who herself benefited from the educational advantages she received in the Midwest, provides a decidedly negative portrayal of the life of domestics and their families in the North. *The Bluest Eye*, which was written at the height of the civil rights struggles although published somewhat later, is the story of a black girl, Pecola, whose mother devotes all her energy to the white family for whom she works. Through her neglect and societal images of white superiority, Pecola develops contempt for her own racial identity. Her obsession is to have blue eyes; this is the only standard of beauty she knows. Then everybody will love her, she thinks, and above all, she will love herself. Through her novel, Morrison effectively shows the harm that institutional racism does to the black family.

Kristin Hunter, in *God Bless the Child* (1964), similarly describes a situation in which a domestic worker is overly absorbed in her service to a rich white family. The maid's granddaughter, the main character in the book, is so determined to rise from rags to riches that she works at three jobs. Her frenzied pursuit of the American dream is her eventual ruination.

Research shows that, for their part, the migrants were generally pleased with the improved labor conditions in the North, with wages three or four times those paid in the South and with the more businesslike working atmosphere (see McElya 2007; and Clark-Lewis 1996). These observations are confirmed in our maid narratives. As we will see, many women of the Great Migration moved from towns such as Durant, Mississippi, to Waterloo, Iowa. Some resumed an education that had been of necessity arrested. Others felt it was too late for them, but not for their children or their children's children, to achieve the dream that for them was forever deferred. Only in Iowa, in these midwestern cities, would these African Americans begin to feel less dependent on individual whites, become more clearly citizens and agents of their own lives instead of people trapped by an economic and political system of racial exploitation.

THE MIGRATION TO WATERLOO, IOWA

The city that took its name from the place where the British defeated Napoleon's army was home to a burgeoning meatpacking industry, a railroad, and farm implement manufacturing. The influx of African Americans to northeast Iowa began as early as 1915, when the Illinois Central went to northern Mississippi and recruited hundreds of black men to replace striking workers (Barnes and Bumpers 2000). The hostility to the newcomers was predictably strong: not only were they of a different race from the native population, but they were also strikebreakers (Kinney 2011). Housing was denied to them except along the railroad tracks, and that is the area where the Waterloo black community exists today. As the strike was settled, blacks retained many of the jobs, and they brought their families up from the South. One of the first things the newcomers did was to build churches. An NAACP chapter formed in Waterloo in 1920 to advocate for the end of segregation. The next generation continued to fight for their rights, and the city offered them much greater opportunities than had been available to the previous generation.

The women of the Great Migration who came to Iowa with their menfolk or at the beckoning of relatives who had made the trip before them experienced considerable improvement in their standard of living, a fact to which many of the migrant women's stories attest. Many of the opportunities provided to the African American men and women, however, came only after a struggle. In Waterloo, segregated housing and school-district boundaries contributed to significant racial segregation in the public schools. Residents of the black community who were active in grassroots organizations such as the NAACP were able ultimately "to bring about some growth in political freedom, local dignity, and economic advancement" (Barnes and Bumpers, 2000, 93). Protests were launched against unequal treatment in employment, housing, and the de facto segregation that kept black students attending black schools and white students attending white schools.

In 1967, in response to demonstrations, the Waterloo School Board issued its first-ever statement of support for school desegregation. One of the initiatives that emerged from this support was the Bridgeway Project at Grant Elementary School (Barnes and Bumpers 2000). This project achieved, through families' elective participation, a student population at Grant Elementary that was nearly evenly balanced between blacks and whites. Increased black student enrollment also occurred at the laboratory school of the local university. Busing, however, was actively opposed by the Anti-Busing Neighborhood Schools Association. Many blacks in the community were dissatisfied with the integration efforts. Dr. Robert Harvey, a black dentist and a member of the Waterloo School Board, began to voice concerns, while others, like the League of Women Voters, the Concerned Parents of Waterloo, and the NAACP, mobilized to advocate for the desegregation of Waterloo Schools. In November 1972, the Iowa State Board of Education issued nondiscrimination guidelines that ended racial isolation in Iowa's public schools. This opened the door for Waterloo to adopt a desegregation plan to be implemented in Waterloo's elementary schools the following year. Many of Waterloo's children, such as Charletta Sudduth, were to benefit greatly from this development.

SHARING THE STORIES

Some of those who participated in the Great Migration are reluctant to share their memories of the past. Although our storytellers were only too eager to share, the religious columnist Karris Golden (2010) reports that her relatives who migrated from the South will tell her little of their previous lives: "One was a 'domestic' during the 1940s and 1950s, and it seems an embarrassing memory for her. I wonder: How many of our mothers, grandmothers, aunts and cousins are ashamed of such work histories? Should such memories cause humiliation or be a source of pride?" (B4).

Fortunately, many others do take pride in the hardships they endured, the respect they received in the community, and the many skills they acquired fending for themselves out in the country. And they take pride in the fact that they were part of a movement that was bigger than themselves, a movement that parallels that of the immigrants who came to America to start all over in a new place.

The black participants in this historic migration to a better and more fulfilling life, however, do not always get the recognition in the history books or media that is accorded to the European immigrants, or the credit given the African Americans who escaped slavery through the Underground Railroad. And, sadly, some among the younger generations of African Americans reportedly criticize their elders today for what they see as passive acquiescence to a cruel system of social control. This accusation is described by Grady, a former maid, whom Howell Raines has memorialized in his Pulitzer Prize–winning essay "Grady's Gift" (1991). Here was a woman who tried so hard to overcome the barriers put in her way, and yet was chided years later by one of her New York–raised sons for "taking it" back in the old days in Birmingham. Grady tells Raines about this in their reunion several decades later. Such criticism of those who survived segregation in the South arises from an ignorance of the realities of the time. Far from "taking it," these men and women from the South packed their bags and said good-bye to all that in their migration north. Many risked their lives in the civil rights movement that ended segregation. No, they decidedly did not "take it." At least two of our storytellers mention being criticized by younger family members for their passivity in the face of injustice. Younger generations need to read the stories that follow.

Part II

The Maid Narratives

(4) In Their Own Words

Black women working as maids in white homes had first-hand experiences to prove money did not guarantee happiness, well-being, or integrity.
—BELL HOOKS, *Sisters of the Yam*

She said, "Baby, Mamma got to leave again." And I would cry.
—TESTIMONY FROM IRENE WILLIAMS

NOW WE COME to the heart of the book—the maid narratives as they were told to us. These are the women of the Great Migration.

We continue the history chronicled in the previous chapters with these stories told from firsthand experience by people who were there. Missing from much of the mainstream historical documentation is the richness of detail and the feeling memories—the sounds, smells, and emotions—that can be obtained only in the personal narrative. Also missing from most traditional accounts is a focus on the social life of women or an emphasis on the roles played by the cleaning lady or cook who sometimes, as we will see, even lived in a back room of the white household. No, the history books are more concerned with explorers, migrations, political leaders, and, of course, conquest and wars. Our concern is with the ordinary people, and given that many of them—these people of the Great Migration—are still living, all we had to do was to locate them and ask for their stories.

Seven out of thirteen of the individuals whose narratives are contained in this section moved up from Mississippi and surrounding states and settled in Waterloo, Iowa. As early as 1900, Waterloo was known as the "Factory City" of Iowa. Once the first group of settlers made the move to work on the railroads, earned decent wages, and brought their family members to join them, wave after wave followed. Our interviewees whose stories follow arrived at different ages, though most came as young adults, and at different times. The most recent wave of African American workers arrived in the 1950s to work for the still-expanding meat factories in Waterloo and Des Moines. Most of these migrant women came from Mississippi and moved in conjunction with the men in their families, but some came to join their sisters and aunts. Our narrators in this chapter are all connected with the Great Migration in one way or another. The one exception is the final storyteller, an Iowa professor who came much later to join the faculty and who, upon hearing of the maids project, contacted the authors and said, "I, too, have a story."

To preserve the richness of the expression and individuality of each contribution, we have edited the transcripts as little as possible, letting the storytellers speak for themselves. Where necessary to account for an abrupt change in subject, we have included the interviewer's questions; elsewhere, we have removed them. The questions are given in italics. We have arranged the thirteen transcripts by age of the interviewees, from oldest to youngest. The women worked as maids and cooks in Mississippi, Louisiana, and Arkansas, and after their move to Iowa, several continued in domestic work. The contrast in working conditions and relationships with the employers is striking.

Threaded through all these testimonials is a strain of collective consciousness—a sense of history as known only by others of the same race and region. Even across the span of years represented by these storytellers—some of whom were children of the Great Depression and others of more modern times—there is much common ground. There is common ground both in what they endured as southern blacks and in the decision they made to get on that train and venture north. They went through so many of the same things and cherished the same things, namely, their families, their church life, and their hopes for a better tomorrow. And now, as you will see, many among them are calling out to the younger generations to hear their stories and not only to hear them but to listen, and through the listening, to understand.

Elra Johnson, from Durant, Mississippi (born 1906). Interviewed by David W. Jackson. "They didn't want no Negroes to have no freedom."

Several years before the present project got under way, David W. Jackson conducted this interview as part of an oral history project on prominent residents of Waterloo, Iowa. Although the focus of that project was not domestic service, we were able to supplement Elra Johnson's interview with a follow-up interview with her son, J. B. McCellan, and a story by Pat Kinney in the January 22, 2006, *Waterloo–Cedar Falls Courier* that featured Johnson's life. As Kinney writes: "She remembers how the whites she worked for distrusted her. How

Elra Johnson from Durant, Mississippi, at age one hundred. *Photo by Rick Chase. Reprinted with permission of the Waterloo-Cedar Falls Courier.*

they made her come in the back door to cook, clean house or babysit. She remembers how they would eyeball her when she left to make sure nothing was stolen—though theft was contrary to her upbringing" (C1). On the tape, Elra Johnson speaks with a stridency in her voice, a stridency that had led her earlier in life to defy the Jim Crow laws and stand for freedom well before such a stand was popular. She died at the age of 102.

I was born January 28, 1906, in Mississippi, and I grew up on a farm. My daddy had a farm. Now I think, if I am not making a mistake, he had 290 acres. We worked on the farm, plowing with a mule. I'd tie him up. And when I'd get to the end of the rope, I'd tie that end of it, and tie that mule to the post.

I worked like the devil! There was no time for play *[laughing]*. No, there was no fun, we had to work! Yes, we did.

My father was a tall, dark man with good hair. He influenced me. He called me "Black Gal." He said "Black Gal, you do that thing that's right and don't let nobody turn you around."

We can fill in some facts here relevant to domestic service from an interview of 2009 with J. B. McCellan, Mrs. Johnson's son. We learn from this son that as this family was hard-working and prosperous, his mother did not have to do domestic work if she didn't want to, and that she would not have put up with any nonsense. She enjoyed working for the McCullaghs, as her son tells below.

> I wasn't brought up by my mother; I was brought up by my grandmother. This is what I know: Mr. McCullagh had about 2,000 acres of land and owned a good-sized store. He had all these people working for him, working on his place. The McCullaghs had one son, and my mother took care of the boy, getting him off to school to the school bus and watching him after school. She worked for them for three or four years. They treated her just like family.
>
> She cooked for the field hands, the people who worked for Mr. McCullagh. When she got through with that, she went back to the house. And then she'd go out and cook dinner, and then she'd go back to her house. Then she'd go fix supper and clean up, and then she'd go back to the house. But she did get paid for the whole day.

One of my first jobs was that I started a sewing business; I sewed for the public. And I can make anything a person wears. The coats, the pants, what they wear. And I don't have to have anything but a machine. I sewed for everybody in the community and some out of the community. I wouldn't sell a shirt for no more than about a dollar. And it had to be a nice one otherwise I didn't get that much.

All the time people came to me. Listen here, it was me, and Georgia Clark, were the two seamstresses amongst the colored race coming up in my towns. And Georgia Clark lived in West. And she took care of West and I took care of Bowling Green and Durant.

Later I got a nursing degree. I wanted to take care of sick people. When somebody was sick, I always wanted to help somebody. I worked at the Durant Hospital. My name's on the record, you can call them up there if you want *[laughs]*. I like helping people. And then a white girl, she was from West, and her name was—oh, I can't think of her name now! *[laughs]*. But anyways, me and her worked together.

I worked only with black patients. White patients did not want to be with us, period. So no, I didn't care. And I used to take care of white people's babies while they go out and do their little thing.

Georgia Clark and I worked in the people's houses we were working for.

We weren't supposed to go in their front door. Yes, the black people were supposed to go to the back door. It really bothered me and so I quit. Yeah, I did! I sure did! *[laughs]*. Let me say one thing. White folks give Negroes hell. I hate to say it like that, but you couldn't come in their front door; you couldn't eat out of their plates. And when they had a dog, they put its food on its plate and let it eat, and then they'd take that same plate and give it to you to eat. We just walked out. Me and Georgia seen them do it and just walked out. And us didn't go back no more.

Interviewer: Can you talk about your involvement in the civil rights movement?

I was the head. Georgia Clark was right side of me. Yes, I get up anyway in Mississippi on that courthouse and tell everything I knew about white folks and what they did. And I wasn't scared. Because I had white folks standing behind me, and sitting there, if they wasn't saying anything, then good-bye to them. And me and Georgia Clark done it. Just broke that civil rights, broke it down.

We weren't scared of the devil. I was a member of the Mississippi Freedom Democratic Party. Me and Georgia Clark decided how they treated our old parents in the front and said now us ain't gonna let them do us like that. When I was asked, "Now, do they let you come in the front door?" I says, "No." They be sitting on the porch and tell you to go on around and come in, and then come back to the front porch.

And so me and her got out and protested. Us got by with it, too, and that opened the door for the next fellow behind me to come in.

That's what us did. And us did it like the devil, too! They didn't want us in there, but us went on in there anyway. And they would tell us, "Go around to the back door." And I said, "I will when I be going home" *[laughs]*. And then when I come in there, come in the front door. They didn't want us to do that. But the police and the law told us, "Don't ever go in a fellow's back door. Go in the front." And us done what the police told us to do. And the police was out there watching to see that us do what they say. And us went right in that front door. And they didn't like it. And so they [the racists] hopped up and moved to Memphis or somewhere. I don't know where they moved. They didn't come back no more.

One man in Durant wanted to kill me and Georgia for getting on the streets, singing, "We shall overcome some day." Yes, we were marching, me and Georgia Clark. And we tried to get some of the other black people. They'd say, "Now I'm living on Mr. So-and-So's place. If I get out there in that march, I got to move." You know we just told them, "Forget it!" But me and Georgia Clark done it.

In the Delta, they'd say "No! No! I'm living on the man's place!" That was in the Delta. And he said, "If I get out there, I got to move."

Interviewer: You mean you're saying that blacks would not join in the fight for fear of the loss of their land?

Right! Now you talking!

Me and Georgia Clark and Reverend Reddiger led the march down the highway. And us got on this side of that road and let the other folk go on that other side. And just was singing as loud as we could sing, "We shall overcome some day." And they ain't all black neither. Sure ain't! Some white people don't believe in mistreating Negroes. No they don't. Some white folks were in the NAACP. And they the ones that stood up on their feet and told us what to do and how to do it. See you get out there in the middle of the road. See the highway is free for everybody. Used to get out there on the highway and do it.

Interviewer: Did you get to go to Washington, D.C.?

Yes sir. The peoples got together, got the money, and sent me to Washington, D.C., to talk to Lyndon Johnson. I also talked to President Kennedy; he was for the blacks. I liked him *[laughs].* He took up for blacks. He listened to me and Georgia Clark. When us got back, some of the whites said they gone do this and they gone do that. But Johnson said, "Anybody put their hand on ya'll, they got to go."

Interviewer: How about other things you did, like your involvement with Head Start?

I was—I worked with the Head Start, with the little children. And what they did then, they put black kids and white kids in the same class. The whites at first had their children going there and our children here. But when they got it going, all of them got together. When I was little, white kids and black children at our mom's and daddy's house played together. And when Mom would get the food ready, she'd say. "Ya'll children come on in." All us went on in there and set down in there. It wasn't no different.

Interviewer: Can you tell about the time when the KKK came to your house?

They had robes, all that stuff on. My husband got out of the way. But I dealt with them! Yes I did. But I tell you one thing, they couldn't scare me.

Interviewer: Did they say anything to you?

Not a word. And I sat there on the porch and didn't say nothing to them. My husband got out of the way. But I dealt with them! Yes I did. . . . [When they first arrived] they hit the ground. And when they hit the ground, then that's when they went to doing that scaring, thinking they gonna get somebody to run from their own house. But I didn't. Nope. They burned up a cross in my yard. I didn't even move. They was acting a fool, and I didn't move. But I had something right here *[motions to her side]*. Yeah, I had a gun, and I bet I had as many shells as they had. That's right! I ain't telling you no story on that! And they got scared. I know they must of seen them or something. But anyway they got scared and left.

Interviewer: Why do you think the KKK went to your house?

They didn't want no Negroes to have no freedom.

Interviewer: Can you tell about your move to Waterloo?

After my husband died, I come to Waterloo. My folks up here; my relatives are in Waterloo. And I just never went back home.

In Waterloo I took care of the old peoples. I love to help sick folks. Because one day I'm going to be sick and I want somebody to help me.

I joined the Payne Memorial A.M.E. Church. I'm the oldest one of them. I done made it to one hundred. And in my daddy's days, his aunts, some of them lived to be 105.

I don't know, it's whatever the Lord going to do. People ask me what it feels like to be one hundred.

I feel just like I did when I was twelve, I reckon. I don't know! *[laughing]*. Nothing hurts me. I don't hurt nowhere. Nowhere!

Interviewer: What would you tell young people on how to live to be one hundred?

You can't tell them nothing. No.

Pearline Sisk Jones, from Taylor and Oxford, Mississippi (born 1918). Interviewed by Charletta Sudduth. "I worked in the home of William Faulkner."

In this interview, Charletta Sudduth got in touch with her great-aunt, her mother's sister, who now resides in a nursing home in Jackson. Sudduth is affectionately known to her aunt as "Pumpkin." Despite her declining health, Pearline Jones sounded delighted to share her memories about "working for white folks," including six months in the home of William Faulkner. By a strange coincidence, Mrs. Jones was interviewed some years ago by David W. Jackson, who was collecting oral histories of African Americans connected to the Great Migration to Waterloo, Iowa. That earlier interview follows Sudduth's.

I was born in 1918 on Hampton's Place in Taylor, Mississippi. We didn't own our land but lived on someone else's land. We stayed in an old barn we had swept and cleaned out, hung some paper up on the walls. We had an old refrigerator, and every time it would turn on, the walls would shake, and my brother, Doc, would laugh. Our sister, Rosie, was a baby then. Them were hard times. A white woman up there at the university [Ole Miss] who was getting her education—a woman getting her education was something—got us out of there, and we moved to Oxford.

The main family I worked for was the Gills. Mr. Gill was so mean. I took care of Eleanor, who was a child, and her mother, Ann. One time Ms. Ann was leaving and had told me not to let Eleanor eat anything before dinner. After she left, Eleanor climbed up on the counter and was getting cookies and her foot hit me in the face. You know, white folks bought good hard, stout shoes. Well, I hit her back before I knowed anything. She started crying.

Pearline Sisk Jones *(right)* with her niece, Annie Pearl Stevenson. *From the family collection of Charletta Sudduth.*

I said, "Oh, Lord," and I started crying too. Her daddy was so mean, and I didn't know what he would do. So when I started crying that stopped her from crying. I said, "Eleanor, we playing, right?" I said, "I'll play doctor on you." I got some water and started rubbing her hands with some lotion and just rubbing her to make sure there was no mark. She did not know what I was doing. I was just rubbing her. I kept telling her we were playing, hoping she wouldn't remember what happened when her mother got home and tell it. She didn't tell it when her mother got home. All she said to her mother was, "Pearline cried, and I cried." I said, "Not hardly." That was it. I said, "Whoa, the Lord heard my prayer." Yeah, we had to talk to the children, read and play with them and be just as good as you can be to them.

Another time I was washing dishes at this same house. They had a coffeepot with one of them glass percolators on top, and that thing slip and fell out of my hands to the floor and broke. When it broke, I thought, "Lord, have mercy; I'm catching it! I'm in trouble now." That evening when Mr. Gill was taking me home, I kept trying to tell him about the percolator. At the time I was saving a jar full of pennies. He said, "You gone have a bunch of money, Pearline," and poking fun. He kept talking and he kept talking and, uh, I couldn't say nothing. Then finally I said, "The percolator slipped and broke." He said, "What good is that coffeepot without the percolator?" We finally got to my home and I was dropped off, and I must have seemed upset because my daughter, Margaret, said, "What is it, Mother?"

Interviewer: How did the white people treat you? What kind of rules did they have?

Sometimes there were some that wouldn't pay you, just give you some ole rags, or something like that, some old clothes. No money to clean up their houses. Many white folks had like a little wash room toward the back of the house for the workers to wash up before entering the main part of the house.

We had to go in and out through the back door. Mr. Gill would say, "Go around yonder to the back door."

I used to take Margaret, my daughter, and Vandie and your mother, Pearl, to show them how to work. So I took Margaret one day. And Margaret said, "The back door look better than the front door" *[laughing]*.

Mr. Gill found out that Margaret and Vandie were going to school. He said, "Them ole gals ain't gone get no education, why they going to school?" Years later after they, Margaret and them, had gotten their education and come back to visit their mother, they rode by the old place in a big car. I sure wished he was there to see they got their education!

Margaret and them can tell you about them ole stories. Sometimes I laugh so long till my mouth gets tired.

When I was working for Mr. Guy B. Taylor, another black lady was working for them. Her name was Annie Murphy; she was the day sitter. I hadn't made it there yet, and Mr. Taylor asked her, "Where is Pearline?" She said, "I don't carry her around in my pocket." Mr. Taylor told her, "Who you talking to?" She said, "I don't know any other way to talk to you but out of my mouth." He said, "You don't know who you talking to. I can get the Klan to come down there." You know, Chile, the Klu Klux Klan! Whoa! *[speaking in a high-pitched voice]* In them days. . . .

Interviewer: That's so scary to hear. Now, on another topic, can you tell about your work at the home of William Faulkner?

I didn't work there that long, maybe about six months. I worked there at that time when I was trying to get a divorce. I cleaned house and sat with who

I believe was his mother-in-law until she died and then with her sister. I remember Mr. Faulkner wearing brim hats, walking very straight and leveled. He loved fried meat and sorghum molasses. Yes, he was a thin, straight man. He enjoyed fried hog, fried soft bacon, biscuits and eggs. He would be sitting in a little screened-in porch in the back of the house off from the kitchen. He would be sitting at a little table reading or writing his works. I didn't talk to him much.

I remember him wearing a black hat, either a derby or brim hat. Mr. William Faulkner's brother was an FBI agent, and he was a writer. Mr. Faulkner used a walking cane, and never tilted his head. He would go to the university and back home. You know he lived right down there in Oxford?

At that time maids were being paid about two dollars an hour, but Mr. Faulkner paid more—about three dollars an hour. Some of the chores I had to do were: I cleaned everything, had to go over them floors, get some oil to make them floors shine, wash the dishes, clean the bathroom with Clorox and Comet, wipe them door knobs and make them shine. I worked so hard. The way I got through all this was I made poems; I wrote poetry out of them jobs. I am old now, but I have some poems at the house, and my granddaughter has some of them on tape.

Interview of 2005 by David W. Jackson

Sitting in her living room in Oxford, Mississippi, Pearline Jones can be seen on the videotape all dressed up for the interview, wearing purple—including purple jewelry—from head to toe. The couch on which she is seated and all the furniture behind her are purple. The subject of the interview was the use of yard art and home decorations by African Americans.

Older people like to have something for company when they're alone. Sometimes you talk to yourself. Sometimes I think of all my poems and poetry, and I laugh. Really, purple is a good color for me. I began to decorate my house in purple about ten years ago. It took a long time because I had a hard time finding pillows to match the couch.

People decorate their yards for any holiday. I would like to have my yard decorated with lights like Ruthie's [her niece, Ruthie O'Neal, whose interview appears in this volume]. I looked at Ruthie's old-fashioned wheel that

William Faulkner's home, Rowan Oak. *Photo by Robert van Wormer*.

Confederate statue in Oxford, Mississippi, town square. *Photo by Robert van Wormer.*

she had in her yard and I thought it made no sense, but then I thought if I had been in a wagon like that, then it would mean a lot.

I worked for a couple of lawyers and doctors. Those people had chandeliers and glass mirrors that covered half the wall. I was shocked at how people could afford all that stuff. They had a white bed upstairs. Today my upstairs is white as well. Ruthie has some things today in her home like the lawyers had. We think alike. We are all made like my father.

Interviewer: Was the color purple for some religious reason—because Jesus wore a purple robe when he was carrying the cross?

No, I just like the color. I used to have purple lights in the yard. I got a lot of things from the lawyers. They got old and were moving. Mrs. Lynch was going to a medicine home, and new people moving in who didn't want that stuff. They were giving these things away. I got a whole set of pitchers and dishes from them, a lot of nice things. But some of the more expensive pieces they thought were too good to give to me, and I didn't get them. Ruthie has her hair purple; I wouldn't want that or to have my walls purple. Ruthie's a sweet girl. I have mine the way I like it, and she has hers the way she likes it.

Vinella Byrd, from Pine Bluff, Arkansas (born 1922). Interviewed by Charletta Sudduth. "The man didn't want me to wash my hands in the wash pan."

This interview with Vinella Byrd took place just six months before her death. A newspaper article that honored her at her passing noted that she was the former director of the Jesse Cosby Center and served on numerous executive boards including the NAACP. She was known in the community as Mother Byrd and described as "a very gracious lady." On the tape she speaks in a quiet, deliberate way.

I worked for two families where I grew up in Pine Bluff, Arkansas. We lived in the country. For the two families I cooked and did housework. I cooked a lot of vegetables and stuff. They ate like we eat now. They farmed and raised their own. We ate corn. I prepared it many ways, boiled and fried.

The women I worked for, the housewives, were fine. I didn't have any really bad experiences. I worked for some pretty nice people. The men were farmers. Some of them worked off the farm, uptown.

Interviewer: What kind of rules did they have?

The man didn't want me to wash my hands in the wash pan. They didn't have a sink. They had a wash pan where you washed your hands. After that, I didn't wash my hands at all. I would just go in and start cooking. He didn't want me to use the same one that he was using. There were no uniforms, and I didn't have to babysit.

I did grow up with one of the white kids. We lived on his farm for a while—Lester was his name. We grew up about the same time. I see him sometimes when I go home now. They let us play together. You know, we were just kids, until we got among other white folks. Then we were separate. That's the way it was back then.

The white folks where I worked learned things from me and I learned things from them. I think the white families learned how to cook from the black workers. I learned a lot of things from the white folks, especially how to cook different things that we, as blacks at the time, didn't cook or couldn't afford. When I was working for the folks and cooking, they ate better than we did. They could buy steaks and varieties of food. They ate a lot of steaks and such. I learned how to get ahead and how to keep house better than what I knew growing up as a kid. We made the beds just the same. We cleaned house the same. Housecleaning is just housecleaning *[laughing]*.

Interviewer: How about education?

The white kids started school in September, and us, the ones who should have been in school, were picking cotton. So that would be different. We didn't get to go to school until the cotton was picked. I think it shaped how I feel about education. I believe education is the most important thing you can have when you are growing up. But you have to also learn to grow up without it. I did not have an education. I went to school at East High after I was married and started having kids. I went to East High at night.

Interviewer: Did any of the white people give you gifts or anything?

Some of them gave me a lot of things and extra money. I think the woman I worked for had a black sister and she was the mistress of the man that owned the store. He was married, but he was into this relationship. Miss Matty, I will never forget her; she used give me a lot of stuff like food that I wasn't able to buy. She lived by herself but it was his house. Looking back now, I think he was better to her than he was to his wife. She had everything. She never had any kids with him.

I didn't experience any sexual harassment. I didn't have that. One thing I would like to add would be, the man that we stayed on his plantation, his father would always be trying to feel on the young girls who went up there after work. Of course we always just pushed him down and went on about our work *[laughs]*. He wasn't any threat. We didn't get in any trouble for it. My mother told me about it; she told me, "Don't pay him no attention." Yes, I'm sure some of the black women had babies with white men. But it wasn't a thing that was talked about. You could just look at them—the babies—and tell.

Mamie Johnson, from Durant and Lexington, Mississippi (born 1922). Interviewed by David W. Jackson. "My mother named me after her doll."

How much worse blacks had it in rural Mississippi than did whites emerges in this contribution by a woman who lived in Mississippi and performed domestic work until she left for Iowa at age thirty-six. Since much of this narrative concerns the Depression era, the whites were poor as well as the blacks, but the black people were clearly at the mercy of the whites for their very livelihood. Ms. Johnson's narrative brings out the exploitation connected to sharecropping in vivid detail. While Mamie Johnson is positive about her life, an undertone of terror is evident as she turns the clock back and shares some of her most salient memories. She wants young people today to understand why people back then took what they had to take, why they did not stand up to the system. It was a matter of survival. The following interview was conducted in Mamie Johnson's home in Waterloo, Iowa. Although this interviewee tended to move away from the subject of domestic service and had to be brought back by reminders from the interviewer, her digressions are significant in their own right.

My home was in Durant and Lexington, Mississippi. I was raised up in a little town in the country from Jackson, Mississippi. I was raised in a town about sixty miles from Jackson. And I went to school there in the country, for all of my schooling I got right there, from Jackson about sixty miles, and it was two little towns, Lexington and Durant. But now, you see, children weren't allowed to do as they do now. We weren't allowed to roam in the country and just go when we felt like it. You had to get permission to go. And you couldn't get with other girls and boys and slip off and go to no place. You had to tell where you be and where you were. Now we had to be in Sunday school on Sunday. We had to go to our church; that was the only place I, and most of us, had to go.

I started working for white people when I was just big enough and old enough to do the dishes, and that was about seven or eight. You could do the dishes. You could sweep the yard. Then we didn't have lawn mowers and all that kind of stuff. We would get out and chop the grass of the yard. Take a hoe and chop it clean. And pile it up and it lays out there in the sun. And you'd pick it up and pile it up and burn it. We'd have a whole bunch of kids out there cutting that grass. Yeah there was a bunch of us.

Mamie was what my mother named me. She said she had an old doll and she loved that doll. She named me after her doll. You spell it M-A-M-I-E. My birthday is April 20, 1922. Wait now, let me tell you, I have my children laughing, my grandson, he would tickle you, he older than your son, though. But he tell me sometimes when I say how old I am, he say "Big Momma, you older than that!" I say, "No, I ain't; you count it and tell me how old I am!" You know when folks get so old—and this is the truth!—it may be funny to you, but when you live in the world and you go and get eighty and ninety years old, you forget! You will overcount or you will undercount! But I tell you, you sure will forget.

Now to tell you my story, my grandmother had a daughter who died. She had six children. And my grandmother had to raise those six grandchildren. Whatever that was needed to be done, we did it together, and we would go to the field—chopping cotton, picking cotton, picking cotton and chopping cotton. You was all out there together, and when we get finished with our crops, we would go help the neighbor. Everybody had to get through. Your parents would tell you, you don't want to be sitting in the shade and your neighbor was working. We all were going to help them. The black people would help. Now you'd find white people in the field, but they were the poor. The poor white people had to do just like we had to do. They lived as sharecroppers. They lived out there and they went in the fields and they chopped their cotton. And they would pick their cotton and we would pick ours. But now when you get all finished gathering yours, that's when you could get a little bit of rest.

The white people who had a little something, they owned the fields. Now we was living on this crop of an old man named Joey Gullich. He was a mailman. He was an old mailman. And he would go out and get up in the morning time and he would go into town, Durant. We lived on the mailman's property.

Now then, you see that later when the Kennedys was living, when they come up and try to help the poor people and everything, you noticed they went up through the Mississippi Delta. Well, they went out all through the country, you know, looking to just see the condition of the people, and they didn't really get a chance to do what they were planning to do because they got killed. But now those little houses out there then that we lived in was sort of like this house here *[points to some rooms in her home]* from the front porch there, to that door there. That was your house. You didn't have a living room. You had three rooms, and that first one was a bedroom, and the second one was a bedroom, and then the third room was your kitchen. That was where you cooked and you ate, in your kitchen. That was when we was going to the field. Now when these black people would live in them, and I'm going to tell you, you can catch onto what I'm saying. These black people were living on this land for these sharecroppers. Well, you see, they lived there and they worked there. And when they worked there, you was supposed to be working on behalf of the sharecroppers. They was supposed to be giving you half and he taking half. Well, you see, they never would let you have no book to see what they was giving you. See what I mean? Now, you know that was crooked, don't you? They was supposed to be sharecropping! When you raised that stuff and he gets ready to sell it up with you, he was supposed to have a book! He was supposed to have this book and pull it up and show you how much money he gone let you have and what you owe, and how much he got for this cotton. But he never would pull out no book!

"So, Mr. Gullich, we want you to settle up, we need some clothes for our kids for Christmas and we want to know when you going settle up." We might say this to him, and then he'd say, "Well, I hadn't ever sold the cotton yet because it wasn't five cents and it wasn't the right price." Well, the workers would wait and wait. And I can remember one time, my daddy went up to the place to talk and get a settlement on their crop. But Mr. Gullich would tell him how much and the others how much they owed. "Next year," he'd say, "you'll do better. You'll do a little better next year."

And there were government checks for the colored people, for all the colored people that were working on the place; they were called paddy checks. But the colored people never knowed it because they didn't get it! The white men got it! And the reason why I can tell you about this, I never will forget this, they went up and he was settling up with them, telling them about how much they owed. And every year he come out, they didn't quite come out, they owed a little bit more.

Interviewer: Can you talk about what being a domestic servant was like in those days?

My mother would sit down and tell us about when she was a girl, before she got married. She would have to get up out of the bed, and it used to be cold! She'd have to get up out of the bed, her and her brother, and get the mule. Her brother would go in the lot and get the mule ready. They would ride together on the mule almost two miles to the white people's house. And her brother would go in and clean out the stove and make a fire. People would burn wood all the way then. And while that was getting hot, she'd be getting ready to fix their breakfast! And she would be getting everything together to cook breakfast. She would come up all the way up there, rode the mule in the cold to fix their breakfast. And then when they get that done, he would be in the house making a fire in the fireplace, clean out the fireplace, make a fire in the fireplace. They in bed; the white folks was in bed. And they get that house warm so when they get up, their food would be ready and their house would be warm.

Now young people ought to be told about this! They should know about this! Their name was Sheehas. At that house, they had an old steam gin. And they had a bunch of black people living on their place. And them people would go out and work that land. And you see what these white people were doing then and what black people didn't really have enough sense to think about this, what they were doing. They'd get that land from the government, when they'd get that land, the black people would be on the place working on the land. Every year, they going to take everything you make.

My mother was about seventeen or eighteen years old when she worked for the Sheehas. My mother, if she wasn't in the field, she cooked, fed them, and cleaned up the kitchen and the house before she went home. She cooked breakfast, lunch, and dinner. My mother would go home and then she'd come back. Them people worked! If it was time, like right now, they would go out there and take the blades, the men would, and clean off the ditch banks, you know, the little ditches going through the fields. If a snake was crawling, you could see them. The men would be out there cleaning off the ditch banks and plowing.

See, they didn't have these big John Deere tractors then like they got now. You got out there and plowed and tore that land up with a middle-buster. Well, they had these great big middle-busters, and it took a good man to hold it. It'd be throwing you from side to side, but you've got to hold it. Well, you see, now a farmer has it good, because he can get out there and he's got a John Deere tractor. And now them black folks will not get out there and work like them old ones did! They got to get some tractors if they want these young blacks to be out in their field. Now you see them sitting up in these big air-conditioned tractors.

If school was going on, you would be out there in that field. You wouldn't be in no school. Now, I know a young man—well, he ain't no young man now; he belongs to my church. Well, back then, he was just a child, and he was going go to school; he was going get an education. He came up to that school that day and that old white man who owned the place where his momma and daddy stayed asked him how come he wasn't in the field. He told him he wasn't in the field because he was going to get him an education. And he went to ask the teacher if he could, he let him talk to him outdoors. And he and this boy had some words. He tried to make this boy leave the school and go back home and go to field. And the boy told him he wasn't going. And this boy went down and picked up a great big sand-rock, and when he throws it up this way, to throw it, the teacher shot him through the arm. Sure did! Now, you know if they'd do that now there'd be some problems. They couldn't do that now. But he shot this boy through the arm.

I'm going to tell you something. When you hear these people talking about uneducated people, now this is why, in the South, so many of them can't read and write their name—because they didn't get no education, and they had to work. Now, you know, when you had a bunch of people, you bringing them up and giving them a house to stay in and then they working, they working for you for nothing!

And now if you got to the place you got tired of working, you just had to get your folks and get your things and move on off his place. People didn't have no other choice. You had to. If you wasn't going to do his work then you had to get on off of his place. My husband told me, he said, "Now when we got married, I'm not going to make the mistake with my family that my dad made with us. I'm not going to have my kids out in no field, farming no white folk's land. I'm going to get away from there if I have to get out there and farm land for myself. If I'm going to farm land, I'm going to farm for myself. I'm not going to have my kids picking cotton and chopping cotton for nobody and they taking everything they get. And he didn't. He didn't.

The young generation of people now will look at the older people and they will say, "Well, why didn't they go to school? Well, why didn't they get an education?" That's the why they didn't get an education—they couldn't! See, you didn't have no money, to buy no land, to work for yourself, you had get on away from them white folks.

And I'm going to tell you, Son *[addressing the interviewer]*, you hear them people down yonder in the South. They were talking about when they killed all them young black men with that bad disease [referring to syphilis], giving shots. And they said, you see right now these white folks will go out here and these doctors will offer all these samples of medicine. I'm not one to go grab a sample. I told my doctor, I said, "Look, if you get some of them, don't give it to me until you going to let somebody else have it." I said, "Listen,"—I'm looking at him in his eyes, "Don't you give me nothing!" Whenever I go out there, he got to go get him a chair and put it up right beside me where he can look at me in my eyes. "Let it kill somebody else! I don't want you to kill me!" And he says, "Oh, Mamie." He pats me, "You know I ain't going to kill you." I said, "No, I don't know what you going to do! But I don't want you to give it to me!"

Interviewer: Can you tell about your work for the white families? What did they call your work?

Well, some people called it a cleaning lady and some people called it a maid. They didn't have nothing for you; they just wanted their house cleaned. They didn't make me wear a uniform. Now, working for them, they wasn't paying you nothing, you could be cleaning in no uniform and stuff like that. They just wanted you to be clean. When I first started cleaning I was about eight years old. The family I worked for was called the Tates. Mr. Tate farmed. He was a plantation owner and he worked his own land. He would just hire somebody to come chop cotton for him. But you see, my parents didn't let us go like that, chopping no cotton out like that. We chopped our own. I would wash dishes once a day at the end of the day, at noon time, on Saturdays. See, I'd be with nothing to do on Saturdays, and I would go clean for Mrs. Tate and clean her kitchen.

You had to go to the back door. It was just a rule and you knowed it! And when the children got to be teenagers, it was Mister or Miss. When I'd be working in the house, they would show me what to say. They would tell me, "When you clean up Mr. David's room, do this or fix his so-and-so, or don't do so-and-so." When they said, "Mister," that is for you to say it—"Mister." And you know them little old children and the teenagers—they loved it for you to say that! Yeah, they loved for you to say Mr. So-and-So. You know one thing, I was so glad when the time come around when black people would talk to white people to say what they thought. Now you talking about a shouting time, I felt just like shouting when black people stopped having to say Mr. So-and-So. And they would say it just for you to say it.

And I'm going to tell you something. Now say you go down there [the South], and you take somebody who's lived up here and you carry him down there. They'd get to talking to him to get to see if he was going to act right. You would have to have taught him. They would get to talking to him to see if he was going to say "yes sir" and "no sir." You would tell him, if you done raised him up here, and you go back down there, "Boy, you keep your mouth shut. Don't you get to saying nothing!" Now, down there when they killed that Till boy, we lived in Durant. I listened to that trial. That trial went on for three weeks.

Interviewer: Let's continue with your story, and we will return to the Till case at the end of the interview.

The Sheehas—I was born on their place. Well, I worked. And they just, I'm going to tell you, they didn't pay you nothing. They pay you what they wanted to pay you. Whatever they feel like you was worth. And if one gives you a little something, he'd tell you, "Don't tell the others what he pays you." Because, you see, they would have meetings on black people, on what to pay them and what to not pay them. They knew if they pay one, one pay them that much, then that one would leave there and he's going to go to the other one, and he's going be looking for the same thing. And they didn't want it to get out! But some of them was a little bit better than others.

My job was to wash the dishes. Now, they just had some common dishes. They weren't all like these dishes people use now—all the flowers, designs, and all that. When you was done, you just put them up. The white people then, they were nobody, had nothing. They were what you call middle-class white people. And I tell you one thing, if you had in your house what black folks have in their house now, they'd have run you off! You wouldn't have had it! You can buy these big color TVs and things. They didn't have nothing like that, just the old cane-bottom rocking chairs and straight chairs in the room. You wouldn't have nothing like this *[indicating her furnishings]*. No, everything in there was something you could just scrub with soap and water.

Let me tell you something, them Sheehas—they were some of the mean ones. But we knew how to handle ourselves around them. And the Sheehas and the Tates—all of them that I'm telling you about is dead now.

The men, they say, would beat up colored folks. And my mother told me they fell on some hard times. So they got to the place where they didn't have bread to eat. So one of them would stand out on the side of the road and try to stop colored people and ask them if they would just stop and cook him a whole loaf of bread.

I cleaned with the Tates for a little bit and, now, they was some pretty good people but I didn't learn much about them. You know, white people at that time, it was some of them had done wrong things, but they didn't let black people hear them talking about one another. If they see you coming, they would hush. Now, these white people now, if they know something about one another and they see you coming, they ain't going to hush. They keep on and they let it get out! But years later I did hear that black people was talking about them, that some old white men was going with black women down there. They done wrong things, but they kept it pretty quiet.

Interviewer: Did the Tates ever take advantage of you in any way?

No. But I'm going to tell you something, the old men was dirty! I had been walking down in Durant after I got grown, and them old men you know, if they see a black woman coming up the street, they would say "Hey Gal! What about a date?" And one Saturday night I was uptown—it was Christmas Eve, I never will forget it. And one of them come out just right up behind me and I'm going up. I said, now this dog is going to say something hard to me. I kept going. I see a crowd of black men. And they was a bunch of black men was standing right in the middle of the street, and I just walked right up to them. I thought maybe that was going stop him, but he just walked head-on. And I cut across the street and was going to the depot where the train was going to come along. And I went across and walked in the depot. Then we had white and black. And I went in the white part and he just walked right on over there and just stood. He was going to watch me until I come out! And my husband happened to come up the street and he was driving his friend's car. And I ran. I hollered at him and waved! And I told him, I said, "You wait! This man's been following me all across that street." He said, "What man?" I said, "that old man yonder." He said, "You wait, I'll stop it." I said, "No, don't you stop it, leave him alone! He ain't done nothing to me, he just following me." He planned on saying something! But you see in that time, if he had said anything, you see, they would have murdered him. They'd murdered him! They'd murder you about your own black woman. That was back in the forties. Back yonder when they killed them three civil rights workers. Me and my husband went right through that little town and got some gas at a filling station there. And, you know, every time I think about that little town, it rubs on my skin. It scares me just that bad because we went through it. And, you know, they got these one black boy and two white boys. And they got them boys.

Interviewer: Can you tell about your work for another family?

I worked for the Morrises. I would go up there and help them milk and help feed the little calves. There was a lot of cows and calves, little baby calves. We would separate milk. They had a separator. You ever seen one of those separators, where you put that cream in there and you turn that separator? And that cream mix up and it separates. The cream goes one way and the milk the other way. And they had a boy, he was a little bit older than me. And they had another boy, was about as old as your son, looked like to be about in that size. And I'd go over there and help them to separate this milk. We would take the milk and separate the cream and put it in one way. And we would take this milk and stand there in this lot and the little calf would come up stick their head through, and we would hold that bucket and they would drink that milk. And we would feed them. They was raising the calves from the cows. See, but them boys was, you know, up-to-date white people. They didn't mess with you, you know? They were quiet people. And her husband was an up-to-date man. He had his own farm. They had a cook. We called her Aunt Jane. She would cook, wash the dishes, and clean up their kitchen. That was all she did. She would come each day. A lot of times she would stay with my mamma. She would cook dinner and then she would have supper. She would fix two meals a day.

I tell you white people, them down there, they ate just like what we eat today, the same foods. They ate greens, corn bread, peach cobbler, blackberry cobbler. But now these white people, now these young ones now, they wouldn't eat that kind of food today. But, you see, those was poor people that come up and raise their children like that.

Interviewer: Can you tell me more about Aunt Jane and working conditions back then?

Aunt Jane would just cook; she wouldn't clean for them. See, because she was an older woman. She would cook dinner and then feed them and clean up the kitchen. She didn't eat with them. Then you didn't eat with no white person. She could eat the meals she made. She waited until they got through eating and then she fixed a plate and ate.

You had then, back there, you had outdoors toilets. All the white folks back there had outdoors toilets. And if they had outdoors toilets, you didn't go to those outdoors toilets. No, you went out there, in the bushes or somewhere. You didn't go to their toilet. Yeah, and she had, this woman, this was with the old mailman. He worked in town. We farmed his land. Now they didn't have nothing fancy. They just had common stuff. She didn't have in her house what you got in your house, what we got in our house. No! You would make her look stupid. But you didn't go in that toilet, and then when you come up, that's my back door there. Now if you come up here in this front, the front door is right there, but you didn't come busting up in that front door. You would come right up to that front door and you'd pass on by that front door and go on by to that back door and come on in that back door. Now, what sense does that make? And you would go out there in town, you didn't come in no bathrooms, you didn't go see a toilet because it's the toilet and you go busting up in there. They had them marked all, white and colored, where you know to don't go in there. That was the public bathrooms.

Interviewer: Was it only at the Morrises where you used the back door?

No, all of them. You didn't go up, come in that door there. You went all the way around, you come in that back door. And these old Sheehas, they had a toilet, it was always out in the back. The toilet was always in the back. She had trees all around her house like I got out here. Now when you cooked for her, you had to cook on the old stove in the kitchen in the back. When them men workers come there, they would come in and they would eat their dinner in the kitchen. Now I cooked. If it would be a whole table in there, you wasn't going eat in there at the table with them. They would sit down and eat in the kitchen. And they'd go on back and go to field. Now you wasn't going to be eat—I don't care who you was—at that table. You wasn't going to eat with them. You find some of these old white folks, done got plenty of them, mixed up from the South, right here in Waterloo. They right round here, you'd be surprised. But they right round here, and when you find one round here, you can know it. Sure know it!

Interviewer: Did you do any laundry for the white people?

Yeah. Well, you see, when I was in the South, I would just do a wet wash for a family. But now it wasn't about nothing! They wasn't paying nothing! But I'm going to tell you something, when you was coming along back in there, you had to work for just what you could get. And that was the way it was. You hear people now, I can sit down and tell people now and they can say, "No, I wouldn't have did. I wouldn't have did." But yes, they would. It was surviving, just the way you had to survive. No, I didn't advertise that I did laundry. No, see, they would come around, talking to you like they had their little cars or they seen you somewhere. They would ask you if you would wash for them. And they would ask you. They'd tell you what they'd pay. It'd take all day to do one family's laundry. All day! I'd wash them, on the washboard. Yeah, these folks talking call these wash machines old "knuckle busters!" *[laughing].*

A washboard was made out of boards and made out of tin. And the tin was made out of ruffle. And you just move your hand up and down, you wash your hand up and down. The ruffle is what washed the dirt out of them, but you was the machine. You squeezed it and you washed it back and forth on that washboard.

You don't halfway know what we have went through. And I hear these preachers telling the people now, some of them that don't know nothing, about the people, making fun of the people from back then. If these ministers was to get up there talking the stuff before them old folks then like they do now, I don't know what the people would have said to them.

Interviewer: Now, I think you wanted to talk about the murder of Emmett Till?

He was in Chicago, was living in Chicago with his mamma. And he come down there that summer! And you know those boys is, they, you know, like way back then they'd call *[does a whistle],* wolf-whistling. Well, that was all the boy did. The boy just whistled at the woman, you know, didn't know the danger he was in. And come down there and stay with his granddaddy one summer. And them old wives had done told their husbands that the little nigger boy come up there and he wolf-whistled at them. And they come back up there, they got that bunch and they went up there that night. They waited until his granddaddy had gone to bed, and they went there and asked for him. Knocked on the door and asked for this boy. Well, the granddaddy told them he was there in the bed. And they went there and got him out of there. Told him to get up, put his clothes on. They went to his old granddaddy's house. I did not know him, but we used to stay right down on the hill from there. We used to live right on that river as we had moved to the Delta at this time. I know where the store is at. I could go down there and show it to you, if they ain't tore it down! Anyway, he went and got that child out of there and made him put his clothes on. They put him in a pickup truck. And they carried that child, they rode that child all around there. And they beat that child. The folks was out on the place; they heard him hollering. They heard that boy hollering and carrying him from place to place just beating him. And they carried him down there on that river where they put him in. They say he was just heard, the boy was just heard screaming. The people around there heard him screaming.

They didn't just kill him all at once, they punished him! And when they found him, he was tied to an old gin wheel. But they never did find him right off, so it was a man fishing and he found him. He saw one of his legs sticking up and then reported him. And they had done beat that child until his head look just like a —. But anyway they beat that child up, just to look at him. Just look like he done took an axe or something and just beat his face up just like you beat some beef up. See, it was intended for him to stay down in that water until the things eat him up! But the police got him out of there and carried him back to Chicago. And oh, you're talking about a mess! It was a mess. But people wasn't saying nothing, you know. People was just whispering, you know, off to their selves, talking about it.

So when they carried him back to Chicago it was a pitiful sight! They carried him back there and they dressed him and put him in his casket. And they had people were just coming by to see him. And they had a Catholic priest coming by. And when he come by, he seen him and he just fell. That Catholic priest just fell, fainted. Emmett wasn't nice to see now—I viewed the body from home on the TV.

The trial went on for three weeks. The three old men, the three old brothers were sitting together in the trial. They was kissing their wives, hugging their wives, and rejoicing. The old womens was on TV; you could tell they was trash. You would see them just rejoicing, you know, hugging one another and kissing one another through the trial.

I didn't know the granddaddy. I just know the store in Greenwood where they did it at. There was three little stores there. And, well, you know how black folks were way back there, you know some of them would buy stuff from them. But the store went out of business after that. They showed that little store on Black History Month, when they was showing black history. It was just, you know, a frame of it. I wouldn't have went there and bought nothing for nothing! But they killed that boy, just killed him for nothing. And his momma's dead now.

[Note: The verdict at the trial was "not guilty." The Mississippi press applauded the fairness of the trial while the world press expressed horror at the outcome. Later the accused publicly admitted their crimes as they could not be tried twice for the same crime (see Whitfield 2009).]

Annie Victoria Johnson, from Ripley, Mississippi (born 1925). Interviewed by Charletta Sudduth. "I worked for white families as soon as I was old enough to walk."

Of all the women interviewed who migrated from the Deep South, Annie Victoria Johnson had the least education; she also in many ways is the most articulate. Although the story is disjointed in places, to maintain the integrity and spontaneity of the interview and the richness of Mrs. Johnson's gifts of self-expression, the transcript is presented verbatim, along with several responses from the interviewer. Mrs. Johnson's interview is remarkable for her memory down to the minute details concerning matters from the mundane (food preparation, quilting arrangements) to the profound (race relations, religious worship). As you read this transcript, consider that this story was told in a lively conversational tone to Charletta Sudduth, and that remarks were often punctuated by the kind of animated laughter that takes place among people who are connecting emotionally, even when the content at times took Sudduth completely by surprise.

I started working for white people as soon as I was old enough to walk. My mother was the kind of lady where color didn't make any difference. She was a missionary. Wherever she went, she took us with her. She would help take care of white babies and black babies. She would help bathe them and feed them. We just did all of that. As I grew older, that taught me. Times back then, people did not have any money. We would wash and iron for white people. They would give us canned fruit, clothes that their kids outgrew, and shoes. When the time came to plant gardens, we all worked together.

Annie Victoria Johnson. Mrs. Johnson lives today in Waterloo, Iowa, where she is very active in church life. *Photo by David Jackson.*

The white women would help us, and we would help them. We would trade stuff. If we had all cabbage and they had all beans, we would trade. We did the same thing with fruit. We would pick apples and peaches. All of us would get together and can fruit and make jelly. We would go out in the woods and pick blackberries and wild plums. Everything we could get we canned and made into jelly preserves. Every season that came in, we had something to can. We would can in the white women's kitchen if she had most of it.

Interviewer: Were there rules about which door black people used or other rules?

There were no rules in her kitchen. We would go in and do just like we did at home. And they would help. During the winter they would have quilting parties. And maybe today they would go to one of the white women's house. They would have food and they would quilt all day. And maybe next week they would go to my mother's house or one of the other black women's house and quilt. The white and black women quilted together. We did everything together. We just didn't go to school and church with them.

Interviewer: What were the working conditions like?

The work conditions were good in Ripley, Mississippi. Well, we had a few that lived back in the hills that were afraid of black folks because they had never seen us.

On Saturdays we would go to town and take all the money we had from raising chickens. My momma made sure we had laying hens. We would save the eggs. That is how we got money for the church. Eggs were like ten cents a dozen. We would save eggs to have money to go to church and Sunday school on Sunday, which would be just a nickel.

This is when the WPA was started, when Roosevelt was elected. Back then, black men didn't have any jobs unless they sharecropped on the land. Some of my people owned land, like family land. But my daddy didn't own any land because he didn't want to pay taxes on it so we sharecropped. Sharecropping meant whatever man you worked for, you lived in his house on his property. And the man's land you lived on, you had to share whatever you made with him. So if we made two hundred bushels of corn, he would get one hundred. He would get half of it to pay for staying there. That was the men; the women would work in the field with the men too. We would chop cotton. We didn't have any playtime, no company time. On a day where it rained, we would be doing something in our house. Because when it rained, you couldn't go out and work in the field. And when we got done in the field in the evening, we went and worked in the garden.

Interviewer: Did you ever go up to the big house, where the white people were?

We went up to the white people's homes and worked if the white woman got sick. We would go up there and cook, clean, and help her until she got on her feet. For breakfast, every morning we would cook homemade biscuits, ham, jelly, dessert, eggs, and sometimes smothered potatoes or hash browns. We had molasses, jelly, preserves, coffee, a big pitcher of fresh-churned milk. For supper, at this time of year, the vegetables would be fresh in the garden. We would get out and pick greens.

Interviewer: What did the white people eat?

The white people ate the same thing we eat today! Everybody had peas, potatoes, and peanuts. We would kill our meat like at Thanksgiving or near Christmas. If it was a big family we'd have two or three hogs killed. We would smoke the ham, grind up the sausage. We would do it by the tubful. They would take corn shucks and roll the sausage up in rolls. Then they'd stick it down in the shuck, wrap it up, and hang it up in the smokehouse. Sometimes they would make little patties, fry them, and put them in a fruit jar. They just fried them like you would for breakfast and then put them in the fruit jar. Then you could just open them and eat them. We didn't have any refrigerators or freezers. Everybody had their own food. If one didn't have something, the other one had it. I worked for a lot of people. We used to go out and chop cotton, like the young ones, if you were twelve or thirteen years old. We did that from sunup to sundown.

Interviewer: When working inside the home, were there any rules?

No, because no one lived next door like we do here. Families lived like maybe ten or twelve miles away. And the white woman would have to come to our house and see about her family, if she had kids. My mother took care of the kids.

Interviewer: How did your mom take care of the white people's kids?

My mom did the same thing she did for us when caring for their kids. She bathed them, fed them, put them to bed. They slept in our beds. Some of the white kids called my mother Grandma. My mother was in her thirties then, and they would call her Grandma or Auntie. She loved them just like she loved us. She whupped them like she did us. The woman would tell her, "If they don't mind, you know what to do." And it was, "Yes ma'am" and "no ma'am" and "thank you." And they do that right now down South.

Interviewer: Yes, they do. When did your mother start caring for the children?

My mother would be there when the white woman's babies were born! She helped make baby clothes for them and feed them. They breast-fed their babies, but as soon as they got to be six months old, whatever you ate, the baby ate. The white women breast-fed and the black folks too.

Interviewer: What! The blacks breast-fed—who did they breast-feed?

The black women would breast-feed the white babies. The black woman's milk would be there for the white baby.

Photograph of African American woman and biracial child from early twentieth century. The photo was purchased in an antique store. *From the family collection of Katherine van Wormer.*

Interviewer: Wow! Where would the black woman's milk come from?

The black woman would have a baby too. They both nursed their babies.

Interviewer: Were the white women in some ways helpless?

The white women were helpless if they were sickly. Just like the some black women be sickly. Some of them could have babies and some of them couldn't. And maybe the ones who did, there would be something wrong with them. And the husband would go get a black woman that was breast-feeding, to feed his baby.

Interviewer: Were there times when any of the white men would go in to the black women?

The ones that were called thugs, that weren't raised right, to respect women, did. They would catch the women and rape them and that kind of stuff. A lot of women back in those days came up with half-white babies. It happened because they were raped. The thugs were just outside men. If everyone went to the field, and they knew a woman was at the house by herself, they would go in there and rape her. It wasn't the white man of the house. It would be like the people around here now who don't work and break into houses and do all that. Well, it was the same thing as back then.

Interviewer: Coming back to your work as a domestic worker, can you say more about that experience?

My grandmother was born a slave. She had to do it [work as a house servant] so my mother watched her do it. Back then, that was the only way they had to get anything. Some black women got married and their husbands didn't allow them to go to the field. They didn't allow them to work in the yard or the garden. They didn't allow them to work for the white women. Some black men back then are just like they are now. They wouldn't have you working for any white folks. And it seemed that they had a harder time because back then, everyone got along and helped each other. But because some of the black men didn't want their wives around white folks, they caught hell because when they needed help, they wouldn't help them.

Interviewer: Can you talk about some things you learned from this work?

I learned a lot about caring for children from my mother. Because whether anyone knew it or not, when we grew up, it was more dangerous then than it is now. I say that because we didn't lie around the house and sleep late. Every time a child got big enough, he had a job: feeding the chickens, slopping the pigs, going and getting the cows to be milked. There was no toilet, so, you know, we had night pots. You learned how to take out that night pot and keep it clean. All that kind of stuff! *[laughs]*. And we went down the hill to the spring to get water before it got dark, before the snakes started crawling. We kept our butter and milk in the spring to keep cool. We didn't have any ice-box or freezer or refrigerator! So we kept our milk and butter in the spring.

Interviewer: What was the education like?

They had black school and white school. Now, we would have to walk at least three miles or more to school. We had to get up in the morning at 4:00 a.m. to help cook breakfast, milk the cows, feed the chickens, feed the pigs, make up the beds, wash breakfast dishes, pack our lunch, and head out to school. This was the kids. My momma would be home. And while we were in school, she would be sewing, making clothes for us. Sometimes if we made enough little extra money, we ordered our stuff from Sears and Roebuck. And she knew how to sew. All the girls looked like paper dolls! *[laughs]*. All of us would be dressed alike! No one complained. Everybody, white and black, whatever they had on was rickrack. Rickrack, I don't see it anymore. It is a trimming that goes on a dress. It is wavy and has designs like X's. There were different colors. All the white women could sew too. The white women and black women would get together and quilt too. When we quilted we talked about the usual things like: "Well, my beans didn't do good this year." One of them would say, "You know my cabbage died." Maybe the other one would say, "Don't worry about it, we got some." Or they'd say, "My peach tree is full so you get all the peaches you want and I can trade you." Or "You can get all the beans you want." They traded goods between the white women and black women. It was like a friendship. If a white woman was out in the town, I doubt she would recognize a black woman out, because like when church time come, they would go to their church. But wherever they would see you, they would speak to you and respect you.

The black folks and white folks were like a community. On Saturday night, my daddy would play the guitar. And we'd have ice cream parties. Black and white people were there. For the ice cream parties, a couple of women would make a big freezer of different ice cream. White and black women made it. And a couple of the women would make a caramel cake and that one would have a chocolate cake. The person who had the biggest yard, that's where the party would be. The men would come too! The whole white family would be there. They would be blowing their harmonicas, and playing their fiddles and guitars, and square-dancing! *[laughs]*.

Interviewer: What kind of jobs did the white people have?

We had one friend that was a doctor. He was what you call a community doctor. My mother and I never worked for him. I'll never forget that old man. His name was Dr. Charley. I guess he was around because we had midwives. And when the midwives see they are going to have a problem with the woman having a baby, one young man would get on a horse. Maybe one or two white men kept horses in the community, most of them were mules. He'd get on that horse, go to town and get the doctor. They had black and white midwives. So he would get in his horse and buggy and come out. The family would take care of his horse. Just like you see in these old westerns! *[laughs]*. He would examine the women and tell the others what he needed. And they would be running and getting water and sterilizing it and all that stuff. All the kids would have to leave and go to one house. The children weren't allowed to be there when the baby was born.

Interviewer: Did the whites have white midwives?

I would see a black midwife helping a white woman deliver. Nobody paid attention to it because we were used to it. When a baby was coming, the white kids and the black kids went to one house together. Dr. Charley was our doctor. He would help the black women deliver too.

Interviewer: Were there any negatives of working as a maid?

The only time that I was called a maid was after I left Mississippi and went to Jackson, Tennessee. I worked at a hotel called Southern Hotel. That is when I was a maid. Before then when I worked in the white people's homes, I was just a black girl working for white folks *[laughs]*. When I went to work in the hotel, they gave you a maid cap, a maid uniform, and all of that stuff. When I worked for the white people before that, they called me by my name.

Interviewer: What were the white peoples' attitudes toward blacks?

It was good. Now my daddy made home brews and whiskey. This man, that we lived with, on his property, he was a sheriff. His name was Sam Ford. And somebody—back then they said nigger—some nigger told this sheriff that my daddy had home brews. My daddy wouldn't sell it, he made it for himself.

So Sam Ford came out, and asked, "Somebody tells me you're making home brew and whiskey?" My daddy said, "I do." He said, "Well, do you sell it?" He said, "No, I don't sell it. I make it for myself." Then the sheriff said, "Well, as long as you don't have over five gallons of each one, you go on and do what you want to do." So for as long as I remember, my daddy kept his whiskey and his home brew.

Interviewer: How was life better back then than it is today?

Life was better back then because we were healthier. We didn't buy all this store-bought food. The only things that we bought were coffee, sugar, flour, extra stuff that we didn't have. We had corn ground. We would shell the corn and my daddy would take it to the gristmill and get it ground. And we had our meat. Folks then used lard; we didn't know then about cooking oil. We had butter; we had milk. The only thing we had to buy was the sugar, flour, baking powder, soda, and stuff like that. We had plenty butter, plenty milk. We maybe went to town for bread or some material my mother needed. We didn't go to other's homes to borrow because nobody borrowed from each other. Everybody had what they needed.

Interviewer: What would surprise or shock people today about life then?

What would shock them is how little money we got paid. If we got any money for what they call "domestic work," it would be like fifty cents for all-day work. You would be there in the morning to wash dishes, clean up the kitchen; there would be no vacuum cleaner. You'd take the sheets off the bed, do them on the washboard, hang them on the line, and everything they wore except their underwear had to be starched and ironed. They made their starch with flour. They put a little kerosene in it to keep the iron from sticking to it. They put in the starch boiling. You would hang the clothes on the line and if it looked like it was going to rain, you'd leave the white clothes out there so that the dew could hit them. You would get up early the next morning and roll them up and start your fire for your irons. And then you'd walk from about here *[points out of the window]* to the sidewalk to get your irons, and you would rub it on sand and on cedar to make sure you got all the smut off of it. Then you would rub it again on a white cloth. Then you would start ironing. You would iron all day long. You would work from sunup to sundown. You stopped to eat. After we cooked, we ate some breakfast.

Interviewer: Did you eat with the white people?

Sometimes we ate at the table with them. You could just do it. We would have conversation.

Interviewer: Did the black men work as hard?

I think the men had to work harder. They worked with the mules, the cultivators, the plows, and all that stuff. The women would be in the house usually.

Interviewer: Do you know of any situations of sexual harassment or of whites getting involved with maids, such as happened with Strom Thurmond?

Strom Thurmond was a senator that lived to be about one hundred. He had got a black maid pregnant. He was a plantation owner. But that was down in the Delta. See, we didn't live in the Delta. We lived up near the Tennessee line. The Delta is way on down near Jackson, Mississippi. Things were different down there. The difference was, down there, even in 1944, those people could not leave off of the plantations unless the owners told them they could leave. They didn't even go to school. Slavery really was just over down there when Martin Luther King started the civil rights movement in the 1960s. Some of them people were still slaves and didn't know it. I've heard a lot of horrible stories from even the 1970s and 1980s, how some of those people were still being treated down in the Delta. They were treated like slaves.

I remember in 1957, I had a boyfriend in Chicago and he had to go down to the Delta. Do you remember when the Till boy was killed? [Emmett Till was a fifteen-year-old boy from Chicago who was tortured to death in 1955 for allegedly whistling at a white woman.] We were down there two weeks after that happened in Greenwood, Mississippi. And my boyfriend—his mother sent a special delivery. She wanted him to come down there and get his brother because they were talking about killing him because he tore up a white man's truck. We went down there and the place where his mother was living was just like a shack on the plantation. I said, "Well, if we're going to take your son back, why don't you come back with us?" And she said, "No, I just want to get my children away from here first, and then I have to slip away." We were going to leave the next morning and she said, "I want ya'll to wait until it gets dark so nobody sees him when you leave." And we had to wait until twelve o'clock at night to leave from down there, from the Delta. This was in 1957! The white men then were having their way with the black women back then in the Delta, but not where I lived. I think it was different in the Delta because they had always been slaves down there. Where I came from, in the hills, those white folks didn't believe in buying slaves. They were more Christian. That part of the Mississippi is dry now [no alcohol]. You don't find any nightclubs or taverns in some parts of Mississippi right now. Where I come from there's none.

The blacks maybe had something to do with them becoming Christians. Because just about everyone, even the sheriffs, the doctors, most of the law enforcement, believed in God. And that's always been. It is just the way the blacks approached the white people, I suppose, like their attitude. We used to get together—not in the churches—but in the homes. There used to be a white man who came to our house, all the time with his Bible. Him and my daddy would sit and read the Bible together. My daddy could read. I don't know how he learned to read, but there is always a way for anything! My daddy used to always say, they had to work instead of going to school. So they were self-taught. He always said knowledge and wisdom. You don't have to be crazy; you don't have to be ignorant. He said, "if you know your ABC's, you can read." And he used to read us Bible stories.

Interviewer: Is there is anything else that you want to add or share?

Well, Mississippi wasn't the only place I worked; I also worked in Humboldt, Tennessee. This was in 1949. Back in those days, wages weren't any better any place you went. First I worked in that hotel, I worked on the elevator. I worked seven days a week for a dollar a day. I worked seven hours a day. When I was a maid making beds and all that stuff, it was a dollar a day. Oh, you had to work!

One day when I heard people saying, "They're paying three dollars a day to chop cotton," I left the hotel. There would be a school bus coming to town every morning. There'd be a whole lot of buses picking up people to go out and work in the field. And I would get up and get that school bus and go out there and chop cotton for three dollars a day. I worked more than seven hours a day then, sunup to sundown. But that was better than a dollar. And some mornings we'd go out there with a different driver. Everybody would get off the bus and he would say, "My wife wants somebody to work in the house with her today. She don't feel good. She's going to have a baby. Does anybody want to volunteer?" And nobody said anything. I said, "I'll go." And she would be lying down. She showed me what to do, showed me where everything was. And I would iron all day. And she would fix me the best lunch. Sometimes it would be fried chicken and potato salad, and homemade pies. They had some kind of pie every day. So then when he came to pick me up, coming back to town, she said, "We're not going to eat that ham you cut yesterday. Give her that ham and that box of stuff I got out there." This was because I had two little boys. She had pickled peaches, applesauce, and canned plums. And, oh, that ham, you could smell it a mile! And I would go and take that in there and my sister would just be jumping up and down! "Oh, I don't have to buy any beets!" *[laughing]*. They would still give me three dollars and that stuff.

I still didn't tell you about Chicago. I think the women I worked for in Illinois were the most prejudiced and hateful women I ever worked for. It was nothing like Mississippi or Tennessee. The people are going to think because you are in Chicago, oh, you're free. No, you're not. This was back in the 1960s. I worked for one woman in Glenview, Illinois, and in Northfield, Northbrook, Highland Park, Winnetka, and Glencoe. I worked for six white families plus some more that I have forgotten about. Now the one I worked for in Glencoe, she was an Italian woman. Now when you find a good Italian, you are the same color as they are. It doesn't make any difference. I didn't have to buy any clothes. When she went on trips to New York or wherever her husband went, whatever she bought for herself, I had. Her husband was an attorney. I did everything for her. I cooked. She taught me how to make Italian spaghetti. Everything she ate was Italian. She liked legs of lamb baked, seafood, and sauces. And she had the sweetest kids. And her and her husband went to the Bermudas and were gone six weeks. The house and the kids were mine! *[laughing]*. And my sister had worked for her before I did and she said, "You don't have to worry about buying any clothes because she's going to buy all your clothes."

The kids minded me. They'd come and hug me and kiss me goodnight and say goodnight. Sometimes they wanted me to read them Bible stories. They would ask me, "Can we have company tomorrow?" And I would say, "Nope." And you wouldn't hear another word. They called me Aunt. And I didn't have to ask them what they were going to eat. Lunchtime would come and I would say, "Come on and eat." They wouldn't say, "I don't want this or I'm not going to eat this." They would say "Thank you, I love you." That is what their mamma was teaching them.

We lived in Glencoe, right on the lake. It was ninety-five steps to the lake. I lived with them. Every evening we would go down to the lake. And I would stand up there with a hundred-dollar bathing suit on and I can't even swim! *[laughing]*. And those little kids could swim like fish! Then we would go back up and take a shower. I would give them their supper and then they were ready to go to bed. Oh, I loved that job! Then they moved to Connecticut and wanted me to move with them. My sister said, "Don't you leave from here." Oh, I hated to see them go. This other one that I worked for in Northbrook, her husband was a United States attorney. And she was nice, oh, she was nice!

Interviewer: Can you tell about a mean woman you worked for?

Oh, there was a mean one. She lived in Winnetka, Illinois. I had been going down there for about two months. So that Thursday I went in and she said, "I'm going to have company today." That didn't bother me. And I said, "Well it won't bother me because this is my day to iron anyways." So I went downstairs, turned the TV on, and did like I always did. When I came up, the women had started to come in. And she said, "You need to get whatever you're going to get right now, because I don't want to see you anymore until I take you to the train." I said, "Okay." So I fixed myself a sandwich and went back downstairs. I was thinking about it the whole time I was ironing. I just wish I could be doing something else to get even with your ass.

My sister had told me some dirty tricks that she had pulled off. My sister went to change out of her uniform. She had a certain place she changed. Up here in the North we had uniforms. So my sister went in the maids' room to change into her uniform and left her purse in there. She said I know how much money I had when I went in that house. When she got ready to go, she got dressed, counted her money, and had less! So she said, "Mrs. Mary, you're not going to pay me today?"

The woman said, "Oh I already did, I already did!"

She said, "No, you didn't because I had the same money that I had when I came here." She done paid her and stole it back.

The woman said, "Well, I have to tell my husband then because I really don't have any money. I'd have to write a check, and the bank's closed." She said, "Okay then I'll get it next week." So she thought, "Yeah, I'll get you next week too!" *[laughing]*. She left that day and told them she had to go to a club meeting. And she left a turkey for her to put in the stove. She said, "When I cleaned the bathroom, I took the toothbrush and cleaned the toilet and stuck it back in the holder." She said, "I took one of my socks and buttered that turkey! *[laughing]*. And she went to her drawer and got a pair of socks and put them on and took the train!" She said, "When they do you dirty, I got some tricks to get it back!" *[laughing]*.

When I left my job that day the woman said, "See you next Thursday!" I said, "Good-bye!" *[laughing]*. She didn't understand what I meant! I never saw that woman again! And she didn't even get to say good-bye! That's the way I did that one. I just left.

We used to ride the Northwestern, and you could hear women on that train talking about what they had done to the women they worked for! *[laughing]*. Because all those women worked as domestics. Some of them would say, "My lady is nice to me." And we would look at each other and say, "My lady?" Instead of saying "Ms. So-and-So, My lady." My lady. I said, "My lady was my mother! I ain't got no lady out here!"

Irene Williams, from Springhill, Louisiana (born 1935). Interviewed by David W. Jackson. "I wish to God I could tell you more, but it's too painful."

Uniquely among the women interviewed for this project, Mrs. Williams found it very painful to look back. Hers was truly a lost childhood, and today, she mourns the loss deeply. She speaks in a slow voice that is full of sorrow.

I stayed in Louisiana with my mother until I got grown; then I got married and left. As a child I lived with my auntie for a while, but then I come back

Irene Williams. Mrs. Williams wants to ensure that her grandchildren know about the hardships she endured. *Photo by David Jackson.*

home again. See, that's when we was working in the fields. I was working in the fields when I was twelve years old. You ever plowed a mule?

My mom, she was the one that had the hard time. See, when I was brought up—I didn't have no father. My father passed away when I was two years old. My mother raised all five of us by herself. And where we were staying, we didn't have no electricity, no running water in the house. We had a well where we had to draw water. We had our outhouse. And the lamp, we had to put on a lamp, you know. We had to fill up a lamp with coal oil in it; that's what we did.

My mom worked for white folks. Sometimes she'd take us to our grandmother's and leave us there. She'd be gone about three or four weeks, away from us because she had to go and work for the white people, she lived with them. And she let us stay with grandmother, her mother.

Interviewer: Let me ask you this. Did you do some domestic work? Did you do some housecleaning, anything like that?

Yeah, for white people. I did housecleaning, cooking, washing clothes, you know, but it had to be perfect, you know. You know how white folks is. Any spot on your clothes is a no-no. You got to get it clean.

The first family I worked for; I don't remember their names. No, been too long, but they had three kids. I was around sixteen years old. I cooked and I washed their clothes, and I hung them out on the fence. Sometimes the clothes would freeze before I could get them hung out on the fence; it was cold out there.

Interviewer: How about your education?

If you go to school, like if it rains in the morning time, then we'll go to school then, and at twelve o'clock if it stopped raining and it get dry enough for you to hitch the field, the white man come get you out of school and put you in the field. I work in the field on through the week, on weekends, and need to clean up their house. We didn't get a chance to go to school. I didn't get a chance. No, never even know how to read or write.

Interviewer: Well, did any of these people call you any names like use the N word, anything like that?

No, but a lot of others called us that. I remember one day, we was walking to school, me, my brother, and my sister. It had been raining, and there was water all out there, and then they call us niggers. They tried to spit on us, and there was nothing we could do; we had to keep walking. When we got home, my mother asked us why we all so wet and we told her and she said, "Well some people just don't know how to act right."

Interviewer: So when you were sixteen and having to work all the time, what was that like?

In those days, us colored people had to take what we could get to try to make a living. You never knew if you'd get paid or not. Sometimes they pay us in clothes. You could take it and go; they wasn't gonna give you no money anyway.

You work in your own clothes. No uniform. You just work. I thought they would call me by my name instead of a maid, but they just called me a maid, saying, "She's my maid." And you didn't go in no white folks front door. You had to go around like when you went to a café, all the sudden you had to go to the back.

I remember one day, there was a bunch of stockings. I didn't think they were no good so I put them in the trash. When the lady come home she ask me, "Well, where are the stockings?" I said, "I thought they had runs and things in them." "No," she said. "I put them out there for you to wash them." I said, "Well, I didn't know that." So I had to pay her for the stockings, for some old stockings. That's the way it was.

They had a big nice house. And they gave you so many chores, so little time to clean, you know, but sometime there'd be two of us—one working the kitchen and one working the bedroom, you know, cleaning. Then when they kids come in, you know by now, white folks don't care what kids come in their house. They come in, they mess up as you clean it up so you had to go back over, excuse me, and clean it again because they say you didn't do a good job. You know what I'm saying?

And I remember when I'd go home and tell my mother how they do and she said, "Well, baby, do your best."

Interviewer: Could you use their restroom?

No, never. At that time my brothers had an old car, and if I told them I had to use the restroom they would come and get me and take me home where I could use the restroom, but I had to go back.

No, they didn't want no colored people using their restroom. And it was tough down there.

Interviewer: Did you have any type of relationship with the wife? You know, like were you friends and you could go to her and talk to her and she would help you?

No. You don't associate with no white folk down there, not at that time.

Interviewer: How long did you work for this family?

Not long, because my mother stopped me from going there. She said it wasn't a good idea for me to go there and work and couldn't use the bathroom. We were just trying to help her because she didn't have no husband. She didn't have nothing but us, nobody but us, and we was out there trying to help her.

After that I went to Minden, near Shreveport, to stay with my auntie, and my auntie went to work one day. There was about three or four white guys out in a car, and her next-door neighbor come to her house and told me that the guys wanted someone to work. Well, you know I wanted to work, all we had was work. So I didn't know no better; so I got in the car and went with him.

Then when we got there, they tell me what to do, but I see all of them standing around one another. You know I don't know what they were saying. I don't know what they were planning. I didn't know what was going on, and it got later and later. I told them, I said, "I gotta go home. My auntie gonna be looking for me." They said, "What's the matter, you scared?" I said, "Yeah I am, because I ain't never been out this late. My auntie don't like me to be out this late."

Then they told me, they said, "Well, we have another place you could go and work." Well, I was thinking what they was gonna do to me, they was gonna try to rape me or do something to me because I don't know. And I said, "No! I wanna go home."

I finally got home. And when my auntie found out where I had been, boy, she was pissed. She slapped me down, and she told me, "I know you don't know, I know you don't understand, but I'm going to sit down here and tell you." She told me, she said, "They are too dangerous—a bunch of men. Weren't no women nowhere, just a bunch of men. Don't ever get in the car with nobody unless I'm there to go with you. Don't go nowhere with nobody in no car."

And later she said to the neighbor, "Don't never let my niece leave here in a car with a carload of white people. They could hurt her. You don't know where they was taking her." I didn't know where I was going myself.

"Don't you ever do that again," she said to me." I said, "I won't," and I didn't.

Interviewer: Okay, so then, you survived that awful day. You survived that awful day.

I was scared, but I made it. Thank God I made it.

Interviewer: Good, okay. So then, you said there were three families? Who was the third person that you worked for? Was there anyone else?

The police. I worked for the police. I worked for him about two or three months. Cleaning. Cooking. Washing. Dusting. Everything you could think of. That's what I did. The policeman had a little house. Let me see, he had three bedrooms, a living room and a dining room and a kitchen.

He would come home to eat lunch, but his wife she didn't come to eat lunch, both of them was working, I don't know where she was working at, but I know he was a policeman because he would come and pick me up in the police car and then he'd take me home in the police car.

He hired me as a cleaning lady. I was paid two dollars an hour, and I worked from seven until four or five that evening.

Interviewer: Did you enjoy the work?

No, because I wasn't getting paid for what I was doing, but I had to take it because there was nothing nobody could do about it. You take what they gave you.

He never did anything for me. I remember one day I was driving, and another guy ran into the car, and I was trying to tell him about the guy running into my car. And you know what he said, "Oh I heard about that." That's all.

Well, the police come to my house one day, and they told me, "You got your license?" and I said "No sir." And he said, "Well, if you got no license you can't be driving the car no more."

Interviewer: Can you say more about what the working conditions were like? Did these people allow you to use the restroom in the house?

Yeah, when they wasn't there. Then I would clean it back up. See nobody was around where I was working, wasn't nothing but white people around there, and I couldn't go to their houses, so I used the restroom there and I cleaned it back up.

No, they didn't like colored people using their restrooms. I don't know if they thought we had some type of disease; I don't know—they didn't say. They just said we wasn't allow to use the restroom.

Interviewer: How about other rules in that place?

I couldn't go through the front door but had to go around through the kitchen door.

Interviewer: Did they allow you to eat at the table with them?

No. I could not eat at the table with no white folk. They not going to have a black person sitting at their table among all the white folks. That's a disgrace to them. You couldn't eat. You could prepare, but you could not eat. You ate after they ate.

Interviewer: Would he give you anything extra like food to take home? Maybe for a birthday present or Christmas gift or Christmas bonus? Anything like that?

I— *[laughing]*. I don't know what that is. It'd be hard to tell you the truth.

Interviewer: Now did he or the other family you worked for, did they ever talk to you about maybe going back to school, getting an education and doing something different?

Are you serious? Only if someone went to school with the white kids. Colored kids, if you was big enough to work, you worked. All but the young kids like five or six years old or seven or eight years old wasn't big enough to work. Other than that we had to work.

Interviewer: Did you learn anything from working for any of these families?

Well, I'll tell you one thing you can't take for granted, you got to take what you can get. And I learned what I did, I did it from my heart. What they done, they . . . they got to pay for what they did, not me.

Yeah. That's what I tell my grandbabies. I don't like to talk about this, it hurts too much. It brings back all the memories and things you know, what you done and where you come from. It hurts *[sounding tearful]*. I used to sit and look at my mother, and I told her one day, I said, "Mom, when I get grown you won't have to do this." But she didn't make it; she passed away, it was this month. I buried my mother Christmas Day. I don't like to talk about it.

Interviewer: I understand. . . . I do want to talk about your mother because I think our kids need to hear it. They need to know that the struggles that black people have gone through to get to the point where we are today because our children are a lost generation. They don't know the history of the struggle and they need a better appreciation of what they have so they don't take it for granted. So your story is compelling. We need it. We need to hear it. People need to know about it, to get them excited about getting an education.

That's what this is all about. Okay. This is important, very important. We can't lose this type of history.

It's a heartache.

Interviewer: Yeah, it happened, it's a reality. It's very, very, very real.

And my grandmother, my mother's mother, she said, "You know I worked for twenty-five cents a day." That's all they would give her. And we would sit and listen to her, and she'd say, "Darling, work happens. We were glad to get that twenty-five cents."

And I said, "What could you do with twenty-five cents, Grandma?" She said, "Honey, you take that twenty-five cents—groceries wasn't high then—and you get you a sack of potatoes—they was a nickel. I said, "A nickel?" And she said, "Yeah." She said that twenty-five cents went a long way, and I believed her.

Interviewer: Let's talk a little bit more about your grandmother. Can you tell me about her?

Her name was Lula Codeman. Grandma told us so many stories, there's so many of them that I don't recall. All I know is that she said she used to work for white folks, and she said how they would treat her back then. I don't remember all these stories.

Interviewer: Okay. What about your mother and what you remember of her work as a cleaning lady?

My mother—they called her a live-in maid because she stayed with the white folks. She left us with our grandmother so she could go off to work. And I remember her coming home, and I was so glad to see my mother. She stayed with us Saturday and Sunday, and she told me, she said, "Baby, Mamma got to leave again." And I would cry. I didn't want my mother to leave, but she did. And my grandmother took me into the kitchen as she didn't want my mother to see me crying and feel sorry because she had to leave me. So I was crying and I didn't want her to go. And my sisters would say, "Sister, it's gonna be okay, it's gonna be okay. Momma be back." I didn't want to hear it. I wanted my mother there with me then. But she couldn't take care of me; she had to work.

Interviewer: Now this is important because it shows the sacrifice that had to be made for the mother to provide when the father wasn't there, that's what she was doing. Did she at all tell you about the family she worked for and if they were good to her?

She wouldn't tell us.

Interviewer: And your father, do you remember what happened to him?

Well, I was too young to remember, but they say he fell off a truck and somebody said they pushed him off. I don't know. I know I growed up without a father.

When my father passed away, Mamma had five kids. She had two girls and three boys. Then she met this other guy. She married him, and she had two girls with him and had five boys with him. But we said that was our whole sister now, we don't go for that half brother and sister stuff, because we all come from the same mother.

Interviewer: Is there something that we think about the youth today and we hope that—what would you hope that they would learn from your story?

You know sometimes I set up here and I tell my grandbabies how we used to have to do. You know what they tell me? "That was back in the olden days." I say, "No, Honey, you just don't understand. This was real." And I tell them how we were being treated, and they say, "No, I wouldn't have took it." But I say, "No, you would have took it, what we did, because there was nothing you could do about it." The kids today, they think it's a joke, but it's no joke, it was real.

I hope they will hear our stories and learn the truth because I don't want them to go through what we had to go through. I know some of them say they wouldn't take it, what we had to put up with, but they would have.

I wish to God I could tell you more, but it's too painful *[long pause]*.

They [the children] don't believe these things because they don't see it. They can't see what you trying to tell them. The think what happened in the olden days is not important to them now.

Interviewer: Now you've told about your life and your mother's life in the South. Was moving to Iowa, your coming here, a way for you to improve your life?

Yeah, because when I was down there I was working for the white people or I was working on the field. Up here the treatment was better. But oh boy, it's been a long time a coming. I didn't get up here until the 1970s. My sister-in-law was moving up here so I come up here and stay with them and my sister's kids, and I never went back.

My aunt was working at Holiday Inn, and she told me I could get a job there; all I had to do was go up there and fill out an application, and that's what I did. I worked at Holiday Inn. The pay was better, and I was working for black people. And they treated me nice. I stayed there ten years, and then I went to Hotel Fort Des Moines, and I stayed there for seventeen years. That's where I retired from.

Interviewer: How many children and grandchildren do you have?

I got three kids. My son, he's fifty. I got a heap of grandkids, but me myself, I got two girls and one son.

Interviewer: So do you think they would be doing better down there or here?

They do better here.

Interviewer: Well, I think we're good, I think we're good. We got through all the questions, and you gave me even more information than I thought I was going to get, so this went really good.

I hope so. It was painful, but telling about it helped me get through.

Odessa Roberts, from Monroe, Louisiana (born 1937). Interviewed by David W. Jackson. "I came from a little nobody to somebody."

The day of the assassination of President Kennedy is one that Odessa Roberts (not her real name) will never forget for many reasons. She made a decision that day that became for her a major turning point and led her to join the Great Migration north. The contrast between her life growing up in Louisiana and the life she was able to provide for her children in Iowa is striking.

I started work as a cleaning lady when I was seventeen, eighteen years old working for Mrs. Ledbetter and Mrs. Ellison. Those were the first ladies I worked for. Also I would babysit for the children and babies. I did all the cooking. I was an all-in-one cleaning lady/maid. I did it all. I worked from eight to four. During that time they paid three to four dollars a day. One lady was four dollars. That added up to fifteen to twenty dollars a week, eight to four o'clock.

The first lady I worked for was Mrs. Ledbetter. She was a doctor's wife. I just cooked regular meals—chicken, greens, and they liked the southern meal like the blacks ate. Then she raised me to five dollars a day. That was what the rich people paid you.

Interviewer: So this woman ate "soul food," as we would call it?

Yeah, she ate chicken, fried chicken, all of that—greens and potato pies. That's when I learned to really cook because I had watched my grandmother. My grandmother was a good cook from her own recipe. She didn't read nothing in a cookbook; she did it from her mind.

Mrs. Ledbetter was rich; all of them was rich. She didn't work at all or do any of the cleaning. I did all of that—the cleaning, the cooking, washing the babies. But she was nice. Gave me leftover things, like stuff—food—we left over, she would give me to take home. That was her kindness.

She was smaller than me so I couldn't wear her clothes, but Mrs. Stevenson, who I worked for later, was my size and she gave me clothes. Later on, Mrs. Ledbetter bought some clothes for me and passed on some for my girls.

Interviewer: Did you enjoy working with this woman?

I did then, because I needed the money and down South we didn't have much, but then things were a whole lot cheaper. You could rent an apartment for fifteen dollars a month.

Interviewer: Could you sit down and eat with her at the table? Come through the front door? Use the bathroom?

I never did eat at the table because I was so busy serving. I could eat meals from what I cooked. And I came through the front door and could use the restroom in the house.

Interviewer: Did you have to wear a uniform?

Yeah. I had to wear a uniform. Usually they were green or white. I had three uniforms that Mrs. Ledbetter bought for me. They had buttons down the front. Snaps in the front.

Interviewer: You talked about how you had a good relationship with her. Did she teach you anything about religion, life, or race relations?

No. She wasn't with any religion. I went to my First Baptist Church then and she was Catholic. I can't remember what religion she was with, maybe Catholic, but I wasn't sure. There wasn't any discussion about race. With the white people back then, there wasn't any discussing about that with us. It was kind of like a segregated discussion. But they definitely stayed in their own race, you know, the white race. They never even crossed over into another religion. They married Catholics, their friends were Catholics.

I want to talk about working for Mrs. Ellison. Her husband was very racist. I would work from eight o'clock until four. That was the hours—early in the morning and late evenings. All day long: cooking, washing, the ironing, cleaning. And I really had to get all that done before I left.

I used to set the table and serve the food. I remember one time I was serving coffee and the lid fell off. It fell on the table. Oh, he had a fit! He was something, I'm telling you.

Back in the sixties it was rough. Anyone from the sixties will be able to tell you the history of that time. But I did it [worked as a servant], and a lot of other folks did too.

Their daughter had some friends who were very prejudiced. They were all dancing one day, and the record was playing, and she asked, "Odessa, can you do the nigger dance?" That's what they said. The daughter didn't say it; it was her daughter's friends who said it. I didn't even answer; I just kept on going to work.

Her father was very prejudiced. I remember one time, I didn't have a washing machine so I brought my bedspread to wash. He saw it hanging on the line; he knows every piece that hangs on the line, and he said to his wife, "Who brought this bedspread?" And she said, "Odessa," and he said, "Tell her to take it off the line; I don't want her hanging her clothes on my line!"

I didn't bring it back again. That hurt my feelings. He was very, a very prejudiced man. That was the time when President John Kennedy was killed. I asked him a question and asked him about the incident. He said, "Oh, as that he was a father, I think that was awful, but as a president that's what he deserved." That's just what he said. But let me tell you what I did to him—I quit working for her. She called my aunt the day I didn't show up for work and asked, "Where's Odessa? Is she coming to work today?" My aunt said, "No, Odessa left the town." I just up and left; I didn't tell her I was leaving. Yeah. And Mrs. Ellison said, "Well, I have all this cleaning and washing to do." My aunt said, "Well if you want to get ahold of Odessa, you've got to go to Des Moines, Iowa." I was on my way on the train to Iowa and I left her! That hurt them so bad! So that was the end of that.

I moved further to a BETTER place.

Interviewer: Good that you are here in Iowa, because I have the opportunity to sit here and talk with you. So were there any other incidents like that?

Down in Louisiana it all wasn't good; I grew up there until I was a teenager, and it wasn't good at all. We sharecropped.

Interviewer: I want to know more about this woman. Did she confide in you at all?

No, she didn't talk to me much, but sometimes her daughter, Katlyn, would talk to me about different things, you know. Sometimes Katlyn would talk to me about things. Not very bad things, just problems she would have with her boyfriend, just teenage talk, you know. She was very nice. She was a very nice white girl.

Interviewer: Let's get back to the working conditions. Did Mrs. Ellison have you wearing a uniform or anything? Or give you anything?

She didn't care so much about the uniform so much as I was there. I had no gifts from there. Except Mrs. Ellison did give me a sofa one time that laid out to a bed. It was pretty nice. In her way of speaking, she was trying to be nice if she could. But she was still prejudiced toward me.

And there she was when I left—she was looking for me on the phone! *[shared laughter with the interviewer]*.

I left her! And, she deserved it! *[mimicking her voice]* "I have a lot of work to do." "Well, you will have to get ahold of her in Des Moines, Iowa" *[both laughing]*.

Interviewer: So were you able to go through the front door or the back door? And how about the bathroom?

I always went through the kitchen door because that was more convenient for me. I had to use the restroom because I worked all day.

Interviewer: Did you ever eat with the family?

No, I never ate with them. But if he was there, he wouldn't have let me. I'm sure she wouldn't have minded. He was something else. I couldn't stand him, but I took off and left him. I'll never forget what he said about President John Kennedy. I thought it was terrible thing to say. But I tricked him! I left him!

Interviewer: Did anyone try to encourage you to get some education or help you out with that?

No. We didn't talk about education because down South, they didn't want you to have it. Because they wanted to keep you under them. Growing up in the fifties and sixties wasn't easy for a black person.

Being a maid was hard; we just had to do hard work. I once had to do work for this other lady; I'm trying to remember her name. She had a beautiful house. The house was white; the outside brick was white; her floors were white. I had to mop on my hands and knees. I had to scrub on my hands and knees.

I had dark spots on my knees when I did it. They changed it to a dark color. It was bad in those days.

Interviewer: Who's the next woman you worked for?

The Ellisons ended the South. I went to Lincoln, Nebraska. That's when I worked for a family, and the mother owned a modern school. Now, they were beautiful people. I would just go in for a few hours in the evening and cook. I was just a cook then. The lady was very, very good to me. She had one little girl and that's when my pay started going up to thirty dollars a week. They didn't want much. I cooked, did a little washing, and dishes. It was when things started looking better.

Interviewer: Did they like your soul food too?

Oh yeah! They loved my fried food. They like my fried chicken, and potatoes. I cooked potatoes, with butter, salt, and pepper. They called them Irish potatoes. They loved my chicken, though. But yeah, that's when things started looking better. Then from Lincoln, Nebraska, I moved here to Des Moines, Iowa, and that when things started really looking good. They were paying five dollars an hour. That was good money! You were treated like you were a person too. Much better. Yeah, that was one lady I worked with, they were my friends. But yeah, when I moved here everything got bright. Des Moines, Iowa, is good for education. All of my kids were put in these schools, and I hope they continue because they will be rewarded.

But I did have some history with the maid work. I remember it was hard coming up as a black woman in the South. Raising my children I pushed them all for an education because I didn't have it. They grew up well, though. My boy is a lawyer out in Washington. I mean, he's an attorney.

Yeah, I made it better for myself. Anyone can do it. You have to make life better for yourself. There is no one out there who is better in making your life better than you.

Interviewer: How much education did you get?

I made it to the tenth grade. My husband was in the service, and service members didn't make any money so I worked to help bring in income. So this was all I needed to do. But I educated myself and did some nurse's assistant training until I retired from it. But I overcame all of it. I had a mind to be better.

Yeah, I went to a nursing home, and they gave me classes. It was at Riverview Manor. I had someone that started me up with education. A girl by the name of Sandy helped me, and I learned from her. I put all the housework down and become a nurse's assistant. They called it a nurse's aide. I was a nurse's assistant for nine years. Then I started to private duty.

I did things nurses did then, and look at me now! I came from a little nobody to somebody. I bought a home and met my second husband when I was fifty years old. He's a deacon in a church, and he's beautiful! So I came from a nobody to a somebody. I always kept a positive thinking frame that tomorrow will be a better day, and this is what kept me going.

Interviewer: What did you do to get yourself through the day when you were living in the South?

I always went to church with my grandmother. I always kept looking forward to tomorrow being a better day, and later I taught my children this. Positive thinking got me through it. They were very prejudiced down there and still are somewhat, but I don't hold it against them because they didn't know any better. But Martin Luther King opened a lot of gates for people to pass through.

Ruthie O'Neal, from Taylor, Mississippi (born 1940). Interviewed by David W. Jackson. "She's twelve years old; call her Miss Nancy."

Known as "the purple lady" for her heavy use of this color in her art, Ruthie O'Neal spent much of her childhood in a beautiful mansion where her grand-

Ruthie O'Neal today. *Photo by David Jackson.*

Ruthie O'Neal in 1999, showing off her yard art. Each piece represents an episode from her earlier life down south. *Photo by David Jackson.*

mother worked as a maid. Her great dream was to one day have a lovely place of her own. Today, she is well known in Waterloo, Iowa, for her elaborately decorated front yard, her bright purple yard art. Each piece of the art carries a special meaning from her long-ago childhood in Mississippi, including even a willow tree to represent the switchings she received from this tree as a child. Through her yard art, she has reconstructed her past in the form of objects of remembrance.

I moved with my grandmother—my father's mother—to Taylor, Mississippi, when I was three years old. That's where I lived until I was fifteen. Then I came to Waterloo when I was fifteen, and then I stayed with my dad until I am where I am today.

My grandma lived on a plantation. It was a sort of a farm owned by Mr. Leland Norris. There were a lot of black people on their place. Well, when Mr. Norris moved out, we moved in his house. And that is where me and my grandmother lived, in sort of a mansion house. I guess she got to live there because she was an older lady and she didn't have any husband, so he chose her to stay there. And she mostly did a lot of washing for white folks.

Her name was Helen Sisk. Yeah, that was her name. And the white people down there called her "Mamma." She worked for Leland Norris, who worked for the Illinois Central Train. She called herself a cleaning lady. She didn't do any cooking. She did house cleaning. Mr. Norris had a lot of land. All the black people worked on his land, which was between Oxford and Water Valley. The lady's name was Georgia Norris. The woman was stingy; she'd growl all the time. She'd say, "No you can't have that." She would have my grandmother to her house to clean or do washing. She would pick her up and take her there, and then they would bring her back. She would wash all day long, because she had to wash, iron, and dry. She washed by hand on a scrub board. They didn't have dryers at that time. They mostly put the clothes on the line. They had to wait until they were dry and then iron them.

They, the Norrises, were close to my grandmother. They lady was the only one who was different. But the man was good; he would give you anything you wanted. He wasn't prejudiced like she was.

With all the children, it was just like my grandmother was their grandmother. They would run and hug, hang on her, and kiss on her. They would have parties, called picnic parties. And that man would come down there and

Helen Sisk, grandmother of Ruthie O'Neal and great-grandmother of Charletta Sudduth. Ms. Sisk worked as a domestic all her adult life. *From the family collection of Annie Pearl Stevenson.*

get in the party and dance. The children would come. They would have fun. The lady never came; she was just a grouchy old lady. She was mean to her husband; he just didn't pay her any attention.

My grandmother worked in the garden all the time. When they planted cotton, she would hoe cotton. And when the cotton would come, she would pick cotton. And she had a big garden so she would get the stuff out of the garden, the vegetables and stuff. She would can a lot. When she would get through with everything, they would come and get it. There were a lot of children out there working hard, pulling that stuff up and fixing that stuff. They would come and get it. That is the way they got their food and stuff, by my grandmother fixing it. She would shell peas and cut corn off the cob. My grandma would pack it all up and can. They would come up and get all that stuff. She did a lot of work. She would say "Ya'll children come and help me do such and such a thing." And we would be mad because we had to do it. We didn't get any of it and it was given to all the white boys. We would be growling.

My grandma lived to be one of the oldest ladies in Mississippi. Everybody was crazy about her, white and black. So they always came to her and got information from her and stuff like that.

Men and women's roles were about the same. If the woman could handle the work, she had to do it. She did everything except for plow with the mule. The men did that. A few women would plow like the men, but not in our area. In our area the men did it.

My grandmother prayed. She prayed more than she sang. She didn't sing that much, but I know she prayed. I heard people talking about how she raised those kids, the Norris kids. My grandmother told me how she raised so-and-so. And when one of the girls turned twelve years old, this lady told her, "Now, Helen, she's twelve years old; you have to say 'yes ma'am,' 'no ma'am,' and call her 'Miss.' Call her Miss Nancy." My grandmother helped raise this child. Nancy was a little bit older than I was. I could call her Nancy and say yes and no. It was okay because we were around the same age. But my grandmother had to say "yes ma'am" and "no ma'am" to Nancy. I guess it was a racial thing because you had to say "yes ma'am" and "no ma'am." Well you could say it to a small kid but once they were a certain age you had to change it.

Interviewer: How did the white people feel toward black people?

I don't know how they felt toward black people. The kids got away with more. They didn't bother kids too much. It was mostly the older folks that they bothered. White folks hung out at a little store. That's where they all sat around and talked. We would go up there at the end of the workday, and they would pay us. They didn't do or say anything to us. Everybody just went on about their business. It didn't look like they were prejudiced, but I presume they were because we were separated. We weren't allowed to do anything, so we did just what our parents said to do. If they said you're not supposed to do that or go over there, we did not. We went on about our own business.

When I was a little girl, we used to make playhouses. We didn't have any toys and dolls and things like they do today. We made our dolls out of sticks, corn shucks, and stuff like that. So I used to have a little playhouse. And I had sticks and got little tops and would make mud pies and cakes. And we'd take the sticks and put the shucks on the head, for their hair. And then I would get these berries that I would get the color from and paint the dolls' hair and their clothes. It gave me the color purple. Purple was my favorite color.

You know kids could do what they wanted. Kids could play with white kids and all that. We played with one another, we worked together, we hit one another, and called one another names, and everything. But they [the whites] knew the difference. We didn't know the difference. Our parents kept us from associating with them because, "You not allowed to do that; that's Miss So-and-So," you know.

So there was a lot of discrimination at that time. The whites went their way, we went our way. We went to our school, and they went to their school. We had our separate buses and everything. In certain areas of Taylor, Mississippi, we were not allowed to go there, you know. They had an area for the white and an area for the black.

Interviewer: Were there any special rules you had to follow?

We had to use the back door, could not go through the front. She could use the restroom in the house. They had everything in the house. She did not wear a uniform. She wore everyday clothes. She wasn't dressed like a maid or anything. My grandmother never mentioned any sexual aggression. When I was old enough to get involved, there really wasn't anyone there but the husband and wife. All the kids were grown up and had their own homes.

When my grandmother got real old and couldn't do anything anymore, she sent me down there to work for Mrs. Georgia Norris. I was about thirteen or fourteen years old. I worked down there for about a year. I lived there in the house. My grandmother couldn't do what she used to do, so I did it. But I never washed the clothes. I guess Mrs. Georgia did all the washing. I remember washing dishes, mopping the kitchen, dusting the furniture, and things like that. I stayed in one of the rooms, in a sleeping room. She gave me change, no big money. She cooked and I ate the food.

When I wasn't working, there really wasn't anything to do because there was no TV and no books. Mostly I just sat there and thought, I guess. I thought about home, what was going on in school, and stuff like that. But I didn't have anything to read or do.

It was lightning, thundering, and raining one night. I didn't know white folks called black people "darkies." That night she was talking on the phone and she said, "Yes, there's nobody here but me and Darky." I thought she was saying Dorothy! And she kept saying, and "Darky this, Darky that." And

"We're doing fine. And Darky's doing pretty good. I kind of like Darky." I don't know what kept me from saying, "My name isn't Dorothy, it's Ruthie!" I went home and was telling my grandmother what she was saying, and my Aunt T. said, "She wasn't saying Dorothy, she was saying Darky!" She said, "That's what they call us." I said, "Why would they call us 'darkies'?" And she said, "Because we're black."

She wasn't cruel to me though. She would always talk to me nice, and try and get me to go downtown. She would give me a little change and try and say you can go downtown. She'd say, "Don't sit down here by yourself all the time. Walk downtown." She was real nice to me like that. She treated me like I was a little girl. But she didn't teach me anything. No, they didn't want you to know anything. They didn't teach about no school, no nothing.

I stayed there for about a year, living there and helping her. Doing dishes there was a part of the arrangement. I don't know if they talked it over or if she asked my grandmother about me doing it. The only thing I know was, my grandma said, "Well, I can't do it now; I'm older. I can't do it." And I had to go down there and help Mrs. Georgia Norris. So Mrs. Georgia came and got me and I went down there. I would come home on some weekends. I didn't get to go home unless Mrs. Georgia wanted to go back up there for something.

Mrs. Georgia's house was a big and beautiful home. I washed dishes there three times a day there because they ate three times a day, breakfast, lunch, and supper. I did not eat with them. I ate later. I ate after they were through and had gone to sit and relax. Then I ate. I would help myself to whatever was left, and then I would clean up. I washed my own laundry whenever I went back home. I took it back home with me.

My grandmother was in her seventies at this point. When I had come to the house when I was a baby, she was about sixty years old. Everybody told my grandma, "You shouldn't have taken those kids; you know you're too old to have those children. Those kids are going to grow up into teenagers and you're not going to be able to handle those kids." She was always tired! *[laughing]*.

I didn't see any young people there at the Norrises' house. I didn't see any black people because the black people didn't live in town. They mostly lived out in the country. Nancy wasn't there then. The only way I got to see Nancy and her sister was when they came to visit Mrs. Georgia.

Mrs. Norris would entertain. She entertained family and friends. She did everything herself. Sometimes her daughter would come over and they cooked. They cooked big dinners. All I did was wash dishes. I did not attend school then. School was not a priority. When I didn't work, I just sat. I didn't have any books to look at, no TV. Most of the time, I would sit outside in the back. They had a big backyard. When her daughter came, she would bring her dog and cat with her. I looked forward to when they came. The family would sit down at the table and eat and talk. They said a prayer, blessings. They ate every day at the same time. The dishes were fancy. They were nice dishes. They had a big dining room. That is how I learned to set tables. I cleaned up in there. It stayed beautiful all the time! The food was bland, but similar to black food. It was cooked, but it wasn't seasoned! *[laughing]*. It looked good but it wasn't as good as my grandmother's. It was plain old food. They had beans, greens, cabbage, and peas. In the morning they had eggs, bacon, and sausage.

When Mr. Norris went to visit my grandmother, he always ate whatever my grandmother ate. He ate it! If she was cooking, he would go in and eat until he was full. He made himself at home. Mrs. Norris—I never saw her eat anything that black people cooked. Now, if she did, she had to be alone because she never ate anything at my grandmother's house.

On the plantation, Mr. Norris had cotton, corn, sorghum, beans, and everything. There were probably forty or fifty people working there. Mr. Norris really liked my grandma. He would come over and have a couple beers and just be partying with us! *[laughing]*. We would have a good time with Mr. Norris. And Mrs. Norris would be angry because he would give himself over to us. And she didn't like that at all! *[laughing]*.

I never experienced any sexual aggression from any of the men. When the kids came to visit Mrs. Norris, I never saw the husband. The only thing I saw was a man that was her son. He was married and out too. He would come there but he never said anything to me or anything. Even Mr. Leland, I stayed there and he never said a word out of line or came into the place where I slept at or anything!

Interviewer: Did the family give you any gifts?

They never gave me or my grandmother anything! The family always said she owed them! So when the crop was finished, she didn't get anything. No money for doing it. They said, "You don't get any money because you owed me this. So it breaks off even." But when I left I don't know what happened after that.

I admired their home and decorations. They had a beautiful home, and a yard, and the flowers. I always admired it. I used to sit around and daydream about whenever I get grown, I'm going to do my house and stuff like that. I always wanted that.

My dad called for me and I moved to Waterloo, Iowa. I was around fifteen then. I attended East High School, and had to work harder than the other kids because I was behind. But I got good grades and did well in art. I got married when I finished school. My husband was a quiet guy, tall, and thin; he didn't talk very much, you know. And he loved doing whatever he did at his job. He loved that. He worked at Rath's Packing Company. We raised two children and lots of foster kids, and when we got married we bought this home.

Interviewer: Now can you describe how you came to make these decorations in your yard?

As a child I used to decorate the front and backyards. But later I had forgot about it, I had said to myself. Until one day I was working in the yard and I was just doing different things and something came to me and said, "You know, this is what you wanted when you was a little girl." This is where I live out my dreams, right here. I express myself right there. And I didn't get involved with this until after my husband died because everything I would put up, he would tear down! So when he died I said, "Now I can do what I want to do!" *[laughing]*.

The house that we lived in in Mississippi was designed with wagon wheels all around it. I loved that house! Oh, I thought it was the most beautiful thing I ever saw in my life. And that is why I got this design, that I was going to paint my house purple and I was going to fix my house just like the house I was raised in. That was my color—purple. When I started dreaming, everything that I want was going to be in purple. I was going to put purple here and purple there and that's how I got into the purple color of my house. I would do my yard this way, and when I got here I started little by little.

Interviewer: What is the meaning of these two German shepherds [referring to statues]?

They mean, see these wagon wheels in the house that I was raised in, they had these two big old white dogs. But they would sit up on these high pillars. I don't have them on high pillars, but they would sit them on these high pillars, and the two dogs sat on each side. They were high, you know. And that is where we played at all the time, around those dogs and wagon wheels and flowers and things, you know. And I said, "Oh my God, that would be so pretty!" We used to go out there and play with them. That's all I did.

Interviewer: How about the oak tree which is decorated with ribbons in your front yard?

That is the way that house was designed. They had a great big old tree right off from the dogs. And they had a lot of stuff on it. I don't know what it was, but I thought it was so pretty. And where they had it fixed, they had ribbons, different things, designs and pictures on this tree.

Interviewer: What is the meaning of the church pew?

That church pew means, well, there used to be a lot of churches at that time down there that had benches on them, out there in the church yard. But they would be under the tree like when church would turn out, people used to sit out there under those trees.

Interviewer: How about the train by the pond?

The train means that when we used to be little kids, there used to be a train that would come down from Taylor store down to the trussels. We called it the trussels. Everybody called it the old trussels, "We're going up to the old trussels." When we were kids we used to run up there every day to see the train go under the trussel. And we stood up over it, and they would wave at us down there. And we loved that!

Interviewer: Moving to the backyard, what about the willow tree with a chair sitting underneath it?

The willow tree is where we used to get whuppings from *[laughing]*. We used to get those trees and braid them together. And they were long. We would run and my grandma could reach and get us with the willow switch and pull us toward her! So that is all that is for. It reminds me of when we used to get whuppings.

Interviewer: How many pieces of art do you think you have in your yard?

You know I never counted them! *[laughing]*. Oh, I think about two or three hundred pieces. I didn't pay very much for them because most of it, I just pick up stuff. Like going out in the country, there is stuff on the side of the road. I just get it and paint it and fix it up the way I want it to be done. People throw away things that were not any good. I would see something there that I could do something with. That is how that works, how I got that. So it didn't cost me very much.

Interviewer: What do you want people to come away with when they view your art?

To learn that anything you start out, you do. You can do it if you put all your mind to it. You can do anything that you want to, because I started as a little girl dreaming and later piecing things together, and I carried it out.

Annie Pearl Stevenson, from Oxford, Mississippi (born 1945). Interviewed by Charletta Sudduth. "You never went in the front door."

In this interview, Charletta Sudduth gets in touch with an aspect of her mother's life she had never quite realized before. This narrative holds significance in that it connects us to the home of William Faulkner as well as to the interviews above of Pearline Sisk Jones (Mrs. Stevenson's aunt) and of Ruthie O'Neal (her cousin). Mrs. Stevenson spent one memorable day working with her Aunt Pearline as a domestic at Rowan Oak—William Faulkner's home. One day the narrator accompanied her aunt to help clean that renowned author's home.

I was born September 23, 1945. We lived on a farm. We grew all our food. That was our living. My father not only farmed cotton and corn. He also

Annie Pearl Stevenson at her high school graduation in Oxford, Mississippi. *From the family collection of Charletta Sudduth.*

Annie Pearl Stevenson with her daughter, Charletta Sudduth, today. *From the family collection of Charletta Sudduth.*

farmed gardens. We always preserved the food. He had his own land at this time. At first, when I was a little girl, we lived on someone else's place. By the time I got old enough to work, we had our own land. My dad used to be a sharecropper. He was a very smart man, though, because he would not allow us to go uptown or to Taylor. Because what they would do is allow people to take up credit. They would allow them to buy food on credit in order to take money out of the crop, when the crops came in. He didn't want us to do that because whether you took up the amount of your profit or not, they would say you had spent all of your money. And you couldn't argue that. So we had to do without a lot because my dad would not allow us to go uptown to Taylor, Mississippi, to that store to get credit. The white men would say, "This is what you've got and this is on the books. You have eaten up all your crop this year." So you worked on sharecrops. So you had eaten up your share. And believe it or not, many people ate up their share! Because that was a trick of the enemy. You could never say, "No, I did not eat up my share." You could never call the white person a liar. You could never dispute, even if you had wrote down what you had got. What my dad would do is, we would raise everything. We would raise all the vegetables. We would even raise all the meat: hogs, cows, and chickens. We had eggs and milk. So all my dad would go to town to buy would be flour because we couldn't raise that and sugar. If we ran out of sugar before the month was up, before the end of the month, my mom would use sorghum molasses to sweeten the cakes. We never got a chance to take up credit at the store. But that was specific to my dad. He always wanted to clear, that's the way he talked, "I want to clear some money out of my crop, out of the cotton that we grew and picked." My dad saved a little bit and eventually he bought the land.

My mother was always on the farm. I think my mother never did domestic work because for one thing she had her hands full at home with nine children. And my dad being a farmer, he was an early riser. Food had to be on the table. Lunches had to be packed because they were going to the field, they took lunch. My mom had to do all that and yet be ready to go to the field. Also, my mom worked in the fields. Now, what I would do is work the fields, but after the fields were done, my dad then would let us go up and stay with my aunt. It seemed to me that after my mom died we had more privileges from my dad.

Interviewer: Is it true that some of the black men did not want their wives to work for white people? Was this the case in your family?

I am sure that my dad would have been one of them. He didn't want us to do that. I think for my dad it was pride. Because he was a very prideful man. I do know that for a fact! He believed in earning a living for his family.

As a matter of fact, I was probably the only one allowed to work domestic. My sister Lilied worked a couple times with me. She did work somewhat as a maid.

I started working for white people at the age of fifteen in Oxford, Mississippi. At first I did domestic work. There were two of us girls that always worked together. We would clean houses, and we ironed all of the husbands' shirts, about twenty or thirty a day. And it was only on the weekends that we would go and clean. It would be like on a Saturday when there was no school. The house was a big house, it was huge. But of course I was a little girl then. I would say there were at least three bedrooms, a formal dining room, a kitchen, a couple—two or three bathrooms, a utility room. It was a big house. We cleaned each room. Me and my cousin would take turns. If she did the bathrooms, then I would do the bathrooms. And together we would iron about fifty big shirts. The man we worked for was a restaurant owner, and he changed shirts at least twice a day because it was hot! He would bring us our lunch from his restaurant every day. Sometimes if he did not bring it, we would go to the back door and get it and take it home with us. I don't remember much about the restaurant because we were not allowed in the front of the restaurant. We always had to go around to the back, and they would hand the lunch out to us. Probably black people were cooking in the back.

The wife worked in the restaurant as well. They trusted us in the house while they were gone. They would come and pick us up. We had a certain place where we would meet them, and we would walk to this place. They would come pick us up and take us out to the house, which was out of town on an acreage. They would leave us there and probably give us four hours to get everything done, and they'd come out and get us. There was no uniform. We went in the side door. We never went in the front door.

The work conditions were really good in this particular setting. If I recall, the owners were Italian people. So they were not quite as hard on us, I would say, as perhaps some of the whites that lived down there who were from there. These people looked like they came from somewhere else. And I never did question them because we weren't allowed to do all that questioning. But they were Italians. We made fifty cents an hour. We were paid cash. I worked for that family and then there was another family in Oxford that I worked for after I stopped working for this family. There were two other ones. I did the same thing. I ironed, mopped, and cleaned bathrooms. I don't recall having to do the bedrooms. I did the dining room and the family room. I did not have to prepare any meals for them. I was just a little girl and they probably didn't trust me. But in this particular house, I had to do it by myself. My cousin had a job. And these people had a store, Nelson's Store, uptown. So they would come get me and take me to their house and I would work for them for about four hours on a Saturday. If they had clothing that was too little or wouldn't sell, they would give them to me, from the department store. This store was located in Oxford, Mississippi. It still is, as a matter of a fact. It is located right next to the post office. When you go around the square, it is about two stores down from the post office. The post office is on the corner. They were nice to me.

One family I worked for, and they were nice people to work for, were college people who came down to go to the university, Ole Miss. They had two children. It seemed to me that I didn't have to watch them that much, but we had to clean. We did cleaning instead of babysitting. They were nice people. They paid me and everything. The kids were pretty nice. I guess I always remember the children would be going uptown to shop, they called it. They looked really dressed up. I always thought that was a fun thing to do, to let your children go uptown. They had their own money, a little purse, and would shop. I think seeing those kids had an impact on how I raised my children. Because I had always wanted them to have the same things, to go uptown and shop. To have money in your purse, not to worry about anything, just have fun. Go to a movie because that was something we couldn't do.

The main rules were to never enter through the front of the house. When we got ready to eat, if we did not take our lunch home, you could not eat it at the main table. You had to eat it in a back room. I recall it was kind of a family room, back where we did all the work like ironing. This room was at the back of the house, this little room was, like a utility room. So we ironed in there and ate in there. And we used the bathroom, if we had to; they had a little separate bathroom you could use. We could wash our hands back there where we ate.

These Italians were rich people. I called them rich people, especially these Italian people that owned that restaurant. I always said they had money. You could tell they had money. I could tell from as many shirts that he had for me to iron, for one thing. And he was not a little man; he was a big man.

I could tell they were rich by them owning that restaurant too. They had the best hamburgers and cheeseburgers that a little child would ever eat! *[laughing]*. I was glad when he let us eat. He always did let us eat either a hamburger or a cheeseburger. We were not accustomed to eating that at all! Because there were certain foods you just didn't have because you couldn't raise it on the farm. Spaghetti, we never ate spaghetti. We lived on a farm and had to travel to town to work. There was a difference in food. Ice cream cones, when we went up town we would get ice cream cones. My aunt lived uptown. And on a Friday, when school was out, I would stay with her so I could go uptown. Then I would catch the bus, the five o'clock bus, and go to Water Valley. And that is where my dad would be to pick me up to take me back to the farm.

Interviewer: Did you think the white women were helpless in some ways?

You know, I never thought of them as helpless. I never put that in my mind that they were helpless. I just thought they had privilege.

Interviewer: Do you think there were any things the white people learned from the black people?

They probably learned how to cook from us. I think most black people cooked for them. My aunt did. They probably learned just how to keep house in general, ironing. They never had to do that work. They didn't grow up doing that.

I helped my aunt clean William Faulkner's home. He lived in Oxford. She took me by there one day to help her. That home looked like a mansion to me because I was a little girl. It was a big, white, beautiful home. The house was so white, I remember that. And the rooms, I would like to go back to that house, even after I got grown. And it's still standing, if I am not mistaken, in Oxford. We cleaned and dusted. I think my job was to probably dust while she changed the bedding. We mopped the floors. It was such a big house. Yes, he was an author at that time. In fact, that is why she took me there. She knew he was an author too. I don't recall seeing him at all. I probably saw pictures of everybody, family members you know. I don't really recall any stories of him from my aunt. She just always said he was famous. She met a lot of people, in fact. She was a good cook!

My aunt would cook for the whites a four-course meal. It would consist of a vegetable, salad, meat, potato, and dessert. I don't remember the items, but I know she prepared a four-course meal pretty much daily. She's ninety-some years old, still lives, and helped me with that. But she is the one that started me in doing, we didn't call it domestic work, I think we just called it housework, day work, or housecleaning, but it was domestic. And she is still alive.

Interviewer: Did you learn anything by working for the whites?

First of all, I learned how to really clean a house. Even in the bathroom that chrome had to be shiny. You could not leave it until the chrome was shiny. I also learned that you cannot pretend you have done something when you haven't. One time I pretended I had mopped the floor, because it looked like it had already been mopped. And I thought, I will just skip this floor. I was trying to get done in a hurry. And when she came home, the lady I worked for, she said, "Pearl did you do the kitchen floor?" And I said, "Yes ma'am." And she said, "Well there's a little grits still left on the floor. Would you do it again?" So I learned not to ever say I had done something when I had not. She didn't scold me; she was nice. I worked for nice people, I have to say that. I learned to be honest and not to say I had done something when I had not. You have to realize, I was just a little girl. I was fifteen or fourteen, something like that.

Interviewer: Did you learn any positive values from white people?

I knew I always wanted to go to college. Always. At that time, I really wanted to enroll in Ole Miss, which we could not because of the color of our skin. We could not go to Ole Miss; only whites could go to Ole Miss College. So then I turned my mind to either Jackson State College or Alcorn. Seeing the couple I worked for who went to Ole Miss College had an impact on me. Also I wanted an education just so I could get a better job. I never wanted to do that kind of work all my life. I wanted a better job so I could provide, like that couple that was going to college, for my family. It just seemed like it was the thing to do at that time. I saw that they were bettering themselves. So at that time it just seemed like it was the thing to do, to go to college and get an education and be able to support your family.

Interviewer: What were some of the negatives of this work?

There were not a lot of negatives. My dad would always say, on Saturday get on the bus and meet me in Water Valley. And the negative part of that was I would get done with my day work, walk to the bus station, and I would be at that bus station at probably one o'clock or one thirty. I would walk up to the lady, the clerk, and then we had to wait for the bus. It was like a hole in the wall. It was dirty—it was filthy, as a matter of fact. By "we," I mean we blacks. There were no chairs. There were crates that pop used to come in, wooden crates. And that is what we had to sit on, wooden crates or a broke-down chair.

I would go to the window when she was not busy, meaning the clerk. I would ask her for a ticket to Water Valley. I would want her to sell me one and I would pay for it. The first thing she would say is, "Well, you wait." And she would use the N word. So then I would go back and take a seat. As a little girl I was thinking, "I have got to get to Water Valley or my dad is going to cut out my job and not let me work." So I would sit back down. I would get back up and she would say, "I'm busy now!" And she would use the N word again and tell me to wait. I did this every Saturday. You would have thought I would have learned a lesson. But when the bus was there to pick up the passengers, and there we had to ride in the back of the bus, I would rush to window again. I would say, "Miss, I have to have a bus ticket! The bus is out." And she would use the N word again, saying, "Don't rush me." By now I was terrified because this driver is ready to go! I could not walk this distance. It was about eighteen or twenty miles. When I finally would get a ticket and get ready to get on the bus, he would set me out, the bus driver would. And he would use the N word, saying, "You gonna make me late." And that was every weekend. It terrified me.

Interviewer: What helped you survive this treatment?

I think the strength to want to earn my own money. I knew if my dad had known that he would not have allowed me to work uptown. First of all because of the treatment, the work treatment. He wouldn't have wanted that. He was a prideful man. That is why if he had known the treatment I was getting just trying to get from Oxford to Water Valley, I would not have gotten the chance to work uptown. So I kept that a secret, and I always was afraid I was going to miss that bus. That was a terrifying thing. That was about the most terrifying thing I ever experienced.

Interviewer: What would surprise or shock people today about life back then?

The pay, that would be very shocking. If I worked in the country, where we lived, we would work all day for three dollars. "All day" meaning from early morning, five or six o'clock to dusk/dark. Like twelve-hour days for three dollars or $2.50.

Interviewer: Is there anything you'd like to add?

I tell you what I'd like to add, and it stuck with me even to this day, was about Emmett Till. That always stuck with me because I always thought it was not true and they killed him because they said he whistled at a white woman. That strikes me because I do not believe he did, and even if he had, it was not anything that would cause death if he had whistled at them. In the South there were certain things that you could not do; and that was one of them. It was just something that you never forget. It did not change my behavior because being a woman, we did not have that to worry about that. But as for the young men, I am sure it probably had an effect on them.

I would not trade my life for anything, though. It was a learning experience on how to treat people today. And by the way, I do not hold any animosity. I wonder why not. I often wonder that because a lot of times you hear people not liking what was done in the South. For me it was just a learning that I will never forget. Number one it was a way of life. Number two it just made me the person that I am today. Because you know after the incident of not doing the floor but from then on I was a good worker. As a matter of fact, when I came to Iowa I was a young lady—eighteen or nineteen, something like that. I was trying to get a job; I want to say at Black's Tearoom. They asked me who I had worked for and I gave them some of those ladies' names that I had worked for in Oxford, Mississippi. They called down. They called the ladies, one lady in particular, because she told me after I went back South. I visited a lady that I had done domestic work for, and she said, "Pearl, I got a call from Waterloo. They asked me how you worked. What kind of cleaning did you do for me? And I gave you a good reference." So I got the job at Black's washing dishes. I was a small girl; the pots were bigger than I. But I got the job.

Interviewer: Did you ever do day work in Waterloo, Iowa?

Yes, I did. Being a black coming up from the South, it was hard to get a job even in Waterloo. My sister Juanita had the job, and she got a different job. And she had me take this job, and they looked to me. They seemed to be rich. I did the same day work. There was no ironing, just the day work. There was no difference in the day work I performed in Mississippi and Waterloo. I could use the front door up North—that was probably the only difference. I forget that because it did not bother me [in the South] unless they had a dog out back. That is the only time going to the back door bothered me. I would be scared if there was a dog. We did not have to wear a uniform up here, but we did get paid more. This was in the mid-1960s. I want to say we got three dollars an hour.

We reminisce a lot about our southern days. We never forget how we stood with James Meredith. We just always remember how we stood by when he integrated the University of Mississippi. We stood by, meaning we had to ride a bus from Taylor to Oxford. A lot of the older people didn't go, and they didn't want us to go as teenagers.

One of the teenagers drove the bus up. And of course all the white students had been in class, and they didn't want people coming in and nobody coming out. When the bus arrived in Oxford, a mob of white folks were on their way to the university to protest and saw our bus stopping and going through the town square. They began to shout at the black students in the bus. The bus driver yelled, "Hit the deck!" as the white crowd began to break windows out with billy clubs and sticks. They were rocking the bus windows. Glass was shattered everywhere. We were all on the floor; only the bus driver's head was up. They were calling us the N word, names, "turn this bus around," "go home." But we said no. We stood up to them. The bus did finally make it through the town square and on to Central High School. Other busloads of young blacks in support of James Meredith and the integration of Ole Miss were coming in from the country. Most of the busloads did not make it. But we did. They either had to turn around or did not come, didn't even start out, like from other places like Abbeville. That was a small town, those small surrounding areas, I don't know if those places made it through or not. I don't remember what happened once we got to the destination. I just remember a lot of the old people not supporting the younger generation. I cannot remember clearly.

Like I said, I wouldn't trade anything for the experience I had on how to treat people. And I love everyone. You know some of the things that we went through, if there was ever a time for people to have some kind of a hate or something in their heart, that would have been the time. But we didn't because that was the way of life, and we adapted to it.

Jimmie Lane, from Springhill and Mansfield, Louisiana (born 1946). Interviewed by David W. Jackson. "It's just the way we lived down south; nobody bothered anybody."

Speaking in a soft, cultivated voice, this interviewee is one to cherish the positive in her life. A college student who filled in for her friend who was a maid, she developed a close and loving relationship with the white family.

I was born in Springhill, Louisiana, and adopted at the age of six and grew up in Mansfield. My mother who adopted me would cook every day. She worked at a Negro housekeeping job, but she cooked for us every day. She'd get off, come in, and cook a fresh meal for my granddaddy at lunchtime. Where she got the energy from, it amazes me now even when I think about it. She was never tired. I'd go outside and hang up a basket of clothes and I was tired.

When I was growing up, my mom was on my butt all the time—"Get your lesson, get your music lesson." I didn't have to do housework. Like I told that white lady when I went to work—"I don't cook." She said, "Oh, I don't want you to cook, just a little light cleaning." And basically that's what it was.

Interviewer: When we look at this type of work that primarily black women were doing, what did you call yourself? Did you call yourself a cleaning lady?

No, I did not. I called myself just a helper. A friend of mine had this job working for this white lady in Springhill. Her husband was the president of the bank and trust. My friend, Nelly, was a maid. I was not a maid, I didn't consider myself a maid, and I was not called a maid. I went in to help them out because my friend got sick. It was more or less preserving her job. Being a maid or whatever, that was something that my adopted mother had to do.

I don't mind working—honest work, that's an honest dollar in my pocket. It wasn't anything dirty or nasty or whatever. Matter of fact, the lady and her husband had children that were grown and gone, and basically, I think she wanted somebody around the house more for company than anything. I didn't have to do dishes; they had a dishwasher. I made one bed. They had a washer and dryer, so I didn't have to go outside. I ran my own kitchen, cleaned the living room, dining room, the bedroom. I cleaned the bathroom, although they kept it very clean. They were very clean people; as Nelly had told me, "They keep a nice clean house and they just want somebody there."

The lady, Mrs. Watters, was retired; she was an old schoolteacher. Her husband was still the president of the bank, and he asked me if I was looking for a job. I said, "Yeah, until school starts." This was in the summer, and he said, "Well, come down and talk to me at the bank. I probably have something for you." I never did.

I had talked to my pastor at the church when I wanted to work at the school, because that's what I had gone to college for. Here is an individual with three years of college, and this [working as a servant] was not what I had gone to college for. But I wasn't doing anything illegal. And they paid me very well. I think Nelly made five dollars a day, and Mrs. Watters paid me ten.

Nelly worked every day. Nelly did windows; I didn't. She would cook a hot meal for lunch. I don't cook. I'm not a very good ironer. Nelly was. She would hang the clothes on the line. I put the clothes in the dryer. And the dishes—I don't wash dishes. I washed the coffeepot. That's all. Everything was always clean; everything was always neat in its place.

What I could do was sit there and take messages and things for her because I was able to read and write. Nelly couldn't. I had an education.

Interviewer: Yeah, tell me about that. Where did you go to school?

I graduated from Desoto High School in Mansfield, Louisiana, back in 1965, and from there I went to Grambling State University. After three years of college, my uncle had a heart attack, and although there is no need for me to quit, I felt like I was a burden. These people had been so nice to me. They put it like, "You're our child and we do all we can for our child." But I wanted to help.

My aunt was the boss of everybody. She said, "Oh no, you need to go to school. Everybody takes care of everybody. You're not a burden, you're family." Yes, she raked my soul over the coals because I didn't go back and get my degree. And that's the way I was raised, and that's the way I feel now about my children.

No, I never went back to school. Always, I regretted that. But I'm thinking about retiring in the next few years, and perhaps now I'll just go back and get a degree for my own satisfaction.

Interviewer: Coming back to your work with the Watters, how often did you work?

I didn't really see any need for me to be there four days a week, but that's what she wanted me to work. I had Fridays off because I told them that I want my Fridays off.

Every once in a while it would be her turn to have a group of ladies over to play bridge, and at those times, I'd just be there. I'd set up the little mats, coffee, put the tea bags out, put the hot-water canister on the table. They did everything for themselves. I didn't go in there and wait on them. I think Nelly wore a uniform, but I didn't wear one. I wore my street clothes.

Nelly wore a uniform—black dress with a white collar. She had a black apron and a white apron. I almost think it was Nelly's idea to wear. I don't think that they were that concerned about it, because I wore my jeans and tennis shoes, whatever shirt was appropriate.

Interviewer: Could you kind of explain your relationship with her? Did she confide in you?

She would confide in me about her kids. She had two daughters. One was okay, and the other one was kind of wild. She liked to party, and she smoked, and she drank. She was a schoolteacher. They didn't approve of perhaps the way she lived or whatever. And I'm thinking, as long as she's not doing anything to hurt herself or her daughter, what's wrong with it? As long as she gets up and goes to work every day, what's wrong with her going out to dinner or whatever, going out to party with her friends or a guy or whoever?

Interviewer: Now, did this woman ever talk to you about like religion, politics, or finances?

She did ask me if I had a bank account. I said, "Yeah, I've had one of those before I knew really what it was." That's because my parents who adopted me saw to it that I had an account at the bank. One thing Mrs. Watters said was, "Jimmie, if you don't have it in your account, don't spend it." That's about it. That's what she was trying to get her daughter to understand. Her daughter was bouncing her checks.

Interviewer: Okay, did you talk about religion, politics, racism, or anything like that?

We did have a discussion about integration. She asked me what did I think about it. And I said, "To be frank and honest with you, integration was forced on black people." I said, "The reason I say that is we pay our taxes, and we get second rate."

I knew this from my experience going to school. My aunt was a principal of the junior high. We had high school and junior high, all in one big school. We would get books from the white high school; we would get their old things and whatever. When I got old enough to really understand a little about politics, I wondered, "Why do I have someone's book? I don't even know who they are, never hear of them. These books would have the N word in them. What idiot would write that in a book?"

Back in my childhood coming up, I would listen to my folks talk about this stuff, and they'd say, "We're going to support Dr. King because we really did like what he is doing." I pay my taxes; I have a degree, and you're going to tell me I cannot vote. And we deserve the same quality of education.

But, as a matter of fact, I think the black kids got a better education, because we were focused on getting that education with all the work that came out of it or whatever. Plus we were doing outside reading. I didn't know black people had so much in the building of the United States until the teacher talked to us in the history class.

Our school was out in the suburbs of Mansfield and covered a whole block. We had a beautiful campus. A lot of money was put in the schools at the time of integration to keep us quiet. They invested I don't know how much money, building us a gym, and a football stadium. They also made us a track around the back. They did put a little effort into it; they'd throw a dollar at you to shut you up.

Anyway, I was talking with Mrs. Watters about integration, and Mrs. Watters said, "Well, don't you think that blacks want to be white?" I said, "No." She said, "Why not?" I said, "I know I don't. I'm quite happy." I was very happy at the school I went to. And the next point was, "Why should we have to go out of our community to go into yours?"

The high schools uptown were landlocked. But in the end, when integration was being forced, they made us all go to different schools.

On the east end of the street where I lived, black families lived up there. On the west end of the same street, white families lived down there. And until they started talking about integration, I don't think anybody was bothered. It's just the way we lived down South; nobody bothered anybody. Your kid's ball went over the fence, and you go around there and knock on their door and say, "I'm going to get my kid's ball out." "Okay, go ahead." There never was an issue, never was a problem.

Interviewer: Are you saying that you did not think integration was a good idea?

No, we had to have integration in order to reap the benefit.

I don't think when I was growing up, I was so much into color. I think I didn't see black or white. I saw people. If you were nice, I liked you. If you were not, I don't care what color you were, I didn't like you and I didn't have anything to do with you. When I was around thirteen, I had little babysitting jobs coming in. I babysat two white kids and took them to the park. The park was segregated. They did not allow black kids to go down and play at the park. I was always down there, playing with that little boy. I'd swing on the swings, I went down the slide, and nobody ever said a word. We went down the road, and nobody ever questioned us or said anything to us.

When the movement for integration really went to touch my life was when

I watched on TV and saw the things that Dr. King and those people were going through, how the police would beat protesters, put the water hose on them, and everything else.

Interviewer: Now for some more questions about the Watterses. Did they allow you to use their restroom?

Yeah.

Interviewer: Did you come in the front door?

Yeah. We always entered through the cupboard room. That's the one I had a key for.

Interviewer: So did you ever eat lunch or dinner or breakfast with the family?

I'd eat lunch sometimes with Mr. Watters. She'd be gone, and he'd come in for lunch and we'd sit down to a little table, sit down and talk. He'd finish; he'd pick his dishes up, rinse them off, and put them in the dishwasher.

Interviewer: You didn't do it? Or he did it?

I wasn't his waiter. This wasn't a restaurant. He'd say, "Wake me if I'm not up at ten to one." I'd say, "Okay." He'd go sit down in his little lounge chair and lie down. They said he went to sleep, but I didn't know. He just went to sleep out there, and I'd hear this ticking noise; I think it was an alarm on his watch. And he'd get up and say, "Got to go. Locking you in." I'd say, "Okay." And he'd leave, and I'd go down around there and watch TV. And I'd leave at one thirty.

Interviewer: What time did you get there?

Eight thirty. I didn't get breakfast. I didn't get lunch. For our lunch, Mrs. Watters would make something. She would always make a fresh pot by the time I would be coming in. "There's fresh coffee." "Okay." That was some good coffee. They were nice. She went to the trouble to make it for me. Every morning, Monday through Thursday, there would be a fresh pot of coffee sitting there waiting for me.

I've always loved grapes. So that became a regular every week. Every week she'd go to the grocery store, and she'd buy me grapes. Sometimes whatever was in season she'd buy. "Do you like kiwi?" I think the first time I ate kiwi it broke my mouth. I called her, and told her I couldn't come in, and I said, "My mouth is swollen; I think those kiwis may have irritated it." So she took me out to the doctor's, and they gave me a shot so I could go back to work the next day. The rash went away. The next day, Mrs. Watters asked, "How's your mouth?" "Fine," I said. "Do you want to sit down? she said. I said, "I got to finish my work." "Oh no, you can leave that until tomorrow," she said. To sum it up, they were just nice people. Perhaps she was lonely; perhaps it was a status symbol for her to have a maid.

Interviewer: Did she ever or did they ever give you anything for your birthday or for the holiday or for Christmas, anything like that?

She gave me a little heart. I still have it. I broke the chain, but I still have the little heart with the diamonds around it. She gave it to me for my birthday. I don't even know why we started talking about birthdays. I said, "You know today is my birthday?" She said, "Well, mmhh." She said, "Why didn't you tell me? Nelly always reminds me of her birthday." I said, "I'm just helping out." Anyway, she went out, and she called back and said, "What time are you leaving today?" I said, "one thirty." She said, "Hold on. Might be a little after one thirty. I need to see you about something." She got there almost two, and she had a couple little roses, and a little box. When she came in the door, I said, "Is that for me?" She said, "Yes." And, oh, she had this big old grin. I said, "Oh, they're beautiful." I didn't see the box. And she said, "I got you a present too," and I said, "This was great, good enough." And she said, "This is from Lou and Jean." I opened it. "Oh, this is gorgeous," I said. She said, "I wasn't sure if you'd like it. If you don't like it, I can take it back. I can take you down to the jewelry store, and we'll try to find something." I said, "I love it."

I still have it. Yes, it's a nice piece of jewelry. Kind of small and dainty little heart, but there's little diamonds around it. Years later my son said, "Oh, Mamma this is pretty; where'd you get this?" And I said, "Well, in fact, a white lady gave it to me." "Mamma, she spent some money on that, didn't she?" he said.

And another thing, being from the South, a lot of the white women my mom used to work for, they were always buying me stuff. Gave me nice pieces of jewelry, bought blouses or skirts, and then they'd buy me the patterns, material for my mother to make dresses or whatever.

Interviewer: Did they give you any clothes to take, such as hand-me-downs?

Lord, she offered me some. I told her to give that to Nelly. She would have given me probably everything in her wardrobe. I couldn't wear her shoes. I couldn't wear her clothes. I could wear nothing, but she was real nice. As a matter of fact, I didn't want much. I just wanted them to be nice, and they were.

Mr. Watters would come in and talk to me, like you and me sitting here talking about whatever was going on. I didn't pay much attention to the news and newspapers after I was out of high school and college and everything, but then this man comes in and he starts talking to me about stock market. What, what are you invested in? And I'm like, "I don't have no money to invest." "Well you should start saving it, saving a little bit at the bank, buy some stocks." He said, "You don't have to have a whole lot to get into it. Save some every year until you get enough." He said, "We had investors here at the bank that can guide you right through it and show you how to invest." He said, "Why don't you come on down there? Come down here to the bank where I work, just come on down there. We'll get you a job there." I said, "Oh thank you, thank you." But I never did take him up on it. That bank only had white folks working there. That's where I began to put my money in the bank there, and I knew the attitude of the women they had at those windows, and I'm like, "I'm not working with these kinds of people." They are prejudiced; they want to talk to me like I'm a nobody. They sit up there and talk to some white person who comes in. Then all of a sudden they split, "Oh, come over here, Ms. This, come over here Mr. That." I don't think I would have lasted there.

Every once in a while, I began to think about talking to Mr. Watters during lunch, and we'd talk about what we saw on the news and everything. He treated me like an equal and expected me to be up on the latest news. The conversations with him got me listening to the news because before that that I used to just hang out with the girls or whoever. I didn't even know what was going on in the world around us. And those were the things that I needed to know so I could sit down and talk to him about them at lunch. I was smart enough to take that hint, and started buying the paper and reading it.

Interviewer: Did Nelly come back to work?

Nelly was off because she had gotten sick. She was a diabetic. When she was able, by the end of the summer, she was able to come back to work. They paid her, and they paid me, because she didn't have any other income.

Interviewer: You talked about gifts you got from the family; how did they treat your friend Nelly?

They were always buying and giving her things. Even after I had moved on and everything, she was a good friend, and I went over to check on her at least once a week. They continued to pay her until she died. They were good to Nelly.

Interviewer: Did they cover Nelly's medical bills when she got sick?

She went on some kind of assistance, but they still paid her, and they would buy her medicine. I know they would give her money for her medicine, because I had been out there a couple of times when Ms. Watters came by, and she had something in a little envelope and she said, "Nelly I'm going to help you out. I put your weekly check in there with you." She said, "I put your weekly pay in there. I didn't give you any more checks because you have such a hard time getting out there to go to the bank or whatever to cash it." She began to give her cash, and she still paid her Social Security, and paid her until she died.

Mrs. Watters would call me every once in a while to see how I was doing. I went up to the bank, and Mr. Watters urged me to get my application in. But a few weeks later, school started, and Reverend Washington got me on there. I worked as a teacher's assistant, and I worked in the office. So then I had a paycheck with benefits.

The Watterses asked me about coming back, and I told them, "No, I have a better job now. I have a job that I like and everything." Mrs. Watters said,

"I knew you wouldn't really come back and help us out." And I'm like, "You all just paid me; I didn't do anything for the money." Because they paid me really well, plus they paid my Social Security for me, and it was really a good job; it helped me out. I didn't have to go get money; I had money every week, and things weren't so expensive then.

Melvina Scott, from Goodman, Mississippi (born 1948).
Interviewed by David W. Jackson.
"I always thought that my brother might have been kin to them [the white family] because he's more light-headed than any of the rest of us."

One of our interviewees of the Great Migration, Melvina Scott has fond memories of growing up with her grandmother in a household surrounded by sisters and cousins. Her keen intelligence and positive outlook shape her perceptions of experiences that might have been regarded much differently by someone of a less robust disposition. The fact that her mother and grandmother saw to it that she got a proper education gave her a major advantage over many of her peers.

I grew up mainly with my grandmother and my brother in Goodman, which was in rural Mississippi. What I recall basically from the time when I was six or seven years old is my grandmother getting up and getting dressed and going up to Mrs. Mary Kirkoff's house to work. When I got to be about nine or ten years old, I wanted to make some money—I had always been wanting to have my own spending money—so I asked my grandmother if I could go and help her out. When I started going with her she let me do the ironing and change some of the diapers on the kids. She let me mop the floor and sweep and clean up around the yard and that kind of stuff to make money. And then when I was twelve years old, some days she would let me go by myself and do the ironing and washing and taking care of the children. Mary Kirkoff's niece had a little boy and a little girl. I took care of them on the weekends while their parents worked in the grocery store. I raised them up until they were really big enough to go down to the store with us, so they were probably nine or ten years old by the time I graduated from high school. As soon as

Melvina Scott. Her dream is for an African American history museum in Waterloo, Iowa. *Photo by David Jackson.*

I graduated from high school, I left and went to Louisiana for about three months, and then came on to Iowa.

Interviewer: What were the attitudes of these kids and the people you worked for?

Well, one thing about growing up in the South and any place, you are going to have people who hate mongrels. But for the most part, we got along great together. Color just didn't make a difference. The only time color made a difference, in fact, was when we went to school. The white kids and my brothers caught the bus at the same stop. The bus picked them all up on Falcon Road. They went off to white school, and my brothers went to the black school, and then that happened about until I left home. We all stood out there together, played until the bus came, and never had any real problems. The people who would burn the crosses and wear the white sheets, they came from other parts of Holmes County.

There were probably five or six white folks that lived right around where I lived. We knew they were not in the Klan, but those were people who came and harassed people who they knew who were part of the civil rights movement in the South. The people who belonged to the United Methodist churches in the South were part of the movement. My mother was part of the movement, and my cousin and my uncle. In fact, I had an uncle who was really part of the protectors, the protectors association. When there was a meeting, an NAACP meeting or a rally, those people would protect the outside of the house while we had meetings inside. No, we really didn't have any problems with the people who lived close to us; the people we had to watch out for were people who came from outside the community.

In later years when I would go back home, I found that Mr. John Kirkoff and my grandmother had become very good friends. He would come drink coffee with her every morning when I would go back home to visit. His sister-in-law was married to a Kirkoff, and his brother was Ray Kirkoff, and those were the people who my grandmother worked for and raised their kids. The kids called her Big Mamma.

If you look at people who raise white kids in the South, a lot of them will call the people who raised them Big Mamma. We didn't, we just call her Mamma, because my mother and grandmother lived only houses apart. I had seven brothers, and all the brothers lived with my mother. We actually lived with my grandmother. And I had first cousins that was raised like my sisters. All of her children were born and grown by the time I was born.

Interviewer: I just don't know this term "Big Mamma." Is it a term of endearment? Or is it just that she was a big woman?

No, it was a term of endearment, because she practically raised them, she changed their diapers and put them on her shoulders and patted their backs when they would cry. She cared for them when they were sick or when they needed to eat. She practically took care of them from the time they were born, so she pretty much was their second mother. That's why they called her Big Mamma.

Interviewer: Do you know how she was paid? Was she paid in cash or clothes and other gifts?

I remember if they killed a hog, they would give her a part of the meat. If they killed cows, they would give her a part of the meat, but I seem to remember them paying her one or two dollars a week. But she didn't have to pay for rent as far as I know, and she actually lived in that house until my brother bought the land and built a house in 1965.

I don't know for sure about the rent, because kids didn't ask questions about this. If you asked questions about finances, you'd get your teeth knocked out! *[laughing]*. You never knew who was on welfare or that it existed, but all I know is we lived well. A lot of people would say, "Well, I have one pair of shoes to wear to school, one outfit to wear to school and have to wash it every night." We never, none of us, ever had that. One of the reasons was because my grandmother's husband died when I was born. I think he died in like 1947, and he was a veteran. And so my grandmother got enough money to take care of herself, because there was something coming in each month. And then my father was a carpenter, a bricklayer, so we actually were rich kids. And so they, my grandmother and my mother, did things because they wanted to, not because they had to. But my father developed a rare brain disorder when he was thirty-six years old and then died when he was forty-two, and so at that time my mother had to work, although she was probably on Social Security. But you never know about that kind of stuff because like I said, they didn't talk about it. But I know I had more than one pair of shoes and more than one church outfit, and a school outfit, and we—my cousins and I—could go down to the grocery store to the McDonalds' clothing store, and we could pick out what we wanted to wear and just tell them to put it on my grandmother's account.

Interviewer: Do you remember when working for the Kirkoffs your grandmother or yourself ever having to go to the back door or anything like that?

The only time I remember was when company came. Mary Kirkoff had a sister and a brother-in-law who lived in Starksdale, and the only time I ever remember me and my grandmother having to go to the back door was when they visited. It was like they didn't want their sister and brother-in-law knowing that we were like part of the family! *[laughing with the interviewer]*.

You look back at that stuff, and you wonder why things changed when they came, but they did. When they weren't there, me and my grandmother would all join May, Ray, Bobby, and Frank, and we'd all sit around the table and eat together. But when these relatives came, me and my grandmother had to serve the food, and I had to set the table. And then we would have to go and eat in the kitchen after they got through eating. Rules got to go in place *[laughing]*. I never thought about this until you asked it, but them was racists *[both laughing]*.

But the kids—Ray and May—didn't want us to know that. Now that I think about it, when we walked in the room, they quit talking, so they must have been calling us names too, but Bobby and Frank and the other Kirkoff kids, we all played together, and then when we got grown up, we still kept in contact. They all, in fact, finally moved away from Goodman. Goodman is pretty much a ghost town now. A lot of the stores that they owned closed, because Walmart came in and a couple of other stores came in, so they couldn't compete. But just looking back, I can see how when company came in from different parts of Mississippi, how the rules changed, and how they treated us then. Being a young kid, you never thought about what racism is and the face of racism until you get to thinking about it later in life.

Interviewer: Was it the same thing with the restrooms?

The same thing with the restrooms. And really now that I think about it, I remember that my mother would say, "You pee and do whatever you got to do before you go over to May and Frank's house; you use the bathroom before we go to work today because you can't use the bathroom." And I would say, "Why not?" She'd say, "You just can't!"

Interviewer: Did you ever have to use it when you got over there?

I'd slip and use it if I had to; I didn't let my grandmother know *[laughing with the interviewer]*. I didn't let her know I used it.

And another thing, when we'd go downtown, if there was somebody in the store when we were shopping down there, my grandmother would say, "Now you make sure you wait until they get through waiting on the white folk." And I never forgot this. When this one white woman came in—she was from some other little town in Mississippi—Miss Lily Kirkoff, who ran the store, was waiting on me. I was buying a dress and then some patent leather shoes, and I had them in my hands. The white woman grabbed the shoes out of my hands. This was the last pair in my size. And to this day I still get mad when I think about it because them was the best-looking patent leather shoes I had ever seen. And the white women took the shoes and bought them. I said, "Miss Lily, them was my shoes." She said, "Get on out of here, girl, I'm gonna tell Phoebe on you!" That was my grandmother.

"But I had them shoes," I said, "Why you gonna give them to her?' She said, "Get on out of here, Girl, or I'm gonna tell Phoebe on you. Otherwise I'm gonna whoop you, I'm gonna whoop you."

I ran home and told my grandmother. And she went down there, and she said, "Lily, I've been knowing you for a long time, been trading with you for a long time, but I ain't coming back in your store; you abused my granddaughter." And it was a long time before we could go back in that store *[laughing]*. My grandmother had a first cousin that lived in Greenfield, or one of them towns in the Delta, and she would take us way over there to shop rather than going to the McDonalds' store. This wasn't like five or six months; this was three to four years before we went back in. We got to be teenagers before we would go there, and my grandmother still wouldn't ever go there to shop again.

Here is another story about my grandmother—one night me and my brother and cousins climbed the tree and then my granddad came up there with a big old switch to whoop us. My grandmother had a Winchester that her husband had bought in the service and given to her, and anytime she had a disagreement with white folks around there, she would pull that Winchester out of there and cock it.

Well, my granddad came out there with that big old switch and she told him, "You ain't raising no black nigger kids. Say if any whooping being done, I'm gonna whoop them. You put your hand on one of them, you gonna wake up dead." My grandmother cocked that Winchester on him and said, "You put your hands on one of my grandkids, you gonna wake up dead." That was her attitude.

Interviewer: Tell me more about your grandmother's work—did she get any gifts from the people she worked for?

Oh, yeah. They gave her clothes and shoes, and they always bought her a Christmas present and a birthday present. So they actually was good to her. And then my brother—I actually used to get jealous—the Kirkoffs took him fishing, on fishing trips, and they and my brother would work the field together. They taught him how to drive the truck because our dad died when he was about seventeen or eighteen years old. So they taught him how to drive the truck and how to drive the tractor. And then when my brother decided he wanted to go to work in the tobacco fields in North Carolina, when he left home around age twenty, they gave him money and a brand-new coat to leave home.

Interviewer: Did the Kirkoffs encourage your grandmother and you to pursue an education?

One thing my grandmother stressed, the only way out of whatever situation you was in, is through education. And a lot of the kids around us and on other plantations was working in the fields. We never got kept out of school to work on the plantation. The only reason my brothers didn't graduate from high school was because they chose to go leave the house and go work someplace else out of the state. This was when they was building the highway system called M State 55 from Mississippi to New Orleans. And from Mississippi to Florida.

Interviewer: Did your grandmother enjoy her work?

Well, yeah, you could tell that she loved to cook, and so she enjoyed having people eat her food. Sometimes, with my cousins and others, she would feed twenty-five to thirty people on a daily/weekly basis. I had other cousins in the community, and each one of the cousins in the family would take a Sunday to have a Sunday dinner. I'm not so sure if she enjoyed it, but I think she enjoyed taking care of the kids, Bobby and Frank.

Interviewer: Bobby and Frank: could you tell me about your experience playing with them?

Sometimes we had fun, and then sometimes when they got older they actually had to get beat up because they wanted to do things. They wanted to do things that boys wanted to do to girls, and so me and my cousin had to beat up on them. We were probably around nine or ten at the time.

Yeah, it was three of them. The one that was more my cousin's age, he was the one that we really beat up on the most. He wanted to experience sex, so me and my cousin had to beat up on him. He'd kiss on you. And they'd do whatever else they wanted to do. We gave him that right hook *[laughing]*.

Before that we would play hide-and-seek and all that kind of stuff; we played it together. When we got to be nine, ten, and eleven, we pretty much didn't play with them because of that. My grandmother said, "Well, since he wants to be mannish, you can't play with him anymore."

Interviewer: Did they ever call you the N word—Nigger?

I don't ever remember them calling us niggers. I'm sure, though, in Starksdale, they probably had those conversations. But the only time I ever remember was when some people found out that my grandmother and mother was involved in civil rights. They burned the cross in my house, and that's when we heard all this talk—nigger this and nigger that. They was out in front of our house, and when my grandmother saw that they weren't going to do anything but burn the cross, she cocked the Winchester and started shooting, and when she started shooting, they took off in their cars and left.

Back then, in the era we came up in, the southern men and boys in Holmes County—most of them were racists. So it was, "Be home by dark because of the Klan." Then things changed; the laws changed, and I had moved away. And now all of them are dead. I visit three or four times a year, but I never went to visit the Kirkoffs, because I figured that some of those folks in the Klan had to be relatives of those others. At that time I thought all the white folks in Holmes County was related some way or the other. So even if they weren't related, they would have been talking to people about the stuff they did.

Did your grandma know of, do you recall any family secrets of the people she worked for?

I learned in later life that the McDonalds and the Kirkoffs were cousins, and Nancy and Don got married when they were first cousins. Also in terms of ancestry, I always thought that my brother might have been kin to them because he's more light-headed than any of the rest of us. But I've never been able to prove it to this day, because, boy, I'd probably be dead if I asked that question, "Whose child is he?"

I have no idea. To this day I have no idea whose child my baby brother is. All I know is all the rest of us is dark. And he's high yellow. And his nose is flatter *[laughing]*. And his daddy act crazy. So it's like he don't belong in the family.

Interviewer: This is common, though? The oldest type of behavior you're talking about?

Yeah. I don't know till this day, um, was anything going on with any of the Kirkoffs and my mother; I have no idea. Let's see if I got anything with his picture in it. Then I could tell you the difference between him and the rest of us.

Put the dots together: He from another daddy. I do know that, um, my mother and one of John Kirkoff's sons—I think his name was Don Kirkoff—I know him and my mother was real close. But in terms of going out on a date with her with him, I don't think so. I don't know, because, like I said, those are things that you just don't ask. But now that I look back on it, my brother was born in '54, and then my daddy was building schools all around Holmes County and the Greenwood area because he was a master bricklayer—he built all the schools when they became attendance centers, all the middle schools. He was a contractor and bricklayer on all those schools. So he wasn't home a lot. And that was when my brother showed up.

Yeah, so that why I'm thinking, Brother, you from another father *[laughing]*. He's so much different from the rest of us.

Interviewer: Did your mother and Mary Kirkoff or these others have any conversations about life or social relations?

Yeah, I know they had a lot of conversations, especially during the civil rights movement and looking at the kind of person that she was and how she treated us as Negroes, as they called them back then, there wasn't any difference except when, like I said, her sister and brother-in-law came to visit.

They were all United Methodist; that was one thing in common they had. The Kirkoffs were United Methodist, and my grandmother was United Methodist, so I think they had a lot of the same kind of values just because of that. And they respected each other, and I know they developed a love for her as a person because in later life, Don Kirkoff would come over every morning, and him and my mother would have coffee together. Sometimes he'd bring the coffee; sometimes he'd make the coffee, and they would sit under the tree and have long conversations about life and people in general. So in terms of answering your question—"Did they teach each other about life?"—I think they did.

Interviewer: Is there anything you may have missed in the way of any highlight moments that were good or bad to remember?

Well, I was good in basketball growing up, and I guess one highlight I remember is when I missed the bus. Mr. Ray, as we called him [Ray Kirkoff], took me to school that day so I could go to the basketball tournament, and usually a black person would ride in the backseat of the car, but he said, "Sister, you can ride in the front seat." And I thought that was something, because usually you didn't get to ride in the front seat with a white man in the state of Mississippi back in that day. And I did! I rode from there to Durant in the front seat with him, and then he pulled up in his Chrysler and dropped me off at school. People said, "What that white man doing in there?" And I said, "That's my godfather" *[laughing]*. And he was, and he was really a godfather now that you look back at it.

People who worked for John Kirkoff, Ray Kirkoff, or Herman Kirkoff, if they went to jail and they worked for them, Monday morning they was out and on the tracks, and that was their philosophy. If you keep your ass out of jail, if you keep your black ass out of the grave, we'll keep you out of jail. And that was the attitude they had about all the people who lived around them or worked for them. They took care of their people.

Interviewer: Any bad or low moments you remember that ended in a good experience?

Only that I hated to see Ray Kirkoff's sister and brother-in-law and their kids. They came to the country to get some country living and country air and country food. I hated to see them come because that was the only time we got treated different.

Hazel Rankins, from Taylor, Arkansas (born 1952).
Interviewed by David W. Jackson.
"[My sister] told me, 'I would not only clean the bathroom but I'd take a bath in the bathtub.'"

Despite her impoverished upbringing and rough treatment at the hands of whites, Hazel Rankins finds much to laugh about as she recalls conversations she later had with her sister about their working lives. As she constantly

Hazel Rankins. Working for a mean white family in Taylor, Arkansas, Hazel's sister found an interesting way around the rules. *Photo by David Jackson.*

moves between past and present tense in her story, you know that the past is still very real to her.

I was born in Taylor, Arkansas, by a midwife and in a house that my father built. I come from a family of seven girls and one boy; the boy was older. The area we lived in was like about maybe fifteen blocks, which was called Rankintown, because the Rankins—my father and all of his brothers had the land there where everybody lived in their little shotgun houses. They all had the same houses, right in a row.

My first job was picking cotton, but I didn't do very well with that *[laughing]*, because I was a kid. It was hot, you know, and they expect for you to work all day long. You'd eat lunch maybe at one or two, but you been up since about five thirty. You've been out there in the field all day, you know, with no breakfast. I remember they give us all a quarter, and we went up to the store. That was to buy our lunch and everything. But they got rid of me. They said they couldn't have the kids eating up the lunch.

I remember at the store they always made us go around to the back of the door, to get our sandwich. If you would be in line to buy a pop or anything or to buy groceries and a white person would come in, you'd have to move over and let them get in front of you. You know they wouldn't serve you until them. And after growing up and we went there to visit my aunts and uncles in the 1970s, things still hadn't changed. I remember going to the store and I got a pop and I was in line, and this gentleman come up and the lady that was running the cash register, she wouldn't serve me. She was waiting on me to move out of the way so she could wait on him.

And the laundromat—they did not change that until about maybe twenty years ago when they removed the "white only" and "blacks only" signs at certain laundromats.

I started working for a white family as a child when I would go with my sister. I think I might have been eight or nine years old. We would sweep the yards and help hang the laundry on the line. My sister used to work really hard. She just always wanted to help Mom and Dad. She would make money to help buy groceries and stuff like that.

She would go to work early in the mornings. The work consisted of cleaning the henhouse, you know, where they kept their chickens. See, domestic work down South for a black woman working for a white family is totally different than what our young people see as work today. Work then was washing the clothes out, maybe by hand, rinsing the clothes in a bucket, emptying that water out and hanging them up on a hanger on the line outside. Once they dry, in the meantime you're cleaning the house and you got to come back in after you've got to get the clothes hung out, get the clothes back in and iron them. You had to iron them and fold them. Then you got to cook, you got to scrub, and you got to clean their bathrooms.

The man—the gentleman that we worked for—always had a lot of kids working for him. You know you really didn't look them in the face; you never said very much. They always just talked to you like you was a small child. They talked this way even to my father, which was not very respectable. But my father was always a gentleman, always respected others and was always very kind and polite to them—to the man.

My sister told me that sometimes the man would come home when the wife was out shopping, and she would be in the bedroom getting things ready, getting the bed cleaned and changing the sheets and stuff. And he'd go in there and pull the bed back and tell her, "Come on," you know, just like she was . . . you know? And she said a lot of times she would just leave the room and go into the kitchen and start doing something else, and he would call out, "Why do you act like you didn't hear me?" And she just totally ignored it. She would go outside and keep doing something else. She said it was always just humiliating.

One thing you need to know is that everybody knew everybody down South. When you worked for a family, it was a neighborhood, you knew everybody. But if something got out, they not going to believe you, they going to believe the white guy. So you wouldn't say anything to anyone about what he had done or what he tried.

You would work all day long and you wouldn't get home until five thirty or six, and then they give you maybe fifty cents, sometimes a dollar, and you done did a lot of work. You done wash, cooked, ironed, made beds, and scrubbed. Kids wouldn't like it today, but you really washed windows. You really washed windows. Not only that but you swept the yard.

Back down South, they like their yards to look a certain way, they're real particular about the way their yards are supposed to look. So when you went there to work, you worked. You know what I mean? You did everything, you did it all. If they had a chicken house out in the back, you cleaned that out, go get the eggs, clean it. Whatever they had for you to do, you did it. If they wanted their canning done or whatever—peeling their apples or whatever—you done all that.

He didn't call my sister by her name; he called her Gal. She worked from six o'clock in the morning until five or five thirty. You worked all day long, and then you couldn't eat out of the same plate. Wait, you might eat out of the plate that the dog might have ate out of. They washed your plate and put it over there where they put their dog plate, and your plate never comes close to where they put their plate. But you clean their bathroom and do their cooking and all that, but you weren't good enough to eat to eat out of their plate or use their spoons. That was separate. And I just couldn't figure out why, you know. I'm cooking your food, but I can't eat off your plates. Well, you already know that you couldn't sit at the table, because if you had to use the back door in order to come in, and you out there hanging their clothes, sweeping their yards, but yet you're using their back door.

Interviewer: Could you use the bathroom?

They didn't want you to *[both laughing]*.

My sister—me and my sister was very close, and she would say they didn't want you to use their bathroom. They would want you to go out to the outhouse. But as soon as they would get gone, my sister told me, "I would not only clean the bathroom, but I'd take a bath in the bathtub" *[both laughing]*.

I said to her, "Sis, if they have caught you, you'd of been gone." I said, "Shame on you."

"Shoot," she said. "I wanted to see what that bathtub felt like." Because we didn't have one, you know. When she'd be telling me about it, I'd just laugh and laugh and laugh. It's just funny stuff. She said that she cleaned the bathroom; why not take a bath in the bathtub? She said, "I'd just take my bath and I'd hurry up and I'd clean it back up, and they never would know what happened."

Interviewer: Did your sister or you have to wear a uniform?

No, you didn't have to wear a uniform. You could wear whatever.

Interviewer: Did she get any gifts or anything for like Christmas or for her birthday?

No, they might give you a candy cane or some apples if they got an apple tree or something like that in the back; they'd give you some apples because you did a lot of cooking for them, for their holiday food, but no extra presents or anything like that. No, not in Arkansas *[both laughing]*.

They would always give her extra clothes, if their kids couldn't wear them or if, you know, they couldn't use them anymore. They would always ask if she could use them. Down South they are really good about if they got extra stuff that they not going to use, they'll give it to someone. They were really good doing stuff like that, but never extra money.

They pay you what they want you to have. It's never a certain fee that's set, how much you would be getting, nothing like that. It's like this: today I might give you seventy-five cents or fifty cents, tomorrow it might be less or a little bit more, but it was never the same thing.

The raises consist of stuff they didn't want, that they were going to throw out. They'd always offer some old shoes or clothes or something like that.

Interviewer: For this family you could not go in the front door?

Oh, definitely no. You never—that's something that you knew and your parents knew—you knew your boundaries; they were white and you were black. Your parents would make sure that you knew certain things, that you knew your place. You knew your place and you did what you were supposed to do, and if you did anything else you would be in trouble. Not only would your parents be in trouble with them, but you know it was easy for them to call the police on you and say you did something wrong, so most of the time nobody got out of place.

I had a cousin who didn't care what people thought; he was radical. Yeah, he lived in jail because *[laughing]* he was his own person. Some kids are going to be their own regardless. You might say "yes ma'am" and "no sir," but they are not going to do it. See, we was brought up to say "yes ma'am" and "no sir" and that's it. You knew your boundaries and you didn't cross 'em; you knew what to do and from being a little child.

You know, they've done some horrible things. You know just being a little girl and sitting around and listening to the older people talk about the stuff they would do, you know, just horrible. Really, really horrible.

For one thing, see, you got to remember, the sheriff knows everybody, everybody. And if you a stranger and you do something and you in trouble you might go to jail or you might end up not in jail but someplace else.

The school was right uptown, and when the black and white kids were put together the town really was never comfortable with it. My cousins were good basketball players, and they had a game, and the white team lost. And they ran them off the road, and those two boys were killed. They ran them off the road. And that's just the way. I think that was just their mentality down South, keeping us in our place. You didn't get out of place; you did not.

One thing growing up in the South is that they just considered you as being ignorant. That you didn't know, certain things you didn't need to know, they didn't take the time to help you learn. They would just come in and give orders of what you were supposed to do and how they want things done and that was that.

Interviewer: Did they ever talk to your sister or you about the importance of staying in school to get an education?

No, when you worked for families back then, you just worked for them; you was just a worker, You wasn't to them no one important. They feel like you was doing all that you would ever do in life, and it's a shame, but you know, when I think about my dad, my father couldn't read but he was, he could with numbers, he was real good with numbers. He could build anything. He worked for a shell plant in Springhill, Louisiana. He could build anything. The house that we lived in, he built it. We would write out the different numbers, and he had his own little plan the way he would do things. My father was a hard worker. But you know, no one ever pushed anyone about getting education or encouraged people or tried to help.

I remember when someone would die and the white people would come. They would always say something like, "So-and-So was a good person; Jesse, if you need something, well, just let us know." But they were not really being sincere.

But the wife at the house was always nice to us. And I remember there was one little old lady, though, that was a white lady and she was always nice and friendly. I just remember her being nice to us as kids, when we would be up town wanting to get some ice. You know back then we used to have to carry our ice all the way back home from town.

Interviewer: Were you or your sister ever called a nigger or any derogatory word while you were working?

I've heard them say it, you know. I would be sitting on the porch and they be talking about somebody else and they would say, "Them niggers down there cutting up." But that's about the only time you would hear it when they would say it right in front of you. I heard it more when I was older and I would go down South and would hear it.

Interviewer: So you said, um, when you were older you heard it more so. When you were going down to visit?

This was around 1969 or 1970. My brother is married to a white woman and my brother would go visit. I remember we was in the store and the man at the counter or another one of them said, "You know Jesse's boy down there got that white woman from the North." And they was just talking about it like we wasn't even standing there, just talking about her. And I was thinking to myself, "That's what he gets" *[laughing]*.

Interviewer: Him messing with life and death, huh?

Yep. When we'd go down there, it was dangerous. It was really—I told brother this wasn't a good thing because really he was trying to show off.

Interviewer: One final thing I wanted to ask you—did your sister ever tell you about any of the family secrets?

I'm sure she probably knew all their little secrets. It seemed like she said that the man played around a lot. The way my sister talked about it, it sounded to me that he was a man just after any woman he could go with. He was a playboy. And he was kind of like the big shot in town.

I remember that he had the biggest house around. She'd tell me things about him and the work as I got older, and I kind of laugh now when she tells me. I really laugh.

But I think, you know, what she really hated was that she didn't get the education that she wanted. She said that all her life she felt like her childhood was just stolen from her, because she worked so hard. When I see kids that don't want to do anything, I think about the kind of work we did, in the fields, cleaning people's houses, then going home where you got to cook a full meal, wash, do all that stuff. We were just real, real poor, but we loved each other. We all lived in a shotgun house, and there were three rooms, and we didn't fight; we got along.

Gloria Kirkland Holmes, Ph.D., from Charleston, South Carolina (born 1953). "I always wanted to be a teacher."

The following piece of writing is a contribution by an associate professor of early childhood education at the University of Northern Iowa who came forward upon hearing of the maids' narratives project to share her unforgettable experience one summer in the late 1960s. During her teen years, not knowing what she was getting into, Dr. Holmes found herself far away from home in a role she likens to that of a slave.

Gloria Kirkland Holmes. *Photo by David Jackson.*

Journey of a Young African American Maid and Babysitter, Turned Ph.D.

Growing up on the east side of Charleston, South Carolina, as a young African American girl was a very important part of my life. While we were considered low-income by any definition of the term, still we were never told that we were poor. Our parents had instilled in us the importance of being grateful to God for every little blessing that came our way. There were many blessings that others may have considered to be unfair, unjust, unequal, and degrading. Instead we looked at life with as much hope as an established and mature adult.

I always wanted to be a teacher. So my gathering of all of the neighborhood's African American children, anywhere from five to fifteen on any given day, was normal for me. I still look back and cannot remember how I learned all of those songs and games that I taught the children. We didn't have many toys other than the ones we made ourselves. I still remember how we made our own dolls with bottles and the rope that they tied around the big ice cubes from the icehouse. Many African Americans had ice boxes (not refrigerators) to help keep food cold and from spoiling. So they frequented the icehouse, and we kept the string.

My neighborhood consisted of all blacks—all of the children and families. But across the railroad track were a few white families. We were taught not to cross the tracks without our families' permission. We weren't ever really told why, other than we were to show love toward everyone. We certainly had no problems with that because, after all, my mother was a very important maid for the Momier family. The name has never left my mind because they were white and seemed rich to us.

They really liked Mamma because she was a hard worker who washed, cleaned, and cooked for the family. They had three children that Mamma would help take care of and raise. So as the children grew out of their nice clothes, she would give them to Mamma for her six children, three girls and three boys. I was the youngest girl, with a brother a year younger. We were so elated when Mamma brought things from Mrs. Momier because we would feel so rich. The clothes and everything that she gave us were all well taken care of.

Little did I know that once I entered the tenth grade I would also follow in Mamma's footsteps and become a maid, babysitter, and nanny. Nanny was not a term used at that time, although because of this family's money, they would certainly rather a term such as that used today. I started working at a very early age. I always felt the need to help Mamma because she and Daddy had separated, and she was left to take care of all of us alone. I must say she was a real survivor, cooking those big pots of lima beans, and okra soup with rice. We ate everything with rice; no wonder we were never hungry. Mamma was a great cook and provider.

I remember working at the Fort Sumter Hotel as a bus girl (helping to clear the tables). They wouldn't let us be waitresses because that meant you would get a tip. They saved those positions for whites. We didn't mind being the bus girls/boys or the dishwashers. Our jobs were just as important in this fancy restaurant that served those with money.

I worked this job after school. This is where and how I met the young couple with one child and growing to two. They needed a young lady to come walk the children on the "battery," a very rich and elite area right where the Fort Sumter battle was fought, and one of the most popular tourist areas in Charleston. They lived right there in one of the most expensive homes, and thought enough of me to ask me to come walk the children on the battery after school. I took my job very seriously and would be there around 4:00 until maybe 6:00 p.m. I did well and taught the children what I knew. So I did this throughout the school year. Then one day right before school was out, they asked me to go with them to their summer home in the mountains of North Carolina. I had mixed emotions about this, being so young, but just assumed it would be similar to the work I did in Charleston. So I agreed to travel with the family after my mother very hesitantly consented. She only did so because there was another young lady one year older than me, African American, who said she had been the summer before. She said the pay is very good. Then there was an older black lady who had been working for the entire family for around twenty years. Mamma thought the older lady would look after us and make sure we were safe.

Well, when we arrived at this secluded place, I immediately went into shock and fear. There was the big house, as it was called, where the family I worked for and the family of my friend would reside. Then the extended family members were there also. We would live in the cabins down below where the big house was. I was so afraid, cautious, nervous, and prayed for my safety. There are these other two African American people there, and Mamma trusted that they would see after me.

As soon as we arrived, the older lady, Ms. Elsie, started to show us what we were to do in the big house. She was so mean, until I wanted to cry, but knew I had better not let her see me. She told us about all of the fancy silverware and dishes we were to use to set the tables at three meals a day. We had to make sure everything was sparkling clean

At times, she would yell at us. I thought to myself, "How could this woman be so mean, knowing we were so far away from home. Lord, am I going to make it here for an entire summer?" I knew how to pray and asked God to please help me.

How was I going to make it in these slave quarters? I didn't imagine that I had agreed to go to a slave quarter where no one could find me. The older lady told me, "You get paid on Thursdays. You can go to town and buy some things that you might need." So I thought the pay and being able to shop would brighten my day. But when we went to town and I saw some other blacks living nearby, but doing the same slave work as I did, I cried inside and outside when no one was looking. I sat down and wrote a few letters to family and church members who asked me to keep in touch. Little did I know that those letters would later open the door back to freedom for me.

We worked from 6:00 a.m. to 6:00 p.m. seven days a week. This wasn't the babysitting job I thought it was going to be. After I would finally get away from that mean woman for a few minutes after 6:00 p.m., here came the children that I had taken care all day from their meals, cleaning and caring for them. They loved me so much they wouldn't go home. "Oh, now, not eighteen-hour days!" I thought. "Lord, please have mercy."

Ms. Elsie would get us up every morning at 5:00 a.m., so we could get our bath, put on our maid uniform (black uniform with fancy silk, white satin and lace around the collar and the little black-and-white hat.) We always went in the back door to the big house. The back door led straight into the kitchen. There was a bathroom right there near the kitchen. We had to go back down to our quarters to use the bathroom. But we were allowed to wash our hands in the one near the kitchen. Ms. Elsie made sure that we washed them often. We never ate with the family. We could have some leftover food with the family's approval and Ms. Elsie's "rationing out" what she thought was appropriate for us to have. We often had to feed the younger children during meal time, but were not allowed to ever act like we were on the same level as the family. They wanted to make sure of that. Our roles were to be understood, with no hesitancy.

We had to be neat for the families we were to serve. We hurriedly would eat breakfast so we could get those tables set, and be prepared if the children woke up. We had to be ready for everything. I always prayed that no one in the family was of a sick mind-frame and would harm us like in some slave situations.

I made it to payday two, and we went to town. It was not the shopping, but the getting away from the slave quarters. I never thought that I would find myself being a slave that I agreed to. I started to cry again. Then a miracle happened. My later to become hero-in-life made a phone call to the big house. I still to this day do not know how in the world she found me other than from the letter I wrote. I was shocked when they came to the "slave quarters" to tell me I had a phone call. I had written to Mamma and all, but certainly was never given a phone number. Telephones were scarce for blacks then and making long-distance calls were even scarcer.

I prayed on my way to take the call and hoped no one had died or became deathly ill. But I wouldn't mind if they told me to come back home because this woman got meaner by the day. I couldn't understand her unnecessary meanness.

Miracle! My aunt had a new baby, and they wanted me to come home and live with them for the remainder of the summer, to take care of the little girl and they would pay me so that I could get school clothes and supplies. They were coming to get me the next day. I couldn't believe the day had come when God answered my prayer. I felt sad that I was leaving the other young girl there. But she had already made it through one summer, and I didn't understand why since she seemed so sad that she had come back again.

I happily told Ms. Elsie good-bye and said farewell to the family that had allowed me to become a maid as a part of their rich family. There were always so many unknowns, but after I left, many thoughts went through my mind. There were many who had come and gone, but Ms. Elsie remained. She knew the system, but she also knew silence! I always still wonder if she was so mean to us to make us tough or if she feared what could happen to us. While I experienced what life is like for some of the rich, I also learned how easy it is and can be to fall into slavery as a maid! Well, those are long-cherished memories as I was able to use that experience as a strength-building experience that played a key role in my long journey to obtaining my doctorate degree.

(5)
The Maid Narrative Themes

I can sit down and tell people now, and they can say, "No, I wouldn't have did. I wouldn't have did." But, yes, they would. It was surviving, just the way you had to survive.
—MAMIE JOHNSON, from Durant, Mississippi

WE TURN NOW to a more in-depth look at the lives of the migrant women of Iowa, drawing on a larger sample of responses that includes both the maid narratives of the previous chapter and a number of additional, shorter interviews. We have organized the content from our interviews with African American elders into eight basic themes: the impact of key events; paternalism; child rearing; stress on education; the sexual vulnerability of black women; southern racial etiquette; the bonds between mistress and maid; starting over up north; and resilience.

As we noted in chapter 3, these women migrants often came with their menfolk, who had been recruited over the years to work on the railroads and in the meatpacking industry. From small towns all over Mississippi and adjacent states, for three generations, black people came to Iowa. Today, Waterloo has the second-highest African American population in Iowa, surpassed only by Des Moines, the state capital and the second city from which we gathered interviews. Most of the African American residents in these cities are descendants of the men and women of the Great Migration (Barnes and Bumpers 2000).

"Tell us about the sharecropping. Tell us about your work up at the big house. What was it like there? What can you tell the young people about that life?" These are among the questions we asked. The stories we got were all different, and yet collectively the story they tell is the same—the exodus from the rural South, where they had no hope of fulfilling the American dream, to a place of considerably more promise. Their stories, preserved in the quotations that follow, are alternately funny, sad, and disturbing.

THE IMPACT OF KEY EVENTS

Our African American narrators led hard lives, and they experienced the ravages both of being second-class citizens and of being forced to serve people who had every advantage of wealth and education, advantages provided to them on the basis of class and race. So entrenched was the position of the servant class in the social order that they would have had little hope that their children or their children's children would ever have a future or that they themselves would be the ones to carry the legacy of the historic past. Think of our storytellers as you read these lines of Langston Hughes (1931): "Children, I come back today / to tell you a story of the long dark way / That I had to climb, that I had to know / In order that the race might live and grow" (155). There is a strange prescience in these lines, which have great relevance today.

Sometimes the younger generations do not appreciate the legacy of the past before their elders have passed on and they themselves are up in years. Narrator Irene Williams from Springhill, Louisiana, shared this frustration with interviewer David W. Jackson:

> You know sometimes I set up here and I tell my grandbabies how we used to have to do. You know what they tell me? "That was back in the olden days." I say, "No, Honey, you just don't understand. This was real." And I tell them how we were being treated, and they say, "No, I wouldn't have took it." But I say, "No, you would have took it, what we did, because there was nothing you could do about it." The kids today, they think it's a joke, but it's no joke, it was real.

One day her descendants will read this book, and they will know these things were real.

Sharecropping

Many of our narrators were brought up sharecropping before they chose to work indoors for the white families. As an economic system, sharecropping closely resembled slavery, and in some ways, serfdom, because the people stayed with the land and lived in small houses owned by the landlords. They also shopped in stores owned by the landlords and bought goods on credit. This was a system ripe for exploitation. Keep this economic backdrop in mind as we discuss the methods of social control whites used to keep blacks in line, and as we consider how blacks having the right to vote might have affected the power structure that emerged following Reconstruction. The sharecropping system supports the observation of the historian Lord Acton that "power tends to corrupt, and absolute power corrupts absolutely." Southern paternalism taught pride in taking care of black people, but there was not much to be proud of in stories like those that follow.

Mamie Johnson, who was born in 1922, described in her own words the typical situation in place when she was growing up:

> These black people were living on this land for these sharecroppers. Well, you see, they lived there and they worked there. And when they worked there, you was supposed to be working on behalf of the sharecroppers. They was supposed to be giving you half and he taking half. Well, you see, they never would let you have no book to see what they was giving you. See what I mean? Now, you know that was crooked, don't you? They was supposed to be sharecropping! When you raised that stuff and he gets ready to sell it up with you, he was supposed to have a book! He was supposed to have this book and pull it up and show you how much money he gone let you have and what you owe, and how much he got for this cotton. But he never would pull out no book!
>
> "So, Mr. Gullich, we want you to settle up, we need some clothes for our kids for Christmas and we want to know when you going settle up." We might say this to him, and then he'd say, "Well, I hadn't ever sold the cotton yet because it wasn't five cents and it wasn't the right price." Well, the workers would wait and wait. And I can remember one time, my daddy went up to the place to talk and get a settlement on their crop. But Mr. Gullich would tell him how much and the others how much they owed. "Next year," he'd say, "you'll do better. You'll do a little better next year."

White Mob Violence

So why didn't the black people, who constituted a numerical majority in many areas of the South, rise up against this system? One reason was they were held back by lack of education. But the main reason was that they were terrorized. In the postbellum South, white vigilante groups singled out black individuals who failed to show the proper deference to the whites. Public lynchings were held, and gruesome photographs were circulated of these events.

Between 1889 and 1945, Mississippi was the site of 476 of the 3,786 recorded lynchings in the United States (Rogers 2006). This type of racially motivated violence was carried out in the Jim Crow era as a way of enforcing subservience and preventing economic competition from minorities, and later as a method of resisting the civil rights movement. The sporadic targeting of individual black men was a deliberate strategy of social control that maintained white dominance by keeping all blacks in a perpetual state of fear. The reports of these mutilations and killings had an impact on every black family in the rural Lower South. Every black mother socialized her son to keep his anger against white folks inside and to never look twice at a white woman.

The psychological impact of the threat of extrajudicial violence figures prominently throughout southern literature. In *I Know Why the Caged Bird Sings* (Angelou 1969), for example, Maya Angelou's grandmother got a warning that the "boys" of the Klan might come by for her son, because "a crazy nigger messed with a white lady" (17). While Mamma fell to the floor praying, the children frantically helped bury their uncle under onions and potatoes in the potato bin. "Even after the slow decay of years," writes Angelou (1969), "I remember the sense of fear which filled my mouth with hot, dry air, and made my body tight" (18). Similarly memorable descriptions of white-on-black violence or the fear thereof occur in *To Kill a Mockingbird* (Lee 1969), *Coming of Age in Mississippi* (Moody 1968), *From the Mississippi Delta* (Holland 1997), and *Francie* (English 1999). This reality also figures prominently in the memories of the women of the Great Migration.

In 1955, the year of the Montgomery bus boycott, fifteen-year-old Emmett Till came down to Mississippi from Chicago for the summer. Isabel Wilkerson (2011) describes a tradition among many midwestern African American families of sending their children to stay with grandparents and other relatives in the South for the summer, thus maintaining extended family ties and connections to the region: "When they saw the cold airs of the New World seeping into their northern-bred children, they sent them south for the summer so the children would know where they came from. . . . But the children did not have the internalized deference of their southern cousins" (366).

Wilkerson describes what happened to Emmett Till and how shaken up people in the Midwest were to learn what had happened to one of their own. By most accounts, Emmett Till, as a child of the North, was oblivious to the warnings he got about the danger to black males who noticed white women. He met a terrible fate. His murder and the trial in which the murderers—who later bragged about their crime—were acquitted horrified the nation and the world. Till's death is considered by many to have been a spark that helped mobilize the civil rights movement. Only three months after his body was pulled from the Tallahatchie River, the Montgomery bus boycott began. The horror of these events still resonated in the voice of Mamie Johnson more than a half century later:

> He was in Chicago, was living in Chicago with his mamma. And he come down there that summer! And you know those boys is, they, you know, like way back then they'd call *[does a whistle]*, wolf-whistling. Well that was all the boy did. . . . They waited until his granddaddy had gone to bed, and they went there and asked for him. . . . They put him in a pickup truck. And they carried that child, they rode that child all around there. And they beat that child. . . . And they carried him down there on that river where they put him in. And they say he was just heard, the boy was just heard screaming. The people around there heard him screaming.

Annie Pearl Stevenson, who was born in 1945, also was pained at the memory:

> I tell you what I'd like to add, and it stuck with me even to this day, was about Emmett Till. That always stuck with me because I always thought it was not true and they killed him because they said he whistled at a white woman. That strikes me because I do not believe he did, and even if he had, it was not anything that would cause death if he had

> whistled at them. In the South there were certain things that you could not do; and that was one of them. It was just something that you never forget.

Perhaps the eeriest account of the murder of Emmett Till comes from L. Walker (who prefers that her full name not be used). She heard of Till's death when she was around eighteen years old and picking cotton along the river on a plantation in the Delta. As she was picking cotton, she could see in the distance that police were searching the river. The boy's body was later found right there, and Walker later learned that relatives of her employer and possibly her employer were responsible for the crime. She never went back to work there after that day.

Elra Johnson was born in 1906 and is one of two of our interviewees to have been threatened directly by the Ku Klux Klan. Her civil rights activities in the early days of the movement had put her at risk, yet if she was afraid at the time, her fears do not show in the way she relates the story. One evening a mob of robe-clad men came up to her house. "Did they say anything to you?" the interviewer asked. Here is her reply:

> Not a word. And I sat there on the porch and didn't say nothing to them. My husband got out of the way. But I dealt with them! Yes I did. . . . [When they first arrived] they hit the ground. And when they hit the ground, then that's when they went to doing that scaring, thinking they gonna get somebody to run from their own house. But I didn't. Nope. They burned up a cross in my yard. I didn't even move. They was acting a fool, and I didn't move. But I had something right here *[motions to her side]*. Yeah, I had a gun, and I bet I had as many shells as they had. That's right! I ain't telling you no story on that! And they got scared. I know they must of seen them or something. But anyway they got scared and left.

Asked why she thinks the KKK went to her house, Johnson simply stated: "They didn't want no Negroes to have no freedom." Melvina Scott, born around two generations later, recalled a similar scene:

> But the only time I ever remember was when some people found out

> that my grandmother and mother was involved in civil rights. They burned the cross in my house, and that's when we heard all this talk—nigger this and nigger that. They was out in front of our house, and when my grandmother saw that they weren't going to do anything but burn the cross, she cocked the Winchester and started shooting, and when she started shooting, they took off in their cars and left.

The Civil Rights Movement

Big changes were taking place rapidly in the South at the end of the 1950s and early 1960s. NAACP membership was strong, and more militant groups such as the Student Non-Violent Coordinating Committee (SNCC) and the Congress of Racial Equality (CORE) were organizing through the black churches and teaching the skills of civil disobedience as a means of moving public opinion.

In 1962, James Meredith enrolled as a student at the University of Mississippi. The enrollment of a black student sparked riots on the Oxford campus, and U.S. marshals were called in to maintain the peace. In the end, two people were killed in the riots, and almost two hundred soldiers and U.S. marshals were wounded. The event received extensive worldwide media coverage. Annie Pearl Stevenson was there and described the scene:

> We reminisce a lot about our southern days. We never forget how we stood with James Meredith. We just always remember how we stood by when he integrated the University of Mississippi. We stood by, meaning we had to ride a bus from Taylor to Oxford. A lot of the older people didn't go, and they didn't want us to go as teenagers.
>
> One of the teenagers drove the bus up. And of course all the white students had been in class, and they didn't want people coming in and nobody coming out. When the bus arrived in Oxford, a mob of white folks were on their way to the university to protest and saw our bus stopping and going through the town square. They began to shout at the black students in the bus. The bus driver yelled, "Hit the deck!" as the white crowd began to break windows out with billy clubs and sticks. They were rocking the bus windows. Glass was shattered everywhere. We were all on the floor; only the bus driver's head was up. They were

> calling us the N word, names, "turn this bus around," "go home." But we said no. We stood up to them. The bus did finally make it through the town square and on to Central High School. Other busloads of young blacks in support of James Meredith and the integration of Ole Miss were coming in from the country. Most of the busloads did not make it. But we did.

Rosie Loggins, the youngest of our interviewees, shared this memory from her youth: "I remember when Martin Luther King walked down Highway 7. The white people, they was always trying to be sneaky, but we knew what they was doing. The white people didn't want to let us see them [the marchers]. You see they were scared we'd quit working, you know, and follow them."

PATERNALISM

The black workers who made themselves well known to their employers had a sort of safety net when trouble called. This fact was evidenced throughout the stories of the white interviewees and by two of our African American storytellers as well. In our interview with J. B. McCellan, Elra Johnson's son, we got a telling description of life in those parts:

> [White folks] didn't mess with any of his [Mr. McCullagh's] help. They didn't mess with his help. He'd go to bat for you, not even a chance for nobody else come out there and get you.
>
> Didn't anybody mess with you. If you get [steal] something and make it back to the farm, he [the owner] wasn't going to go out there looking for you; he was going to go up to Hugh McCullagh. He'd tell everybody, and that's as far as it would go.

Similarly, Annie Victoria Johnson explained:

> Some black women got married and their husbands didn't allow them to go to the field. They didn't allow them to work in the yard or the garden. They didn't allow them to work for the white women. Some black men back then are just like they are now. They wouldn't have you working for any white folks. And it seemed that they had a harder

> time because back then, everyone got along and helped each other. But because some of the black men didn't want their wives around white folks, they caught hell because when they needed help, they wouldn't help them.

CHILD REARING

The women who participated in the maid narratives shared a lot of details about their upbringing and about their experiences raising white children. These descriptions are contained in the full transcripts, but a few samples will suffice to reveal two facts about black childhood socialization in the 1920s through the 1950s—children in the rural South had to work in the fields from early childhood, and when mothers took care of white children, their own families were often neglected.

White families, as we'll see in the narratives of part 3, were absolutely dependent on black women for help in child care; the black women often were expected to socialize the white child into white southern norms for proper behavior. This tradition is emphasized in novels such as *To Kill a Mockingbird*, in which Calpurnia is the moral educator as well as the maid, and in Abileen's raising of Mae Mobley in *The Help*. By many reports, the attachments were very strong between the caretaker and child but took on a different form as the child matured. In the words of Abileen in *The Help*, "How we love they kids when they little . . . and then they turn out just like they mammas" (128).

Connected to this theme is the extent to which all the attention lavished on the white child takes away from attention that could be given to the servant's own family. We see this in African American novels such as Toni Morrison's *The Bluest Eye* (1970), in which the mother comes to compare her own child unfavorably to those she works for, and Alice Walker's *The Color Purple* (1968), in which Sofia, who was forced to work for the mayor's wife and family, was denied a meaningful life with her own children. In African American autobiographical accounts as well, family neglect emerges as a theme. Anne Moody (1968), for example, in *Coming of Age in Mississippi*, remembers: "That white lady Mamma was working for worked her so hard that she always came home griping about backaches" (31). And when her mother went to work for another family, she left her small children home alone until their older sister got home from school. Once they were found playing outside naked, and the entire neighborhood laughed at them. "I got mad at Mamma" Moody said," because she had to work and couldn't take care of Adline and Junior herself" (28).

All of the women interviewed expressed great respect for their forebears and appreciation for the suffering they endured. The women who were interviewed for this book showed little resentment of the time lost with their mothers who were busy catering to the white children. There was one notable exception, however. Irene Williams, who grew up in Louisiana in the 1930s and 1940s, still gets depressed today as she recalls her mother's absence. In a voice tremulous with emotion, she shared one of her most painful childhood memories:

> My mother—they called her a live-in maid because she stayed with the white folks. She left us with our grandmother so she could go off to work. And I remember her coming home, and I was so glad to see my mother. She stayed with us Saturday and Sunday, and she told me, she said, "Baby, Mamma got to leave again." And I would cry. I didn't want my mother to leave, but she did. And my grandmother took me into the kitchen as she didn't want my mother to see me crying and feel sorry because she had to leave me. So I was crying and I didn't want her to go. And my sisters would say, "Sister, it's gonna be okay, it's gonna be okay. Momma be back." I didn't want to hear it. I wanted my mother there with me then. But she couldn't take care there, she had to work.

Many of the women were brought up by their grandmothers. Most did not feel neglected or lonely as they were in the company of siblings, cousins, aunts, and uncles. In any case, with the exception of Irene Williams, no interviewee expressed a sense of being a victim of child neglect. More typical of the attitude we found is this quotation from the narrative of Annie Victoria Johnson:

> My mom did the same thing she did for us when caring for their kids. She bathed them, fed them, put them to bed. They slept in our beds. Some of the white kids called my mother Grandma. My mother was in her thirties then, and they would call her Grandma or Auntie. She loved them just like she loved us. She whupped them like she did us.

Every one of our maid narratives presents a picture of hard, sometimes backbreaking work, often in the fields. Childhood was described as a time of heavy work and little or no play. The oldest of the storytellers, Elra Johnson, states: “I worked like the devil! There was no time for play. No, there was no fun, we had to work!”

Similarly, L. Walker, born in 1935 in Batesville, Mississippi, describes the situation she faced from an early age: “We had to go to the field. They would pull us out of school in March so they could run the tractor. In April we'd be chopping the cotton, cutting the vines. In the fall, we'd pick cotton up until Christmas. So we went to school about three months out of the year.”

Children did get to play some of the time, however. Ruthie O'Neal grew up in Taylor, Mississippi, in the 1940s. She tells how they had fun making mud pies and dolls out of sticks with corn shucks for the hair. In the South, white kids and black kids were often playmates, but only as small children. Nancy Hickman, who grew up in Holly Springs, Mississippi, in the 1920s and 1930s, reported, “I was raised up with white kids; they'd go to my house and I'd go to their house. They were our neighbors.” Ruthie O'Neal similarly remembers: You know kids could do what they wanted. Kids could play with white kids and all that. We played with one another, we worked together, we hit one another, and called one another names and everything. But they [the whites] knew the difference. We didn't know the difference. Our parents kept us from associating with them because, ‘You not allowed to do that; that's Miss So-and-So,’ you know.”

A legacy from slave days, discipline was strict. Rosie Loggins, like most of the others interviewed, seemed to have no problem with this aspect of her upbringing: “Oh, I was about nine or ten years old. Some kids were working when they were five or six, you know doing cooking and in the fields. It was hard work! Young people don't know how it is! But we were disciplined. I used to get some good whoopings! *[laughs]*. No one is disciplined now! Kids need it. That's why you got so many kids in jail and doing drugs and things now—there's no discipline!” Mamie Johnson recalled from her growing up in the late 1920s: “I started working for white people when I was just big enough and old enough to do the dishes, and that was about seven or eight. You could do the dishes. You could sweep the yard. And then we didn't have lawn mowers and all that kind of stuff. We would get out and chop the grass of the yard. Take a hoe and chop it clean. And pile it up and it lays out there in the sun. And you'd pick it up and pile it up and burn it.”

Annie Victoria Johnson provided a detailed description from her childhood: "I learned a lot about caring for children from my mother. Because whether anyone knew it or not, when we grew up, it was more dangerous then than it is now. I say that because we didn't lie around the house and sleep late. Every time a child got big enough, he had a job: feeding the chickens, slopping the pigs, going and getting the cows to be milked. There was no toilet, so, you know, we had night pots. You learned how to take out that night pot and keep it clean. All that kind of stuff!" *[laughs]*.

A major problem with the work pressures on these children was that they were not getting the education they needed. But this is not to say that their parents did not value education.

STRESS ON EDUCATION

Trudier Harris (1982) deplores the fact that black domestics are so often overlooked in U.S. cultural history when they have occupied such a central position in black life. A large percentage of blacks who today are doctors of philosophy or medical doctors or lawyers, according to Harris, are so because black women in their pasts scrubbed floors or washed or cooked for whites.

Of course, the whites stood to benefit by having a class of uneducated people with low expectations whom they could have to perform the dirty work of society, work that no one else wished to perform. Still, the black workers would see how white children were socialized to get an education to get ahead in life, and they had to wish the same for their own children. Occasionally, the lady of the house would impart some of her teachings to one of the child maids. Mrs. Truett, for example, went out of her way to instruct L. Walker concerning ladylike behavior: "She always told me to save your money. Don't buy stockings with wiggly lines in the back; whores wear those kinds of stockings. To this day, I have never worn those kind of stockings. And when you sit down, she said, keep your legs closed. Always be neat; keep your hair looking pretty. And don't be missing school. It's important to learn to read and write and do arithmetic. She was kind of like my mom."

African American poet Langston Hughes, in his poem "The Negro Mother" (1931), adopts the point of view of past generations of house servants and sharecroppers all embodied in the mother of the Negro race:

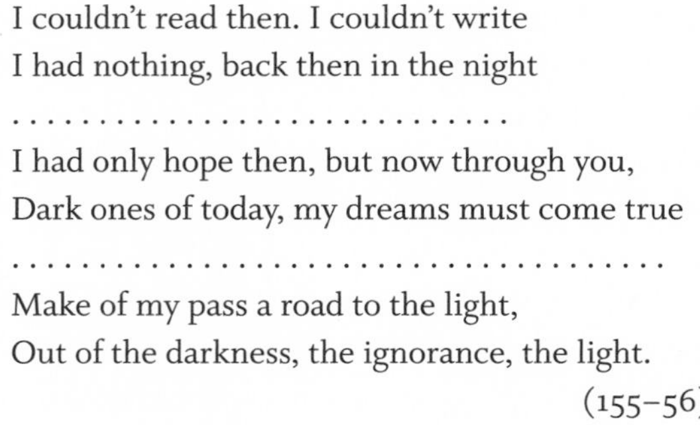

I couldn't read then. I couldn't write
I had nothing, back then in the night

. . . .

I had only hope then, but now through you,
Dark ones of today, my dreams must come true

. . . .

Make of my pass a road to the light,
Out of the darkness, the ignorance, the light.

(155–56)

Hughes could have been speaking directly to the following women from Waterloo, Iowa. Vinella Byrd, born in 1922, provided this general description: "The white kids started school in September and us, the ones who should have been in school, were picking cotton. So that would be different. We didn't get to go to school until the cotton was picked. I think it shaped how I feel about education. I believe education is the most important thing you can have when you are growing up." As Annie Pearl Stevenson shared: "I know I always wanted to go to college. Always. At that time I really wanted to enroll in Ole Miss." Rosie Loggins, who went from working in the fields and white homes in Mississippi to becoming a master's level social worker, described her background:

> Yeah, we went to country school. Sometimes we didn't go to school, though. It depended on the crops. The teachers knew and just made sure you were caught up. You see, because that was your income. Back then you had kids to work! Lots of parents would keep their kids out of school to work. My Mamma valued education a lot, though. I wish she could have seen me graduate—she would have been so proud!

"You didn't go to school down there," said Louisiana native Irene Williams, continuing, "If it rained you went to school; if dry, the man would come to get you to work in the field. I worked in the fields and then on week-ends go to the house and clean."

Transportation was often a major difficulty. The black children might have to walk past a white school near their homes to attend a "colored" school miles away. L. Walker, who lived ten miles from her school, remembered, "We'd leave at five in the morning to arrive at nine, and we didn't get home until nine at night unless a wagon or car came by and gave us a ride."

Mamie Johnson shared a harrowing tale about a boy who left the fields in the hope of attending school but was shot in the arm for his efforts. Then she added: "I'm going to tell you something. When you hear these people talking about uneducated people, now this is why, in the South, so many of them can't read and write their name—because they didn't get no education, and they had to work. Now, you know, when you had a bunch of people, you bringing them up and giving them a house to stay in and then they working, they working for you for nothing!"

THE SEXUAL VULNERABILITY OF BLACK WOMEN

Long-term U.S. senator Strom Thurmond had a secret in his life. As a young man he had engaged in sex with a black teenager who was a servant in his household and she had borne a child. Six months after Thurmond's death on June 26, 2003, Essie Mae Washington-Williams publicly revealed that she was Strom Thurmond's daughter. At her birth in 1925, her mother was sixteen years old and Thurmond, twenty-two. Although Thurmond never publicly acknowledged Washington-Williams when he was alive, he supported her financially and paid her way through college. Some commentators perceived a contradiction between die-hard segregationist Thurmond's aggressive fight against civil rights policies and his sexual affair with a black woman. However, as a reading of southern history reveals, white male access to black women was integral to the segregation ethos, which combined personal intimacy with the notion of caste. Paternalistic affection for black mammy figures, as Micki McElya (2007) suggests, rested on intimidation of black communities through the "soul murder of lynching and rape" (162–63). Psychologists might say that since white males often started life nurtured by warm black women, it would be natural for them to feel drawn to black women later. In *Killers of the Dream,* Lillian Smith (1949) refers to this phenomenon—white men seeking in black women the "tender and tragic relationship of childhood" (128). The rituals of segregation were to Smith a symptom of a grave illness; racial and sexual oppression she saw as twin-born. White women were to be protected at the expense of black women.

As white men pursued young black women sexually, their sense of entitlement was profound. In her autobiography, the American literature scholar Trudier Harris (2003) tells how young white men from "good" families might turn to the maid or the maid's daughter for sexual initiation. She recounts how one of her mother's cousins' children was "coal black" and the other "high yaller." It happened, as was explained to the author, after Mr. So-and-So "had had his way" with their mother (43). Virgin white men in the part of Alabama where Harris grew up visited the black side of town in search of black females to pay for sex. They could even use force and get away with it.

At the age of sixteen, Irene Williams got herself in a vulnerable situation, one that she still finds highly disturbing to think about.

> My auntie went to work one day. Three or four white guys wanted somebody to work. I didn't know no better. I got in the car with them. . . . Then when we got there, they tell me what to do, but I see all of them standing around one another. . . .
>
> I said, "I have to go home." They said, "What's the matter? Are you scared?" . . . Then they told me, they said, "Well, we have another place you could go and work." Well, I was thinking what they was gonna do to me, they was gonna try to rape me or do something to me because I don't know. And I said "No! I wanna go home."
>
> I finally got home. And when my auntie found out where I had been, boy, she was pissed. She slapped me down, and she told me, "I know you don't know, I know you don't understand, but I'm going to sit down here and tell you." She told me, she said, "They are too dangerous—a bunch of men. Weren't no women nowhere, just a bunch of men. . . .
>
> "Don't you ever do that again," she said to me." I said, "I won't," and I didn't.

"These things were not talked about"—this same comment was uttered by several of our narrators. Black children growing up did not figure out what was happening until years later, often because of having a family member who was several shades lighter than the rest of the family or because of somewhat extravagant gifts received. For example, as reported by one Arkansas interviewee, "My grandmother worked for a pretty good white family. The man she worked for owned a locker and for years brought to my grandmother's house all kinds of extra meat. Something must have been going on there." Melvina Scott was more explicit about her suspicions:

> Also in terms of ancestry, I always thought that my brother might have been kin to them because he's more light-headed than any of the rest of us. But I've never been able to prove it to this day, because, boy, I'd probably be dead if I asked that question, "Whose child is he?"
>
> I have no idea. To this day I have no idea whose child my baby brother is. All I know is all the rest of us is dark. And he's high yellow. And his nose is flatter *[laughing]*. And his daddy act crazy. So it's like he don't belong in the family. . . . He from another daddy. . . . But now that I look back on it, my brother was born in '54 and then my daddy was building schools all around Holmes County. . . . So he wasn't home a lot. And that was when my brother showed up.

Vinella Byrd, who was in her late eighties, referred to sex at the end of her interview:

> One thing I would like to add would be, the man that we stayed on his plantation, his father would always be trying to feel on the young girls who went up there after work. Of course we always just pushed him down and went on about our work *[laughs]*. He wasn't any threat. We didn't get in any trouble for it. Well, she told me about it; she told me, "Don't pay him no attention." Yes, I'm sure some of the black women had babies with white men. But it wasn't a thing that was talked about. You could just look at them—the babies—and tell.

Although the majority of our interviewees denied that they were exploited sexually at their place of work, several described situations known to them, and one barely escaped from a white man who targeted her as she walked along the street. When with relief she met up with her husband, she made the mistake of telling him what was going on. He was ready right then to go after this man. She then quickly changed her story, minimizing the situation and passing it off as nothing. He could not protect her; he would have gotten himself killed, she said.

An even more terrifying situation befell L. Walker at age thirteen, when she was sent by her employer to the store to purchase ingredients for a cake. The man behind the counter tried to pull her over by her arms. When she resisted, he said, "You can be made to do anything." Fortunately the bread man came in just then, and she fled out of the door. Later some bodies were found of girls who had been raped and killed. This same man was charged with this crime. "This affected me so bad, I never really got it out of my head how close I had come," Walker said.

Rosie Loggins described working for a disreputable family in Mississippi:

> The Hopgoods were known for whooping black people. We were the only ones who would work for them. We didn't have any problems with them, though. . . . We didn't know it then, but Mr. Hopgood got my mamma's niece pregnant! And you know they sent her away. They sent her off to Flint, Michigan, 'cause they wanted to get rid of her!

Loreatha Smith-Reid, who grew up in Cotton Plant, Arkansas, in the 1940s, referred to occasions when people were caught engaging in forbidden acts. Smith-Reid, who was only nine years old when she went to work, was known by her employers as "the little maid." In her words:

> I was working for a husband and wife, and in their home I did the dishes, I made the beds, I mopped the kitchen floor, and I fed the chickens. So that was my first job. The man was real mean. He would beat dogs to death and all kinds of things like that. He would beat his horses because he some pretty horses and would beat them and scar them all up and stuff. So he was really a mean man. He didn't bother me though because I was a little girl and my mother was always around when I was there. She didn't take no mess off of him. He did go after one of my sisters one day and he wanted to rape her. They were in the guest room. She, you know, the Mrs., came in and stopped it. He was really a mean man.
>
> One secret I found out about was that his wife had a niece who lived with her, and her name was Lonnie, and he was going with her. I walked in on them one day [having intercourse], and he told me if I would tell he would kill me. I knew better than to tell.

SOUTHERN RACIAL ETIQUETTE

At times, our African American narrators described certain aspects of life that made it sound as if they had grown up in a foreign country. White activist writers who grew up with maids have been horrified in their adult lives as they contemplated the senselessness of the rules of racial etiquette in which they had been indoctrinated (see, for example, the autobiographies of Lillian Smith [1931] and Sallie Bingham [1989]). In her autobiography, Maya Angelou (1969) reminisces about a time when her dignified grandmother had to demean herself to get help for Maya, who had a toothache: "Now the humiliation of hearing Mamma describe herself as if she had no last name to the young white girl was equal to the physical pain. It seemed terribly unfair to have a toothache and a headache and have to bear at the same time the heavy burden of Blackness" (183). In *Coming of Age in Mississippi*, Anne Moody depicts a wretched scene in which the black children are scolded by their mother for trying to join their white friends downstairs at a movie theater, which was off-limits to colored people. Blacks were restricted to the balcony in movie theaters.

Sometimes the rules were strictly enforced, other times, not. We see this in the literature as well as in our narrative collection. For instance, for our seventeen African American interviewees who grew up in the South, we compiled the following list related to the enforcement of the cultural norms sometimes called the black codes. They range from the paternalistic to the unnecessarily restrictive.

~ Could not enter through the front door: 14
~ Could not use the white family's toilet: 11
~ Could not eat with whites at the table: 15
~ Given gifts such as leftover food instead of a living wage: 13
~ Mentioned a sexual situation involving self or other domestics: 7
~ Called by one's first name: 17
~ Addressed white adults as Mr. and Mrs. (or Ms.): 17
~ Said to be like a "member of the family": 2

In many ways, these daily insults are the most memorable when they are described in interviews by the people who experienced them. Although we can learn of these prescriptive norms in books on southern history and from the memoirs of white southerners, blacks' narrative accounts reveal the emotional impact of such practices, as well as the humor that sometimes arose in situations that seem utterly absurd by today's standards. But always the undertones of humiliation are there. The following are just a few samples from our recordings.

From the narrative of Mamie Johnson:

> They would tell me, "When you clean up Mr. David's room, do this or fix his so-and-so, or don't do so-and-so." When they said, "Mister," that is for you to say it—"Mister." And you know them little old children and the teenagers—they loved it for you to say that! Yeah, they loved for you to say Mr. So-and-So.

Similarly, Rosie Loggins remembered:

> We always had to call the white people Mr. and Mrs. Everybody called the white kids mister and misses too. I didn't, though, to them. I would say "Mister So-and-So and Mrs. So-and-So" to the white people, but not the kids. We weren't allowed to eat at their table. We couldn't ride in their front seat. And we couldn't use their front door or sit on their front porch!

From Vinella Byrd of Arkansas we hear how one man tried to protect himself from some form of contamination: "The man didn't want me to wash my hands in the wash pan. They didn't have a sink. They had a wash pan where you washed your hands. After that, I didn't wash my hands at all. I would just go in and start cooking. He didn't want me to use the same one that he was using."

Annie Pearl Stevenson summarized the unwritten rules:

> The main rules were to never enter through the front of the house. When we got ready to eat, if we did not take our lunch home, you could not eat it at the main table. You had to eat it in a back room. I recall it was kind of a family room, back where we did all the work like ironing. This room was at the back of the house, this little room was, like a

> utility room. So we ironed in there and ate in there. And we used the bathroom, if we had to; they had a little separate bathroom you could use. We could wash our hands back there where we ate.

Sometimes whites would bend the unwritten rules within family circles but then jump back into role playing when visitors came to call. Melvina Scott, who worked with her grandmother and others, enjoyed almost equal treatment until company came, when the southern formalities were called back into play.

> The only time I remember was when company came. Mary Kirkoff had a sister and a brother-in-law who lived in Starksdale, and the only time I ever remember me and my grandmother having to go to the back door was when they visited. It was like they didn't want their sister and brother-in-law knowing that we were like part of the family! *[laughing with the interviewer]*.
>
> You look back at that stuff, and you wonder why things changed when they came, but they did. When they weren't there, me and my grandmother would all join May, Ray, Bobby, and Frank, and we'd all sit around the table and eat together. But when these relatives came, me and my grandmother had to serve the food, and I had to set the table. And then we would have to go and eat in the kitchen after they got through eating.

Use of the toilet, one of the central themes of the popular novel *The Help*, was an overriding issue in all these homes. Some servants had a separate toilet to use, usually in the back of the house. Others had to go home or, even worse, find someplace outside in the woods where they could relieve themselves. As Loreatha Smith-Reid describes the situation she endured in Arkansas:

> They had a separate restroom. They had men who worked in the barn, and you would use that. The sign on the door said "Colored." It was really muddy in there. They wouldn't clean it out. The floors were so loose, and they had boards laying across there. They would just lay limbs across there and wouldn't clean it out. They would just let it sit there, and during the summer it would get really bad.

THE BONDS BETWEEN MISTRESS AND MAID

The sociological and historical literature, as discussed in previous chapters, devotes a great deal of attention to the intimate ties that formed between the white woman and her household maid. Although we will see this theme woven through the interviews with white employers, our African American storytellers did not echo this theme to the same extent when describing their work in the southern homes. One reason undoubtedly was that many of them were young teenagers when they did this work. Jimmie Lane, who had a college education, worked as a housekeeper for a couple in Louisiana, and they did draw very close. The workload was so light that she felt she was hired for companionship more than anything else. African Americans who worked as mature adults in white households in the North did describe forming close relationships with the white families for whom they worked.

Tyrone Hunt, originally of Fairhope, a coastal Alabama town, volunteered to be interviewed to share the story of his grandmother, Elmer Smith, "a full-figured lady" who sounds as if she was mother to everyone, white and black. Hunt's story goes back to the 1950s, when he was growing up. Because he drove his grandmother back and forth to work for several years, and because he had so much respect for her as the matriarch of the family—even the dogs obeyed her instantly—he was well aware of the conditions of her work. She worked for a prominent doctor and his wife. "She was sort of extended family to them," he said.

> She helped raise the kids. Sometimes the kids would ask her to intercede such as when the son was forbidden from going to a football game. She said she wouldn't get into it; they were the parents. Her opinion was consulted on matters concerning the children and on what kind of car they should buy. . . . She worked for them for around twenty-five years, and when she got cancer, they paid for all her medical expenses. When she died, they were heartbroken.

L. Walker, one of the many narrators who worked for the white families as a child, referred affectionately to the women she worked for as "all of them Christian ladies." While Mrs. Truett took a deep interest in her and provided her with lots of motherly advice and new gifts such as dresses for Sunday

Elmer Smith, Tyrone Hunt's beloved grandmother, who worked as a servant in Fairhope, Alabama. *From the family album of Tyrone Hunt.*

school, the white woman also learned some things from her young maid. As Walker laughingly recalled: "A lot of whites couldn't cook really. All they could do was make peanut butter and jelly sandwiches and stuff like that. Now at this one house [the Truetts'] all she could do was, she could hardly boil water. She had me show her how to fry chicken and make cornbread. When her family raised her up, they didn't teach her how to cook."

L. Walker also describes a close relationship she had with Mrs. Brown, a woman who always walked around the house in her robe and slippers. She even drove dressed in her nightclothes with Walker in the car so that Walker could run in the store and buy what was needed.

Another story that we have come by indirectly is told by Melvina Scott. She also was already working for white families as a child. She provides much detail about her and her mother's experiences. Her mother, she said, did confide in her employer. "They were all United Methodists," she said, "so I think they had a lot of the same kind of values. They developed a love for her as a person." There was a lot more to the story than that, in fact, for one of her brothers was suspiciously lighter than the rest of the family. "Don Kirkoff and my mother was real close. . . . He'd come over every day later in life, and he'd bring her coffee every day. They'd talk about life, and they learned from each other."

A case of woman-to-woman bonding took place between Nancy Hickman, who migrated up from Mississippi to Iowa, and her employer. The woman she worked for was from Texas. In all probability, this employer felt free to let go of the old southern rules of maid-mistress decorum now that she lived in the North. Hickman described what sounds like a fairly egalitarian relationship: "I worked for a lady from Texas, and she was just like I was. We'd have a cigarette, watch a story on TV—*Another World*. She thought she was no better than me, and I was no better than her."

STARTING OVER UP NORTH

Judith Rollins (1985) suggests that because of a common understanding of cultural expectations in the South, the mistress-servant relationship was psychologically uncomplicated because people knew what was what. Northern employers, on the other hand, having had less experience with blacks, had to struggle to draw the boundaries across class and racial lines. Common cultural traditions between white and black in the South were uniting rather than divisive, according to Rollins. As a result of these factors, Rollins suggests, the women she interviewed actually preferred the warm and personal relationships they developed with their southern employers to those they experienced in the North.

Micki McElya (2007), on the other hand, asserts that white southern employers were clinging to "fantasies of paternalism and mutual affection" (225), and that white northern employers sought to hire southern mammies who were faithful, ignorant, and speaking in the southern colloquialisms of their slave ancestors. What we found in our analysis of the twenty-three maid narratives was that bonds of mutual affection in many cases did develop across racial lines, and that this was true in all geographical regions.

Our interviews revealed much diversity in the treatment these women received, but on the whole they were glad to leave their masks behind and to do an honest day's work for an honest day's pay. Leora Henderson, whose story of domestic service in Oklahoma was told by her son, much preferred her work as a nurse's aide in Iowa to the heavy work required of her in the South. When she developed dementia in old age, her mind would turn to the past.

And every time it did, she would say, "Damn whites. Those damn whites." Her bitterness and hatred never left her, and feelings unexpressed earlier came out in her old age.

We did find, in agreement with Rollins, that the northern families who had full-time maids tended to be better off financially than their southern counterparts. But we are also talking about a later and more prosperous period of time since the oldest of our narrators grew up during the Great Depression. Also the narrators were older during the northern period of their lives. Unlike in Mississippi, where the domestics were seldom given uniforms to wear, but like in New Orleans, where they often did wear uniforms, maids in the North were provided with uniforms, according to our interviewees.

Rollins makes the important point that the economic differences between white and black were not as pronounced in the South because even southerners with fairly low incomes could afford household help; besides, it was the custom for whites to have servants. In contrast, maids who worked for white families elsewhere often were working for employers of some means.

The racial etiquette characteristic of southern life did not exist in the North, according to our reports. "You were treated as a person," reported Odessa Roberts of Monroe, Louisiana. From her account, although the domestic workers tended to be called by their first names, they often used the familiar form of address for their employers as well. They came in the front door, and they used the toilet facilities in the house. The humiliating rituals, not being a part of the culture of the Midwest, were absent. The employers would have known, in any case, that their servants would not put up with such treatment; they didn't have to.

Odessa Roberts, who had some unusually bad experiences, even for the South, saw a huge difference in the treatment she received up North. In the South, she was forced to clean the floors on her hands and knees to the point that her knees were permanently scarred. And when her employer, a man who celebrated the assassination of John Kennedy, berated her for hanging her own bedspread on his family's clothesline, she packed her bags and got on the train headed north.

In Iowa, Odessa Roberts was paid five dollars an hour for her domestic work, far more than she had earned in Louisiana. And she found that in Des Moines, unlike in the South, education was stressed for all children. So she pushed her children to get the education she lacked, and they were educated

Dorothy Weathers, who thrived in her move to Iowa, where she was more private secretary than domestic servant. *Photo by David Jackson.*

all the way up to professional levels. She herself eventually went "from a little nobody to somebody" and became a nurse.

Every now and then, a story came along that seemed almost too much out of the ordinary to be included. So it was with the story of Dorothy Weathers. She worked for a remarkable family—the Piggotts—in Des Moines, who acted more like parents than employers. No, her story is not representative, but it is too good a story to miss.

Dorothy Weathers was a well-educated person married to a college-educated man. Her opportunities for nondomestic work in 1950s Des Moines, Iowa, were not that good, however. In her interview, she offered the following insights into how race relations were played out in that city:

> At the time possibly every older woman that I knew was doing day work. There were very few office workers. I shouldn't say it, but possibly if you were not of light color you didn't work in the department stores or anything. . . . There were a few when I came up North to Des Moines. There was a factory called a bag factory, and a lot of the younger girls worked there. And the older women were doing the day work, as we called it then.

Another interviewee, Jana Bragg, confirmed Dorothy's observations. Born in Arkansas, Bragg followed her mother into domestic work in Des Moines.

Dark-complexioned women like her mother, she said, didn't work in the department stores, and only lighter-skinned women worked in the elevators. Only in the late 1960s did good opportunities come for black people; this was to prevent riots, according to Bragg.

Other options being scarce, when a friend suggested she do domestic work for the Piggotts, Dorothy took the suggestion. This family turned out to be very prominent as well as prosperous; the lady of the house was close friends with the governor of the state. Moreover, they were very generous. As she spoke, Dorothy brandished a diamond ring, one of her many keepsakes from this family. Dorothy's story is completely out of the ordinary because she actually did become a member of the family for whom she worked. Mrs. Piggott, whom she addressed as Patricia, was a former English teacher. On discovering that Dorothy was bright and eager to learn, she set out to teach her how to grasp symbolism in literature. Mr. Piggott taught her how to manage things and build up her credit for investments. In her work, Dorothy rose from maid to housekeeper to caterer for social events. And above all, she was a loyal confidante of Mrs. Piggott.

> I don't know what it was about her but she was the kind of person you weren't afraid to say anything to. Very, very helpful in my young life. In advising me about what to do and when to do it. And we began to grow together because you got to remember for forty-four years I was with this lady, so there was a lot between us.

In fact, the Piggotts saw to it that this housekeeper, if she could be called that, was financially secure for life. "Well, I never left the Piggotts. I still have not left in my heart," she said. "I will never lose the Piggotts; they will always be in my life because they have done some things that you wouldn't even believe."

Among the things the Piggotts did for her was to help her buy a new car, establish good credit through the bank and a retirement plan, provide her with an expensive wardrobe, purchase a paid-for funeral for her to spare her children the expense, and give her valuables such as a Chinese urn. Finally:

> Patricia considered me her daughter, she had a son and an adopted daughter, and she was allowed every year to give a ten-thousand-dollar

gift to each one of us without having to pay taxes for it, so that's where that ten thousand dollars came in, and then when my husband died, they said the ten thousand dollars they gave me was to bury him with and whatever was left I was to keep.

We agree with McElya that many women of the Great Migration were delighted to exchange the intimate mistress-maid relationship for an employer-employee relationship. If the work is not to her liking, according to Trudier Harris (1982), the northern worker makes it known. Consider, for example, what Millie Safford said to her Iowa employers:

I told them what I would do and wouldn't do. And if they put anything else on me I just told them it wasn't in the agreement. Most of them would have dogs, little old puppies. And if they left and that dog did something that needed to be cleaned, I'd go back in the room to get my clothes to go home, like my purse and my coat. If I saw that he'd done something on the floor, you think I cleaned it up? I looked at it and walked on out. I said, "It ain't my job. I ain't cleaning up after any dog."

Mamie Johnson reflected on the norms of the South and how some white migrants brought these same attitudes northward:

Now you wasn't going to be eat—I don't care who you was—at that table. You wasn't going to eat with them. You find some of these old white folks, done got plenty of them, mixed up from the South, right here in Waterloo. They right round here, you'd be surprised. But they right round here, and when you find one round here, you can know it. Sure know it!

Annie Victoria Johnson at first sounded quite negative when she generalized from her experience. "I still didn't tell you about Chicago. I think the women I worked for in Illinois were the most prejudiced and hateful women I ever worked for. It was nothing like Mississippi or Tennessee. The people are going to think because you are in Chicago, oh, you're free. No, you're not. This was back in the 1960s." Yet she had one lovely experience there with an Italian family who affectionately called her Aunt:

> Now when you find a good Italian, you are the same color as they are. It doesn't make any difference. I didn't have to buy any clothes. When she went on trips to New York or wherever her husband went, whatever she bought for herself, I had. Her husband was an attorney. I did everything for her. I cooked. She taught me how to make Italian spaghetti. . . .
>
> I lived with them. Every evening we would go down to the lake. And I would stand up there with a hundred-dollar bathing suit on and I can't even swim! *[laughing]*. And those little kids could swim like fish! Then we would go back up and take a shower. I would give them their supper and then they were ready to go to bed. Oh, I loved that job!

Visits Back Home

Wilkerson (2011) came across the phenomenon of the cultural shock experienced by black children reared in the North when their parents took them down South for visits. In Wilkerson's account, this "homeland" was a foreign country: "The homesick migrants loaded up sleeping children in the dark hours of the morning for the long drive to the mother country when there was a death in the family or a loved one needing tending or just to show off how well they were making out up North" (366).

Jessie Nicholson (2010), an attorney and the director of legal aid services in St. Paul, Minnesota, is a child of the Great Migration. In a keynote speech at the University of Northern Iowa, she describes her family visits home to Mississippi:

> I was raised in Waterloo, Iowa. I was raised in the Antioch Baptist Church and sang in the choir. This is my background: In the 1940s, a lot of African Americans were coming to Iowa from Mississippi so my Dad came to Iowa to give us kids a better opportunity. We would go back to Mississippi summer to visit my grandparents. We traveled in the dark so we would not be pulled over. One of the most fun parts was that we would bring fried chicken and a loaf of special bread which we would eat along the way. We would eat and drink; the trip was around twelve hours long so we would have to stop to go to the bathroom. When it came time that we had to go to the bathroom we would go in

> the back door of a gas station, or we would stop on the side of the road. I remember when I was around seven years old asking myself, Why is that? Why are people like that? Later I figured out that by traveling at night, we could preserve our modesty when we stopped. So, asking these questions later brought me to sociology at the University of Northern Iowa. (344)

As a married woman, L. Walker would have to go back to Mississippi periodically with her mother. At this time, she was married to a fellow Mississippian and had gone with him to Iowa, invited up by his brother. They really thrived in Iowa, but she was always haunted by her narrow escape from being murdered by a store owner who later was found to have killed other black girls who came into his store in the Delta:

> This really bothered me. The terror of that day came back—all the way down there I would get a terrible pain in my back, and the pain stayed with me the whole time. I would go with my mother to church, and people would come up who remembered me from before. "Oh, this is your daughter! I remember her. She is so pretty," they would say. But I never went anyplace else, not fishing or anything, couldn't wait to get back home.

RESILIENCE

Resilience, like oppression, is both a psychological and sociological phenomenon for an individual growing up in a racially hostile environment (Greene 2008). Ethnically and racially diverse families and communities can help children cope with discrimination by teaching them a means of resisting the oppression and by helping them to avoid internalizing the message. As we have seen in the excerpts from these stories of African American women who worked as maids in the Deep South and who endured conditions of economic and social oppression during the era of segregation, these black women put their families first.

And in their stories of growing up under conditions of gross economic exploitation and disempowerment, these women demonstrated remarkable resilience. Their later success in rearing a family and participating in church and community life in an integrated midwestern city further attests to their ability to prevail over personal hardship. In addition to the value placed on education, several major themes related to resilience among older African Americans surfaced in the interviews.

Respect for One's Family and Elders

All our interviewees showed respect for their parents and for the hard times they had endured. Annie Pearl Stevenson fondly recalls her father, a hardworking farmer: "When I was little, my dad was a sharecropper. But he was a very smart man. . . . He was a prideful man. He believed in earning a living for his family." Annie Johnson, similarly, has fond memories of her parents—her mother sewed clothes for her and her sisters, made quilts, and baked for her neighbors, and her father taught himself to read and read Bible stories to the children.

Resistance to Oppression

Collectively, the stories obtained for this book tell of resistance to oppression of all sorts—racial, economic, and personal. When they could not triumph over the evils of segregation and could not even vote, they packed their bags and boarded the trains. Some of the younger migrant women experienced what was to be the transformation of the southern social system, but they could not have known how far it would go at the time. We learned from Annie Pearl Stevenson's reminiscences about her participation in the historic event in 1962, when James Meredith enrolled at the University of Mississippi in violation of Mississippi law and in defiance of the whites who rioted there.

Annie Victoria Johnson, who grew up in the 1930s, had to be more devious. In her youth she was involved in a wild rescue of a man in the Delta who was held there against his will and in considerable danger. And later, working as a maid in Illinois, she set her employer straight when the woman tried to trick her out of her money. Elra Johnson's resistance was the strongest as a nationally recognized civil rights leader who directly confronted southern white racists at the risk of her life. Unlike the others who resisted by leaving, she remained in rural Mississippi until much later in life.

Strong Religious Faith

Annie Pearl Stevenson was raised a Baptist and attended Antioch Missionary Baptist Church for most of her adult life; today she is Pentecostal and attends the Church of God in Christ. Mamie Johnson, who regularly attends the Gift of Life Church, provided the most detail on this subject. In answer to the question of whether black people learned from the whites about religion, Mrs. Johnson was emphatic: "No! The whites learned from the blacks. The blacks maybe had something to do with them becoming Christians. . . . We used to get together—not in the churches—but in the homes. There used to be a white man who came to our house, all the time with his Bible. Him and my daddy would sit and read the Bible together.

A Positive Attitude and Belief in the Meaning of Life

When asked what the attitude of the white people was toward black people, Johnson said simply and rather astonishingly, "It was good." Stevenson was more reflective: "I wouldn't trade anything for the experience. I learned how to treat people. It was a learning experience, and by the way, I don't hold any animosity. I often wonder why not. It just made me the person I am today."

We saw how Rosie Loggins went from a domestic worker in the South to a master's level social worker in Iowa. Odessa Roberts of Monroe, Louisiana, similarly, spoke with pride of how she went from cleaning houses. In her words, "We have a beautiful home. I kept that positive thinking—tomorrow will be better. Don't look back." Thankfully, she was willing to look back for us so we could record her story for posterity.

Resilience, such as that demonstrated by the lives and philosophies of the older African Americans who participated in this study, had its roots in their upbringing in the rural South during the days of segregation. The women whose quotes highlight this chapter not only endured the oppression in their early lives, they prevailed over it.

Compared to the childhoods that these women had to struggle to overcome, some of the white women in Mississippi and nearby states could be considered to have lived "in the lap of luxury." To what extent they benefited from their privileges of race and class and to what extent they did not is revealed in their narratives.

Part III
The White Family Narratives

(6)
In Their Own Words

The history we are born into always seems natural when we're young, but it seems misshapen and grotesque as the winter years come upon us.
—PAT CONROY, *My Reading Life*

ALTHOUGH THEY COVER much of the same ground as the previous narratives by the domestic workers themselves, and they pertain to the same time period, the flavor of these contributions is remarkably different. Seven out of the fifteen women whose narratives are included in this chapter preferred to submit their memories in written narrative form; the other contributors chose to tell their stories in a personal interview. With one exception, all of these writers and interviewees were solicited and interviewed by Katherine van Wormer, consistent with our plan of using same-race interviewers. The exception was the one man whose memories were recorded in an interview taped by David W. Jackson.

As with the maid narratives, we order these reminiscences from the oldest to the youngest of the storytellers. Unlike so many of the white participants whose briefer statements are quoted in chapter 7, all but three of these contributors agreed to use of their own names. Significantly, seven of these participants were solicited shortly after the release of the movie *The Help* through an announcement on a LISTSERV for social work educators. The response was impressive; the participants we chose were those who could write their stories or be interviewed right away.

Elise Talmage, from New Orleans and Amite, Louisiana (born 1922). "It's just not done."

When invited to contribute her reminiscences of what she calls "our dark past," Elise Talmage, who is Katherine van Wormer's mother, submitted two narratives. Although the quote we chose to characterize the theme of her writings is not contained in these particular stories, it effectively captures the essence of what she tells us about the rigidity of the era in which she was brought up. When the young Elise asked her mother why the maids couldn't come in the front door or socialize in various ways with the whites, her mother would always say, "It's just not done."

Nicey and Gladys

It was 1932, and I was ten years old. The Depression lay hard on the land, but I and my little sisters didn't know it. We saw nothing unusual about tired, worn men coming to our door to get food. Mother was kind, and she and our cook packed small brown bags of sandwiches to pass out. Surely our house must have been marked. Other homes in New Orleans couldn't have had so many beggars.

But now I am leaving this everyday scene to visit my grandparents in Amite, Louisiana. Daddy drove me to Carrollton Avenue to catch the Illinois Central train going north. Big Mamma, my grandmother, was waiting for me in the big Hudson with crystal vases inside, and I rode along with a sense of importance.

As soon as we reached the house, I dashed into the kitchen to see Nicey. I loved Nicey. There she stood swaddled in a white apron with a wide grin on her brown face and arms outstretched. I tried to purse my lips so Nicey wouldn't see my new braces. They looked so awful! My mouth was filled with wires and even rubber bands between my jaws.

But Nicey spotted them anyway. "My, 'Lise," she gasped, "What are those pretty gold things on your teeth?" Her eyes sparkled with admiration.

Nicey lived in a cabin that looked just like a slave cabin in the field back of the house; it had no conveniences. The big house had two and a half bathrooms, but I saw Nicey crawling under the house to use the toilet. There was an old outhouse on the side of the home, but it had fallen into disrepair since Papa had installed the first modern bathroom in Amite, Mother said.

About the time the war broke out, Nicey disappeared. I don't recall why she left or where she went, but all over the South I knew colored people (that's what Mother said was the polite term) were on the move. Even servants were better paid in the cities than in small towns, and some got jobs in war plants while the men headed off to service. Those working on the docks probably were excused from military service along with the PT boat workers in New Orleans. But now women were grabbing the soldiers' jobs.

Gladys, our cook, walked out, much to my mother's consternation. We were totally dependent on servants because we had not caught up with the times. We had no washing machines and no dryer and sported a drop kitchen behind the house. Mother thought it cute. This was to keep cooking odors out of the home. Now food had to be carried up through the butler's pantry, the breakfast room, the hall, and into the dining room.

One day there was a knock on the front door. Servants had to come and go by way of the back door. But there stood our former cook, Gladys, coming to visit. She was arrayed in blue organdy billowing around her heavy body.

Gladys perched on our living room sofa to brag about her new job. Gladys was now a foreman in the war plant.

We knew a lot about Gladys. Her husband had a way of acting up and chasing skirts. She took care of things in her own way. As she told the story, she threw him over a heater and broke his leg. When the ambulance came, he said he had fallen down the steps. Gladys was standing over him with her hands on her hips just daring him to open his mouth.

She would tell us about her home life while she was cooking dinner. How her husband opened his eyes one morning to see a cold hatchet blade on the pillow with him. No wonder she was made a foreman.

Violet

"Put on your navy-blue silk dress, Elise, while I am getting the girls ready." My two little sisters were being scrubbed and brushed, two ribbons being tied in their bobbed yellow hair. We would wear our black Sunday school shoes—Mary Janes—to walk with Daddy to the church to the wedding.

Violet, our young cook, was getting married. We adored Violet, with her handsome brown face and her warm white smile. She told me she had Indian blood, but I could see she was also part French as well as African.

Violet lived with her Aunt Mamie just around the corner from our home on Meadow Street. She and I were pals, would have long talks sometimes while Violet shelled the black-eyed peas and mashed the potatoes. She told me about bad people who lived near their place in the country. Her aunt, who had no children, had brought her from a farm in the bayou country to look for work in the city. We called her Aunt Mamie just like Violet did. There was a fine mulatto seamstress who lived next to Aunt Mamie who had sewed my navy-blue silk dress with a lovely handmade lace collar.

In the summer, Violet would live in our house on the Mississippi Gulf coast. Her aunt saw that she had very pretty clothes, which she would wear in the evening sitting on the seawall. I'm sure the mulatto seamstress made them.

Aunt Mamie had been the cook in one of the large upper-class homes in the university section. Upon retirement, the family had given her a neat, small house on Audubon Street near Magazine for her long service. Now she was helping to teach her niece Violet fine Creole cooking. In no time she would be serving what we considered to be your basic dishes: gumbo and stuffed mirlitons, shrimp creole, red fish coubion, and oyster soup.

Aunt Mamie's home was well equipped with the best kitchen utensils, and when Mother needed a certain kind of pot she didn't have, which she frequently did, Violet would quickly run around to her house and lend it to Mother.

Now we three trotted along with Daddy to the wedding in Aunt Mamie's neat living room. Violet was marrying a man from their hometown in the country. Aunt Mamie was pleased with the match as he owned a barber shop and was better fixed than most in their parish.

However, we three were very upset about losing Violet to anyone.

The room was crowded, but we glimpsed the groom, and he wasn't handsome like Violet and had acne scars on his face. Violet didn't even look like herself in her wedding dress with white powder on her pretty brown face. (There wasn't yet makeup available for people with dark skin.)

By the time the services started, the three of us were crying pretty loud while Daddy struggled to get us quiet, but we just sobbed louder and louder, and Daddy was helpless. When it was over, we three cried all the way home.

We loved Violet.

Flora Talmage Landwehr, from New Orleans (born 1929). "I don't remember experiencing any tension or problem resulting from this custom [segregated streetcars]."

The younger sister of the previous storyteller takes the Talmage family into a somewhat later time period. This narrative describes the family maid, Elizabeth, who would have been a fairly young woman at this time when she replaced Gladys, who left to take a well-paying job in the war factories, as described above. You will be reading about this prominent figure again in the

Elizabeth Griffin in the garden. She worked in the same home practically all of her life, for two generations of the same family. She lived around the block. *From the family album of Flora Stuart.*

narrative of Susan Hudgens, who grew up in the same house on Broadway Avenue with the same maid a generation later.

Memories of Early Home Life in New Orleans, 1929–1960

My father at this time was able to buy his first home, a very small bungalow in a neighborhood bounded at one end by the great levee and the other end by a beautiful park named for John Jay Audubon. The levee made a crescent-like bend and protected the city, below sea level, from the Mississippi River. The people on our street were white people; however, around the corner were several small "shotgun" houses where some colored people lived. My parents always instructed us to refer to these people as "colored" or as Negroes. We were never to call them "niggers." One of these women was Naomi, who was light-skinned and who lived with a young girl who wore a Catholic-school uniform. We took notice that this family was a little different from ours. My mother respected Naomi and sometimes would go to her home to have her sew or alter clothes. Mother considered Naomi a good seamstress.

Along the foot of the levee there were rows of small unpainted houses where the colored people lived and found jobs doing domestic work and labor. They furnished the help for the white neighborhoods doing the laundry, cleaning, and cooking. I remember that my mother depended on these women to help her; running a household was very labor intensive. I also remember that my mother taught these women skills in the kitchen and in the laundry work. Mother was a very conscientious mother and did not leave her child care to her maid or servant.

When I was eleven years old, my father bought a much larger house on Broadway, about eight blocks from our first home. At this time a new maid came into our lives. She lived around the corner about three blocks away and could walk to our home. Tall and slender, she had a very winning personality and knew how to cheer us up and share our joys and sorrows.

My mother said Elizabeth had learned her skills from a prominent New Orleans family. She knew how to iron beautifully men's white dress shirts and all the tiny tucks and pleats in baby clothes; she could remove stains and produce bed linens sun-dried and snow-white. She knew how to sew for herself. A highly skilled cook, she knew how to make the Creole sauces and gravies, how to make eggplant fritters, how to broil and fry fish, fry chicken, and make red fish coubion.

New Orleans had a very good public transportation system, affording the poor and the wealthy alike the means to shop and travel to their jobs. But society was segregated by race, and so were the buses and "streetcars" (electric trolleys). The small signs saying "no colored" were movable and could easily be transferred from seat to seat as the passenger load required. The passengers of both races took on this responsibility themselves. I don't remember experiencing any tension or problem resulting from this custom. My mother often traveled on the Broadway bus and knew many of the colored maids, who were friendly and called her "Miz Talmage."

Elizabeth always came to our backyard and entered through the back door. She would use the toilet in a building in the backyard, and she always wore a uniform and white apron.

Elizabeth had a sister who had moved to California and would come back occasionally to visit. She would bring her two daughters with her to visit their beloved "Auntie," who had no children of her own; they spoke of their very pleasant California life. They also came in the back door and stayed in the kitchen to chat. We were very interested in these girls; they were different and quite charming. Elizabeth had visited California but was not interested in moving away. Elizabeth had a "husband" named Richard. I remember that he had a kidney illness and went to Charity Hospital often. I don't remember ever meeting him.

Our new home was a half block from our school until we went to high school, which required catching rides and taking the buses and streetcars. Elizabeth was always in the kitchen when we came home. We could tell her our troubles and perhaps get a snack. This pattern continued through our years of high school and college. One by one, my older sisters married and left home. When my mother died, Elizabeth was there to continue preparing the dinner, doing the laundry, cleaning, cheering us up, and helping my father.

While cooking and ironing, Elizabeth enjoyed listening to the radio in the laundry room. She sang along with all the gospel music she loved. My sister Jane and I thought the music was awful. Little did we know that this music was the precursor to the music the whole world now loves, including our grandchildren!

Elizabeth silently observed our social life during these years. However when "Mistah Joe" started coming around, she was delighted and sensed another wedding. Later on, Jane and I started going back home with our babies. Elizabeth loved playing with them and could make the baby stop crying while we ate dinner.

When I visited home, she taught me some of her cooking skills and laundry skills. I will always be indebted to her for all the love and care she gave each of us.

These vignettes belong to a very young child and to a young woman and mother. They reflect a life that was very happy and secure. The many injustices in our society are only suggested here; however, as we matured, we were sympathetic with the great changes around us, and the struggle for social justice, which came slowly. When the transportation system was desegregated, I said, "Elizabeth, now we can sit together." But she could not accept sitting alongside me, and insisted on sitting in the seat behind, much to my objection.

Anne Noell Rowan, from Comer and Athens, Georgia (born 1933). "Putting these thoughts on paper made me remember so many things!!! Thanks for the memories."

Most striking from this interview is the discrepancy, revealed in the portrait of Bill, between the whites' description of the maid-mistress relationship as one based on mutual caring and the way "the help" characterized this relationship.

Bill

In the spring before my fifth birthday, a black man in our small town asked Daddy if he could use household help. It seems that his fourteen-year-old daughter had dropped out of school and had run away. His two older daughters worked for families in town, and he wanted this one to also have a job. This was very good timing since my mother had decided to accept a job teaching school in the fall and needed to go to summer school for some needed credits. So Bill came into our lives. I don't know why her family did not use her given name, Georgia Mae, but her personality was not that of a frilly girl, and Bill suited her better. To an almost five-year-old, she was "grown up," but in reality she was still a teen.

We were living on my grandfather's farm when Bill came to work for us. Bill learned to keep house, wash and iron clothes, cook breakfast and lunch, and keep up with me. She had a good sense of humor and seemed to be always smiling.

I remember one morning my daddy asked her to cook him two pieces of bacon. She replied, "Yes, Mr. Willis." My mother said, "No, he doesn't need but one piece of bacon." "Yes, Miss Jeannette" was her response. In a few minutes she brought their plates to the table and on Daddy's plate was one piece of bacon cut in two!

Bill would sometimes pack a "lunch" for the two of us and we would go exploring in the woods. When cotton-picking season arrived, Bill's father needed her help in the field. I would go with her and pick cotton with her younger siblings, who were about my age. We younger ones had small picking sacks instead of the big ones the grownups used. At the end of the day, her father would weigh what each person had picked. I would tell my daddy how many (very few) pounds I had picked, and he would pay me for my "work."

Bill stayed with us for about seven years when another family offered her more money. By this time I was able to be of some help with the housework, and we did not need any "help."

Many years later, I met Bill again. At this time, my husband was in graduate school, and we had a new baby. I was so delighted to introduce our baby to an old friend. Before she left our apartment Bill said, "Miss Anne, what do you have to give me?" Then I realized she did not really consider me as a friend, but as a part of a family on whom she had depended. This pretty much sums up my feelings of hurt and disappointment that I was not as special to her as she was to me in my memories. After she visited our apartment, it was likely clear that our living arrangements were not superior and that there was nothing that I could give her.

Helen

When my husband was in graduate school, we had a new baby and I needed to go back to work. At the time when we were in grad school, having a maid was cheaper (and more dependable) than paying for child care. In fact, I don't believe there were many options for child care at that time. I asked a woman who was a cook at my sorority house if she knew anyone who would be interested in the job. She sent her friend Helen to us. Helen's main duty was to care for the baby, but she also cleaned our very small apartment, did laundry, and prepared the noon meal for my husband. Helen took care of our son as if he were her own. One day some cousins of mine dropped by to see the baby. Helen did not know them, and I had not told her they were coming (I did not know either), and she would not let them in the house.

This apartment was in an old house that was very drafty in the winter. Helen would not put the baby in his playpen but put toys in his bed for play. She said she was so glad when my husband came home each afternoon so she could go home and get her feet warm!

The wall cabinet in our kitchen fell, breaking nearly all our plates and glasses. We bought for replacements only what we had to have. Helen was not satisfied with this. She put the baby in his stroller and walked about two miles to a store to buy Jim a BIG glass for his iced tea!

At the end of the year we moved to another city since Jim had finished his studies and had found a job in another city. We will always remember Helen's fierce loyalty to our son and her faithfulness to her work.

Jane

We next needed "help" when my husband was back in graduate school, and I needed to go back to work. We moved into student housing and encountered a new situation: There were a number of women who worked for student families. As one family graduated, these women would find work with a new family just coming to school. Jane and her mother were part of that work force. Jane looked after our two children, cleaned the small apartment, and prepared lunch for us. She was efficient, pleasant, and dependable. She sometimes surprised me by cooking a dessert for our dinner. There were times when there was room at the table for her to eat with us, but Jane was ADAMANT that she would eat in that tiny kitchen.

As I have spent time remembering these women, I realize how amazing and resourceful they were. Putting these thoughts on paper made me remember so many things!!! Thanks for the memories.

In response to follow-up questions, Anne Noell Rowan stated that none of the three women wore a uniform. As Rowan explains about other issues pertaining to the time period:

There was only one toilet in each instance, except when Bill first came to work for us—at that time we had no running water, and we all used the same "backyard convenience." I don't recall gifts to take home. They were called by their first name and called us "Miss Anne" and "Mr. Jim" or "Miss Jeannette" and "Mr. Willis." They ate in the kitchen, which was the only place to eat for Helen, but she would eat at a later time, finding other things to do while Jim ate (playing with the baby, folding clothes, etc). Bill and I ate together when we were "adventuring."

Hal Chase, from Des Moines, Iowa, and Frankfort, Kentucky (born 1943). Interviewed by David W. Jackson. "You have to talk to them, and really listen to them."

This narrative offers a fascinating contrast between the social environments of the Midwest and the South. Dr. Chase taught and researched African American history from 1967 to 2009, the last twenty-two of those forty-three years at Des Moines Area Community College. Upon hearing of our project, he came forward to share his memories of his relationships with three remarkable African American women who had a great influence on his life.

Interviewer: Dr. Chase, if you could, please share with us your experience growing up with a maid or cleaning lady.

There were two that I can remember. The first one, Elsie Mae Jackson, lived

In this photo, Elsie Mae Jackson has baked a birthday cake for Hal Chase's mother. Not much attention is being paid to Elsie, however, for all her work. *From the family album of Hal Chase.*

in our home on Grand Ave. in Des Moines, Iowa, where my two older sisters and I lived with our mother and father until they divorced when I was six and a half. The second was Mrs. Leora Mitchell, who came into our home in Frankfort, Kentucky, after our mother remarried a man from there a little more than a year later.

Elsie Mae Jackson was hired by my mother and father because her older sister, Georgia, worked for my father's mother, who also lived in Des Moines. They came out of Oklahoma. Elsie was a young woman, mid- to late twenties. She was primarily a cook. The child-care part was tertiary. It was cooking, cleaning, including laundry, and then taking care of myself and my sisters if our mother went out. Most of that time I was not yet in school.

I remember Elsie Jackson always being in the house, and I have a couple of vivid memories of her. She was a spirited woman, for sure, and attractive. She was a medium build, not thin and not tall. What I can also tell you is that I followed her around a lot as my two older sisters were already in school. When my mother would go out to do some errands or have lunch or attend a meeting, Elsie and I were in the house together. That's how I remember it. She was my buddy; she was the kind of older person that you knew everything was safe and sound as long as she was around. In this sense, I would say that she was my protector.

Interviewer: Did she discipline you?

Not that I recall excepting once that I remember vividly. It was a weekend morning and I was in my pajamas that had the feet in them. What I remember was that no one was up in the house except me, so I went and opened the door to her room, and there she was in her birthday suit. She shrieked, and I remember that it was like I exploded out of her room.

The other vivid memory of Elsie Jackson was in Frankfort, Kentucky, which was still legally segregated in the early 1950s. I was in the second grade and was walking home after school so it was a little after 3:00 p.m. on a spring day when I saw her car. It was a sharp, pale-colored convertible. She was behind the wheel and visiting with a young woman about her age. I was happy to see her and went up and greeted her. When she turned and looked at me, I asked her, "What's wrong?" as I could tell something wasn't right between us. She said, "Well, I'm late" to her friend. The implication was clear, and I said, "You're leaving? You're not going to be with us anymore?" because she was dressed up and there were suitcases in the backseat. "No," she said, and drove off. I went home wondering what had gone wrong, and when I asked my mother about it, she said something to the effect of, "It didn't work out between your stepfather and Elsie." He was a man of his time, and I guess he saw Elsie as "uppity" or whatever you want to call it. Here's my educated guess on why she left. Elsie made more money in Des Moines than what she was paid in Frankfort because you and I both know that the wage scale in the segregated states was lower for African American help than it was, generally speaking, in the North.

Interviewer: When we look at the type of work she was doing—you said she was doing the cooking and the cleaning. Was she there all day?

Yes.

Interviewer: Did she eat with you?

Not that I remember.

Interviewer: Do you—could you say that she enjoyed her work? Were there any vibes there that made you feel that she didn't enjoy it?

I'd say she did not enjoy her work. The servant role, if you will, wasn't Elsie Jackson. No, clearly she had more ambition. I think because of her sister she got to Des Moines, where there was a job that gave her access to a nice car, nice clothes, and so on. That's what I think. She definitely had ambition to be more than a domestic.

Interviewer: Do you know whether she could use the restroom in your home?

I would say absolutely yes.

Interviewer: Did she use the front door of the house?

Here's my guess. One of the things that didn't work for my stepfather was that she probably came through the front door because the back door was out of the way so you'd have to go all the way around the house. When she living with us on Grand Ave. in Des Moines, she lived in the house on the second floor with the rest of us, not in some room in the basement, attic, or over the garage.

Interviewer: Did she wear a uniform?

Yes. What I remember, gray normally, a gray dress, and when there was a dinner party, a white dress.

Interviewer: Do you know if she was ever called the N word, a nigger? Was she ever called that?

I never heard that. Those are words that my stepfather did use, but not in her presence.

Interviewer: And you two formed a bond together?

That is the way I felt.

Interviewer: Yeah, that's what I'm gathering. You formed a bond together. What was her reaction—can you recall—when she said she was leaving?

She was distant, and I remember feeling disappointed in that. What I did, as children will do when something goes wrong, is feel that you did something wrong. Long ago, I realized that it was nothing that I did as far as I can tell, but rather the segregated environment of Frankfort, Kentucky, my stepfather's upbringing, and her strong will. It just didn't fit. She was probably thinking, "I'm gone. I didn't leave Oklahoma to be back into that situation." There are so many questions this experience has raised for me. It would be wonderful if I knew what did happen.

Interviewer: So her absence, was it an easy adjustment for you? Were you sad? Were you okay with it?

It was not easy. No question about it.

Interviewer: Let's move on and talk about the second person. You said there were two.

Mrs. Leora Mitchell worked for us next. She was from Kentucky. She was from a large family. Leora Mitchell was Roman Catholic. Leora Mitchell was, I would say, at least twenty years older and clearly understood the system, had lived under it for fifty years, and Leora Mitchell was the person from whom I learned a lot about life; some may call it race relations.

She only came on Tuesdays and Thursdays unless my parents were going to have a dinner party. At that time, people had other people over for dinner, usually for a Saturday night. People would come at 5:30 or 6:00 p.m., have cocktails, and then sit down and have dinner. Afterwards, they would play bridge.

Leora Mitchell had her own car, also a convertible, and she parked it in front of our house, but walked around the house and came in the back door to the kitchen. She'd usually come about 4:00 p.m. to have dinner on the table by 6:00 p.m. I was one of those children that had a lot of questions, and she was the soul of patience.

Interviewer: What did you call her? Did you call her Leora? Ms. Mitchell?

If I'm not wrong, I think she asked us to call her Ms. Leora, which was part of the system. No last names, right? My stepfather called her Ms. Leora, and I'm pretty sure that my mother and the three of us called her Ms. Leora, too.

Interviewer: Would you know anything about how much she was paid? Can you recall?

David, I cannot think that it was what we could call a wage. I would call it a segregated wage.

Interviewer: Did she ever eat with your family? You and the family sit down and have breakfast, lunch, or dinner?

I don't remember that, but I would say particularly when it was a dinner party, my sisters and I would eat earlier, get us out of the way, and she would be busy fixing the rest of it. Here's the one bit of memory I have of eating together. It was between my sophomore and junior year of high school. It was late summer. I was sixteen and working on the farms owned by a friend of my parents. The watermelons were ripe, and I had brought home a couple as there was a large patch where I worked, and the tenant, Tommy Donovan, had told me to help myself. I cut one open and asked her, "Would you like a piece?" You could see from the emotion on her face that she was surprised. That reminded me of the system, and I asked if she would like to take some home. She smiled as she said, "Yes, thank you." I gave her the whole other melon.

Interviewer: Did she wear a uniform?

Yes, it was gray with a white apron.

Interviewer: Do you recall her ever being called a nigger at any point in time?

Again, no. As I said, my stepfather would use the term, but generally, as I remember it, when other men, white men his age and friends and associates were in the house. They would use that term, and it wasn't right.

When I moved to Frankfort, Kentucky, and started school, on the first day as I remember it, I went home and asked my mother, "What's a Yankee?" When she asked me why I was asking her that, I told her that people in my class were calling me a "Yankee," "Damn Yankee," or, pardon their choice of words, "Nigger lover." I don't remember her saying, "Well, you know, Hal, one hundred years ago there was a civil war that ended slavery." I don't remember that approach at all, but David, it was very clear that my classmates were telling me, "You ain't one of us."

My most vivid memory of Leora Mitchell is a conversation we were having about "right and wrong" when I was still in grade school. When I asked her how she knew what was right, her unforgettable answer was, "A right's a right, and a right doesn't wrong nobody."

The third person and the one who had the greatest influence on my career as a professor was Ora Jane Caise. She cooked, cleaned house, did the laundry, and took care of an elderly couple around the corner and is the person who taught me the most. In addition to her full-time job for the Ironses, she was an elementary school teacher at Mayo-Underwood, the segregated 1–12 school for African Americans in Frankfort. She never had any children of her own, so she took into the Ironses' home a series of young men she met in her class, and John Sykes was living there when I moved to town. There he was in an all-white neighborhood and me a "Damn Yankee," so both of us were on the margins, right? John Sykes is one of the most honest people you'll ever know, and we became buddies who played together in the afternoons exploring the State Capitol and the Old Capitol that had been turned into a museum and playing football or baseball on the Capitol grounds. When John and I would go into the Ironses' kitchen in the late afternoon, there would be Ms. Caise. She was tall, broad-shouldered, middle-aged, attractive in a strong way whose steely eyes and mind would stare down at us and start asking us questions faster than we could answer. "Where you been?" What you been doing?' Basically, she asked us to give an account of ourselves. It was okay to be boys, but don't be doing something you shouldn't be doing. And always be learning about the world. She was always that kind of teacher. I mean she was always teaching us, and, literally, sometimes, she would ask us about some current event, its who, what, when, where, and why. There is no question that Ora Jane Caise was a positive model for teaching and learning. So I think that was one of the reasons that when I was in high school, I decided that I wanted to become a teacher.

Ora Jane Caise, who worked full time as both fourth-grade teacher and domestic servant for a white family in Kentucky. Hal Chase credits her with directing his path toward teaching. *Photo by John Allen Sykes, from the family album of Hal Chase.*

Interviewer: This woman, this Ora Jane Caise, she influenced you to go to college?

Absolutely. No question. Like Elsie Jackson, but Elsie Jackson was angry, thinking that the way we were living here [segregation] was totally unacceptable. Ora Jane Caise was very clear that segregation wasn't right, yet she was far more sophisticated in how to deal with it in terms of defiance and her dignity in the world. She was always superior in the sense of being above some others who used the term [nigger] or said, "You have to go to the back of the bus." She would walk. There was no way she would sit in the back of the bus. People like her were the reason young people got involved in the in the so-called civil rights movement in the 1950s and 1960s.

Interviewer: You've talked about Ora Jane Caise, Elsie Jackson, and Mrs. Leora Mitchell. In particular, did you stay in touch with Ora Jane Caise?

What I remember is that I had something, and I am going to guess that it was a Christmas present. It was during my graduate school years because that is when I began to focus on African American history. I took her something related to that, and what I remember was, I went down to her house on Logan Street, and she invited me in and was happy to see me, and we hugged. I gave her the gift, and we sat down and we talked about African American history. I remember particularly asking her, "Was anybody in your family part of the

Great Migration who got out and went up North during World War I or in the 1920s?" I learned she had a younger brother who left home at sixteen for the steel mills in Pittsburgh, where he died tragically in an industrial accident. Clearly, she had been very close to that brother. His death was a lifelong loss for her. So for me, what I learned from our conversation was that to really understand the person behind the uniform, you have to talk with them, and really listen to them.

Margaret Smith (not her real name), from New Orleans, Louisiana (born 1944). "It was what it was, and now is no more."

Now we come to a very different style of writing in the story told by a woman who also clearly has agonized over the servant-employer situations that were commonplace when she was growing up. The writer states here that she assumed she would always have a maid. Today, as she shared in private correspondence with Katherine van Wormer, indeed, she has a Latina housekeeper.

There were no maids in our home in Gretna, Louisiana, in the 1940s. There were also no cars in our driveway, radios, TVs, or air-conditioning. Home was a shotgun double owned by my great-grandmother, and there were seventeen family members living there. Prejudice found a home there, too.

My family was poor and undereducated. In order to be better than somebody else, my family, although kind in many ways, felt superior to black people, called Negroes back then, or worse. There was a lot of derogatory talk. My family members were equal-opportunity bigots; they also called Italians "dagos," and oriental people "wops." But they were proud to be called "Coon Asses" themselves, so they may not have thought their name-calling was particularly insulting.

One night as I lay in my granny's bed, supposed to be asleep, I overheard a conversation among the adults around the kitchen table, accusing the black boy who delivered our groceries (yes, there were no supermarkets, only corner stores that still delivered) of stealing a football from under our house. How they thought they knew he took it, I do not know. There were no fences around our house or gates, and under our house was just that—a completely open area under our raised house. There were a lot of angry words and racist talk that had nothing to do with one boy and one missing football. I was not even six years old, but I knew that what was being said was unfair. I cried.

My mother, who was a pretty woman, attracted the attention of a man above her class and economic circumstances, and when I was six she remarried, and we moved to the uptown section of New Orleans. We were not home owners but rented half of a double house from a relative of my stepfather. My stepfather was the vice president of a small insurance business and owned some land in Mississippi and Louisiana where tung trees were grown for the oil they produced, oil that is useful in paints and varnishes. We were middle-class now, and we had a maid named Rita. My mother for the first time in her life had some power, and like people born into ignorance do, she abused it. Mother loved to tell the story of how Rita would never let her drive her all the way home, so Mother decided to do some detective work. She followed Rita and found that she was living in the French Quarter with only a cloth covering for a door. She, who had just escaped from poverty herself, would then add importantly, "I couldn't have someone who was dirty working in my home, so I fired her."

My stepfather had many black people working for him during the gathering of the tung crop. He called them "darkies," and outside of that, always treated everyone well.

I believe that there was one woman hired after Rita, who stayed only a few days, and then came Evelyn. Evelyn remained with our family from then on until arthritis took its toll to the point that she could no longer work. By then I was married and had been gone from the family home for many years. It is Evelyn who lives in my memory, and I am her only storyteller if her story is to be told, since all the rest of the players from her home and ours have passed on, even my baby brother whom she loved so much.

This is what I know of her life and times. It is not much, but it is all I know. Evelyn was the granddaughter of a slave, and she knew that she had white blood somewhere in her heritage. Her son, whom I will call John, was light-skinned and, according to my mother, "lived up North and passed for white." She warned me never to have anything to do with John if he ever came to the house (he never did). She told me he was crazy and to stay away from him. John did call the house once by phone. I was older at the time, probably an older teenager, and after the conversation I realized that it was possible that my mother may have been right. He engaged me in a weird conversation, and

Evelyn, who was there, overheard, and sensing that it was he, got upset and took the phone from me. I remember only her voice screeching at him, and questioning him about what he was saying to me, etc. That was my only experience with John.

Evelyn's daughter, who was raised in a basement apartment and then in a housing project, was a pretty woman. I never understood why she never married. She lived with her mother all her life and took care of her when she was old. Sometimes, if there were a large party at our house, she would come and work along with her mother. Maybe it was because of her mother's marital experience that she never married.

Evelyn was married to a man I will call Will. His last name was a typical New Orleans French name, so I can assume that his roots were on a plantation somewhere in the French South. Will fathered his two children, then moved on to greener pastures. Evelyn raised his two children by herself on a maid's pay, which in 1950 was twelve dollars a week. She worked in our home five days a week, from 10:00 a.m. to around 7:00 p.m. She was responsible for all the cleaning, laundry washing (we had another woman come in to iron), and cooking. She also kept an eye on us kids when my mother was not home. She was off on Thursdays and Sundays. Every day she followed the same routine, and she became a fixture in our home, like a washing machine or dishwasher. We became used to having an outsider in our home daily.

Since my younger brother and I never had any responsibility to do any work around the house or care for our own things, I guess you can say we were spoiled. We were certainly thoughtless. It never occurred to me to consider Evelyn when I put my dirty clothes in the hamper or left my books or stuffed animals tossed about the room. It was her job to pick them up. I never considered it unfair. I never felt privileged, just accepted our lives as what they were. I never felt that it should be any different, and when I thought of the future and dreamed of being married myself, I assumed that I would have servants. Evelyn never complained or suggested that I should clean up after myself. I wonder now what she was thinking and feeling. I guess I will never really know. I think she was happy to have a job, and I was not unkind to her in any other way; my family would not have tolerated unkindness.

Sometimes, if it was particularly late because the family had asked her to work overtime, or if it was raining, we would give her a ride home. Otherwise and most often, she left our home at 7:00 p.m. and rode the bus home. It was not too far from our home to hers, only two buses were involved and not a long distance for the first ten years. When I was sixteen, my mother and stepfather bought a home on the Lakefront, and the bus ride home became significantly longer. Evelyn was probably in her fifties then, and arthritis was starting to set in. It could not have been easy for her. My mother would allow her to "tote" leftover food home, and she would carry her sack on the bus with her to feed herself and her daughter.

My brother was born after Evelyn came to work with us, and she adored him. He was a cute kid, but oh so undisciplined. My brother and Evelyn were very close. She hugged, kissed, bathed, dressed, and fed my brother from the cradle to the day he left home to move in with his father (my mother and he were then separated).

Evelyn and I rarely spoke. Our conversations were limited to issues relating to her household duties only. We never chatted that I can remember. Even when I got my driver's license and was willing to drive her home just to be behind the wheel, we would ride home in silence and say goodnight when we arrived. What I know about her is what I overheard in conversations she had with others. When Evelyn retired on Social Security, Mother continued to send her money weekly until she died.

We had other black servants in the home. They were not full-time employees so I did not come to know them well. As time wore on, the black people who came to work in my mother's home became more confident in themselves and friendlier, less formal.

Then there came a time when my mother could no longer afford a full-time servant and had a cleaning girl on Saturday. Evelyn had always worn uniforms, which my mother provided. The cleaning lady hired after Evelyn wore street clothes. The day pay was significantly better than the full-time pay had been for Evelyn. As a matter of fact, I now remember that Evelyn started doing day work in our home when my mother could no longer pay her full-time, before she retired fully and Mother brought in others.

There were many stories about blacks who stepped out of line and what happened to them. I believe there was much fear behind the formal relationships of maids and their employers. And economically times were hard for black women in the 1950s without much opportunity for advancement. There were also horrible stories of gross injustices. But their day-to-day understated humbling is what really kept blacks in the yoke of slavery for so many years after they were freed. Perhaps most in our African American community have been like the circus elephants who are chained when young and can be kept under control long after they are able to break their bonds because they are still held firm by the belief that they are not free, or like hostages who side with their captors. Whatever the cause, it was what it was, and now is no more. Thank God.

Mary Hart, from Camden, Arkansas (born 1945). "To realize not only that segregation, discrimination, hatred, and violence existed was one thing, but also to realize that my family was a part of it was humiliating."

Mary Hart became a civil rights activist after reading *Black Like Me*, which totally turned her life around. Two years after the Civil Rights Act was passed in 1964, the Student Non-Violent Coordinating Committee (SNCC), influenced by the Black Power movement, voted to remove all the white members. Mary Hart was one of them.

It is a joy to remember some of the good times. And, of course, always difficult to think my family was a part of what I have worked so hard to change.

My most vivid memories of a maid are of my paternal grandparents' home. We went there every Sunday for dinner (served at one o'clock). They lived in Prescott, Arkansas, about thirty-five miles from Camden, where I grew up. Mother had "help" but not in the same way as my grandparents. These memories cover a period from 1949 to 1960. I was born in 1945.

Grandmother's maid was named Austine. She was single and as far as I know lived with her family (parents) until they died. Grandmother and Granddaddy married in 1895, and I suspect that Austine came to them sometime in the 1920s or 1930s. She did all the cooking and cleaning, serving meals—Sundays were best china, crystal, and silver (which Austine kept polished) with linen tablecloths and napkins (which Austine had washed in a wringer washer, dried on the clothesline, and ironed). She bossed Prince, the gardener and handyman, around. Prince was married, and he and his wife had an adopted daughter named Queenie.

One of my favorite memories was Austine teaching me how to make biscuits. My mother never let me or my sister into the kitchen, so cooking was like magic. She taught me how to add the flour to the lard, how much salt and baking powder to use, but most of all how to knead the dough until it was just right and then roll it out and cut the biscuits with a clean Campbell's soup can. I adored her. And she thought I was wonderful—at least I believed she did.

Austine was a terrific southern cook. It's a wonder we didn't all die of a heart attack by age twenty, given that most things were fried in lard or boiled in fatback. She made the best cakes and pies in the world. I have no doubt that she made enough to take home for her family. I have no idea how much she was paid back then, but I would guess somewhere around a dollar or two a day—plus toting.

She and Prince ate after we had finished dinner. They would usually eat in the backyard at a table except in the winter, and then they would eat in the kitchen—standing up. They had their own silverware and dishes that were kept in a separate cabinet. After they ate, Austine would start a pot of boiling water and boil their dishes. I remember asking why, but I don't remember the answer.

When Austine's mother died, my aunt went to her house to be sure they had what they needed for the wake and the funeral. I remember that when she came back she was smiling and said—"I shouldn't have been concerned. Austine had toted some of the sheets in the linen closet, and her mother is laid out in all of mother's fine linen," My grandmother bought a dozen sets of sheets and pillowcases at the white sales in January every year, and they lived in a huge closet off the upstairs hall.

Toting was something that was understood. It's not that gifts and hand-me-downs were offered to Austine. She took home leftovers and things that Grandmother told her to throw out. Grandmother was a Victorian lady, and while she was about four foot ten inches and maybe ninety pounds, she ruled the house and family with an iron hand. NO ONE contradicted her. If she was annoyed with you, she would call the family lawyer and write you out of her will. You were put back in as soon as someone else was written out. However, Austine bossed Grandmother around. She would tell her what to eat, help her dress, when to take her medicine. She did it gently, but Grandmother was utterly dependent on Austine to organize her life.

Once, Grandmother decided that Prince should dig up all of the daffodil bulbs—I'm talking a field of daffodils. Austine told her that was a bad idea because "Miss Mary liked to pick them on Sundays." Now, Austine probably didn't care whether I picked them or not, but she knew that as soon as Prince had dug them all up, Grandmother would change her mind and make Prince replant them. Prince didn't talk back to Grandmother; he would just shake his head. In fact, I don't remember Prince saying much of anything.

I really don't remember which door Austine used. Even when I would spend weeks in the summer at my grandmother's, Austine was always there. I am sure she used the back door when she came and went, however. As for the bathroom—I talked with my sister after both of us had read *The Help,* and neither of us can remember anything about anyone having separate bathrooms for the maids. I don't remember anything about bathrooms and Austine at all. But they didn't talk about such things in front of the children—little pitchers have big ears, you know.

Austine did wear a uniform some of the time. Grandmother probably told her when she was supposed to wear it. My recollection is that she wore it on Sundays and when we had company. Everyone called Austine, "Austine." She called all of us by our first name preceded with "Miss." Except for Grandmother and Granddaddy. She was Miz Hart, and Granddaddy was Mr. Hart. But my father was Mr. Hugh and Mother was Miss Mildred. I was Miss Mary.

Austine died in the late '50s or early '60s. I remember when she was no longer at Grandmother's but nothing about an illness or her death.

I went to college in 1963 in Atlanta. We were assigned to read *Black Like Me* for a freshman discussion book. For me it was one of the two or three most important events in my life. I had lived with "colored" restrooms, waiting rooms, back of the bus, etc. I didn't think much about it. It was just the way it was. To realize not only that segregation, discrimination, hatred, and violence existed was one thing, but also to realize that my family was a part of it was humiliating. I experienced white guilt for several years, during which I was a part of the civil rights movements in Atlanta. When I got thrown out of SNCC because I was white, I realized that feeling guilty wasn't getting me anywhere—so I became a social worker!

Lettice Binnings Stuart, from New Orleans, Louisiana (born 1946). "Viola was my second mother."

The author of the following narrative is a professional journalist living in New York City who is known to Katherine van Wormer from the years when they both attended Louise S. McGehee School, in the New Orleans Garden District. Margaret Smith, the writer of a previous piece, also attended this school. Stuart's and Smith's stories are striking in both their similarities and their differences.

Viola

Growing up in the South in the 1950s, back when housekeepers were maids and blacks were colored people, we had a maid named Viola, whom I loved dearly.

For eighteen years, Viola cleaned our home, washed and ironed our clothes, polished the silver, cooked and served dinner, and at 8:00 p.m., when the dishes were done, walked or got a ride back to the housing project where her seven children waited in a run-down, two-room apartment. She worked Monday through Saturday, with Thursdays off, for twenty-five dollars a week.

Viola was my second mother. My real mother was the gracious soul of our antebellum home that was filled with antiques, silverware, porcelain, and portraits dating back to her great-grandparents' plantation, which at one time had one hundred slaves or more. After the Civil War, two of the slave women, now free, were "passed down" through the family, helping to raise my grandmother and later my mother. Mother loved Mammy and Ella, and so it was that she passed down to us a respect for all people, regardless of their skin color or station in life.

Viola and the maids who followed her entered through the front door with their own key, used the family bathrooms, and ate our food. Lethia, the last maid to work for my parents, said when she drove up to the house for the first time, she thought, *There ain't no way I'm going to work in that big house.* "But," she said, "when I rang the doorbell, Miz B invited me into the parlor and served me iced tea, just like I was one of her friends!"

Treating people kindly, however, did not imply equality. My father believed that blacks, though good people, were basically lazy and had smaller brains than whites. He would say this at the dinner table while Viola waited in the kitchen for Mother to step on the floor-bell that called her to pour more water from the silver pitcher on the sideboard. Mother and I would shush him, but he was unaware or insensitive to the fact that Viola could hear him. Once when I referred to Viola as a lady, he reprimanded me, saying, "Viola is a woman. Your mother is a *lady!*"

Even as a small child, I was troubled deeply by the inferior status of colored people. Both blacks and whites seemed to accept the fact that blacks had to watch movies from the balcony, use separate water fountains and bathrooms marked "Colored Only," and ride at the back of the bus or streetcar. My father said that it was the natural order of things. I never heard Viola say anything that indicated she felt otherwise.

Viola was a jovial soul who laughed at herself and her large belly. One summer Mother made Viola a tentlike bathing suit so she could get in the river when she came with us on vacation. We were so excited when she lowered herself into the five-inch-deep water along the bank, but somehow she rolled over and was not able to right herself. We were terrified, but when Mother was finally able to sit her up, Viola was laughing and sputtering water. "Lordy, I almost drowned myself!" We teased Viola good-naturedly about her attempt to swim and other mishaps, but we never made fun of her or said an unkind word to her. That was not allowed in our house.

Viola was defined by her deep Catholic faith. She arrived at our house in her starched white uniform at 10:00 a.m., somewhat breathless from her daily trip to church to make a novena to various saints. Sometimes she'd tell me what these petitions and prayers were for—usually for one of her children who was having some kind of problem.

Viola had never married, and her seven children were from several different men. She told me that with some shame when I was older. She loved her children and devoted her life to providing for them, but one was slow, several got pregnant, and one—her only son—went to prison. One Saturday a month, Viola would take off from working at our house and ride the bus three hours to Angola Prison to see him, then three hours back. On several occasions, Mother drove her and sat in the waiting room while Viola visited.

My most poignant memory of Viola is sitting in the car one day when I was driving her to see her doctor about her high blood pressure. She was sad that day, and when we parked I asked her why. She said she was worrying herself sick about her son. A friend of his had no money to feed his children and, in desperation, decided to hold up a bar. He asked Viola's son to go with him. They got ten dollars and ten years. She wept describing the prison conditions. She said he was always hungry and that she had to make that six-hour round trip so she could buy him a hot dog. "I'm his mother," she said, "and all I can do for him is buy him a hot dog once a month. For that one day he won't be so hungry."

The last time I saw Viola was an October afternoon forty-one years ago. My husband and I had returned home a few days earlier from an eighteen-month stint teaching school in South America, and I was eager to see Viola. Mother had written me that Viola had fallen getting off a bus. There was something about her diabetes and high blood pressure and a badly hurt knee. She wasn't doing well, Mother said, and by the time we returned, Viola was at home in a semi-coma.

Mother and I drove the twenty or so blocks to the projects where Viola lived. Though I had driven her home many evenings, I never could pick out her apartment in the row of dingy, sad-looking, identical brick units. I had been in her tiny apartment a number of times over the years, but I was always shocked. The one bedroom and small living room with its sunken sofa, TV, Formica table, and kitchenette at the far end could fit into my large, airy bedroom. How could she and her seven children live in this space? Where did they all sleep? I never asked.

Her kids had freshened Viola up for our visit, probably fluffing up her pillow and straightening the covers and pinning back her wiry grey hair, but she lay expressionless as I kissed her and told her I loved her. On our way out, we noticed the corner curio cabinet displaying bowls, silver candlesticks, and other knick-knacks from our home—many that Mother had discarded or given Viola over the years, along with some that were just missing.

A week later we were sitting in the second row, behind Viola's children, in a small, wooden church sending Viola off to her glory. Her children wept and wailed with upraised arms. One daughter keened in grief, calling "Muh-dear, Muh-dear" as she threw herself on the coffin. I could feel that my own sobbing was embarrassing my parents, and I was embarrassed myself to realize that my grief was somehow inappropriate, that I didn't hold the place in Viola's life that I thought I did. We never saw her children again.

Flora Templeton Stuart, from New Orleans, Louisiana (born 1948). "If only I had been able to appreciate her when I knew her as a child."

An attorney in Bowling Green, Kentucky, where she specializes in personal injury cases, Flora Templeton Stuart shares the following account of her New Orleans childhood. Her memories of growing up with a maid also reveal how the easy life of one segment of the population depended on the hard work of

Teen (Celestine) Holmes, Flora T. Stuart, and Elizabeth Griffin. Flora posed for this picture upon her return to New Orleans in 1973 as an adult. *From the family album of Flora Stuart.*

another whole segment whose contributions were so often taken for granted. The narrator is Katherine van Wormer's sister.

My Nanny, Teen (Celestine Holmes)

My first memory of Teen was when I was six years old in 1955. My friend Coco from down the street was hiding in the closet with me in our "secret club." Teen opened the door, and we relished the moment to spook her. She shook her head in that funny way and muttered in disdain, "Nasty . . . Nasty!"

Teen was more a nanny than a maid, watching out for us when not cleaning or cooking. Coco's nanny, Bea, was often seen running down the street calling her name. Teen had a deep southern accent, being from Mississippi. I can still hear her say about her trip to Chicago, "My yars was frozen," referring to her ears. Teen seemed to always be at our home since she was only off on Sundays. Teen always wore a neat starched white apron with her hair pinned back. Teen was proud and took her status from her white family, like my mother's family maid, Elizabeth. Teen referred to me as Miss Flora and my mother as Miss Elise. Even when married, black nannies had nicknames given to them by the white folk like Teen, Bea, and even my grandmother's maid, Nicey, who lived in Amite.

There was always a wonderful smell emanating from the kitchen. Every night we ate rice, our staple, often with red beans, gravy, or as shrimp creole. Other delicacies that Teen prepared came delivered from a local market such as veal, okra, and fresh shellfish. Grocery stores as we know them today were nonexistent. All of our shopping was done in the neighborhood store down the street while our meat was cut by hand and delivered to our home.

We did not see our first air conditioner or television until I was a young child. We would huddle in the den close to the coolness of the air conditioner watching the few shows available like the *Lawrence Welk Show, Dragnet,* and *Roy Rogers.*

One very memorable day, my mother, who was always breaking some social code, arrived with several young black children who were covered from head to toe with mud in their tattered clothing. They arrived for food, and after Teen fed them, she put them in the bathtub. Teen was disconcerted, somewhat embarrassed while exhibiting a sense of superiority. She even referred to their hair as "nappy" as we giggled in a girlish way, being fascinated with the entire spectacle. From that day forward, at least in private, we called her "Nappy Teen."

As strange as it seems now, I never saw the home where Teen lived although it was close to our neighborhood, nor do I know which church Teen attended or anything about her family. I asked my mother, now eighty-nine years old, to tell me about Teen's family. She knew very little about her background.

My mother told me other things about those times. She did recall being asked to keep her old schoolbooks so the black kids would have books. When she asked why the black kids could only have used books, her mother told her, "That's just the way it is." She also told me that black medical care was at the Charity Hospital, and they had public assistance when they needed money. There were only a few responsible families who provided for the black servants in retirement and sickness.

Growing up, we seemed to take little interest in the lives of our nannies. Unlike in the North (we referred to northerners as Yankees), the blacks lived in close proximity to the whites. I never saw a black person in our snobbish Presbyterian church; even the public swimming pool and all public facilities with "White Only" signs did not allow blacks. When we rode the streetcar, blacks had to enter and sit in the rear. There was a dichotomy in

New Orleans—we lived a few blocks from our nanny, yet our lives were totally separate, never worshipping together or attending school together. Our lives were apart, and as teens we were never allowed to mingle.

An eerie feeling comes to me as I remember the graveyards in New Orleans. The tombs were above ground, and we enjoyed roaming the graveyards at night. Some of the graves were often left open with bones exposed. I later learned that these were the graves for the black people so not well tended and left to deteriorate. Even in death, resting until eternity, they were separate, apart and unequal.

When I was twelve, we moved to bayou country, and there I befriended our black gardener, Felton who was a handsome, proud, self-educated black man. Felton was not allowed to own property or vote in Plaquemine and St. Bernard Parish without serious consequences. I enjoyed Felton's companionship. One day I asked to accompany him to the store, and after hesitation he granted my request. I jumped in the passenger seat and off we went. It wasn't long before a sheriff stopped us and attempted to arrest Felton for being with a "white girl." I vehemently opposed the arrest, and this was my moment of realization. My next was while visiting friends in Mississippi for the summer. When we were going to bed we learned that there would be a Ku Klux Klan rally that evening. Searching for adventure, we sneaked out the window and hid in the bushes watching a KKK rally. It was a moment of horror I will never forget.

In New Orleans things were changing. The streetcars were integrated in the late 1950s without much fuss, but school integration was another matter. Some of the white parents put up a lot of fuss and brought negative publicity to the city. When the Catholic schools were integrated, a few parents were excommunicated for their resistance. On our way to school, we passed by one of the public schools where black children were being enrolled. There we saw a mob of angry whites shouting and chanting, "Two, four, six, eight, we don't want to integrate." Many whites in the city put their children in private schools that were springing up everywhere.

Eventually we left the old city and moved to Chapel Hill, North Carolina, which was in the throes of the civil rights movement in 1963. In Chapel Hill, my sister, Katherine, and I immersed ourselves in the civil rights movement, which was organized through the black churches. We would sing "We Shall Overcome" while holding hands. We even protested in the streets, blocking traffic.

Later, as a grown woman, I returned to New Orleans and found Teen in a very simple home between rows of houses close to the levee. It should be noted that the richer white folk built their homes on higher ground so when hurricanes came it was the poor and black families who suffered the brunt of the floods.

Years later, with fond memories, I returned to find Teen and my aunt's cook, Elizabeth. And there we were hugging. It was a new day and age.

Teen is a part of me forever. If only I had been able to appreciate her when I knew her as a child.

Jeannie Falkner, from Greenwood, Mississippi (born 1951). "I grew up during Freedom Summer."

An associate professor of social work at Delta State University, Jeannie Falkner is a first cousin once removed of William Faulkner, whom she remembers as a somewhat strange relative known as "Little Bill." Dr. Falkner is a great storyteller herself who has contributed greatly to this project in referring interviewees from her region.

Baby Ruth

My favorite maid—whom I called Baby Ruth because, in my childlike view, she was short, fat, and black, like the candy bar—left to work in the civil rights movement and moved to Chicago. When this did not work out, she returned and wanted to return to work for us. I begged and cried. Mother said no, she abandoned us. As far as I know she never worked for another white family. I do not know what ever happened to her.

Hazel

Hazel was my Grandmother Falkner's (The Honorable and Mrs. John Wesley Thompson Falkner II) maid. She lived in their backyard in a small house just behind 706 South Lamar, one block from the Square in Oxford, Mississippi. I don't have many memories of Hazel, just that she was always there. My parents divorced when I was five, and we moved back to my mother's home in the Delta. I visited my grandmother on occasion.

My memories and stories are of Hazel's living situation. She worked seven days a week, with Sunday evenings off. I remember that she was married, but that my grandmother did not allow her husband to live with her. He was allowed to visit on the night she had off, but was expected to be gone by the time she was to return to work on Monday morning.

My grandmother kept a formal dining room for all meals. She had a sterling-silver bell which she rang from her place at the head of the table when she wanted Hazel. I do remember that as late as the 1960s Hazel cooked on a wood-burning stove in a terribly hot kitchen. I'm sure she was to use whatever toilet facilities were in her home and would have never considered using the ones in the house.

When I think of this today, I can only sigh and know that I lived in my social context as a child. Perhaps it is rationalization, but I can imagine that her home in my grandmother's backyard and her station as a housekeeper/cook was far better than many of the African American women who had to live and work in the fields. Neither was free from the oppressive society of the time.

Ironically, her house today is remodeled and is prime real estate for student rental at Ole Miss.

Nellie

Nellie was my Grandmother Scruggs's maid in Doddsville, Mississippi. I do have vivid memories of Nellie. She was paroled from Parchman Penitentiary to my Grandfather Scruggs, who served on the board of directors for the penitentiary. Her predecessor was Frances. When Frances was too old to work (she may have passed away), Nellie arrived. Nellie was a tall woman, very dark, with a wide grin. I was in the fifth or sixth grade when I met Nellie. My grandmother called her into the kitchen and introduced her to my girlfriend and me. She told us Nellie wanted us to go to her house with her. Now this scared the dickens out of us as we knew Nellie had murdered at least one husband (legal or common law).

My grandmother was a kind, well-bred, southern matriarch. So it did not make sense to send her granddaughter off with the ax murderer—and to the maid's house, which was across the backyard, through the gate, next to the chicken coop, and out of sight of our protector. But off we went. As we followed Nellie with trepidation, holding hands and trembling, we tried to be brave. As we entered the sparsely furnished cypress tenant house, Nellie said she wanted us to have something, and proceeded to bend down and pull a large box from under the bed. The gun? The ax?

It turns out it was a gift. We got to each choose a stuffed animal from the collection she had made sewing during her time in the penitentiary. Needless to say, Nellie was harmless to us grandkids. She spent the next years of her parole, and afterwards working for my grandmother. I ate many a meal prepared by Nellie. Her kitchen was a happy place.

Nellie did continue to have men problems. On Saturday nights, Doddsville, like many of the plantation towns, became a haven for "coloreds" on the one night they had some freedom. The blues were born just up the road at Dockery Plantation, so I imagine the music was mighty fine and corn whiskey made on the Eastland Plantation added to the revelry. Nellie had a thing for Uncle Sam, an older man who worked on Granddaddy's land. On more than one occasion, my grandmother would hear of Nellie's altercations with Uncle Sam downtown, get in her 98 Oldsmobile (one year she had a green Cadillac) and head to town in her robe and hairnet to "fetch" Nellie.

Now Nellie may have murdered a man or two, but she was no match for my grandmother, who feared losing her cook. I never saw this firsthand, but heard the stories from my cousins who were on the scene. The vision of my stately grandmother in robe and hairnet, stopping the 98 in the middle of a "colored" street brawl, and demanding that Nellie get "in this car this minute" and heading back to the house with Nellie complacently in the backseat, makes me laugh to this day. Southern womanhood is a powerful weapon when used correctly!

The advice I had from Nellie on men was this: "You can love a man, you can even live with a man, but you marry them, you got to kill 'em." The older I get, the wiser I think she may have been!

Nellie would have never used the toilet in my grandmother's home. She would have to use the outhouse behind her home. I used it once—decided I'd go back in the house next time. Way too many wasps.

The Toilet on Grand Boulevard

When I moved back to Greenwood in 1992, I purchased what was known as the Frasier House. It was built in the late 1940s, when everyone had a maid and a yard man. I acquired, along with the house, a small tool shed in the backyard, complete with "the toilet." It was for the maid and the yard man. The Frasiers had both. (I also got the bomb shelter from the Cuban crisis/ Kennedy era. Never could figure out what to do with that.)

Carrie's Bathroom

Carrie helped raise me. She is a friend, mentor, mother, and wise woman. She was the maid for my best friend, Anna. She worked for Mr. and Mrs. W. M. Whittington Jr. Carrie was the afternoon maid for as long as I can remember and stayed working at the house after both Mr. and Mrs. Whittington had passed away. Carrie retired when the house at 1000 Grand Boulevard was sold. I have many Carrie stories and still see her today. She is a very private person. Her children and grandchildren are very successful professionals.

There was a bathroom (toilet and sink) in the back of the kitchen, past the laundry room. I always called this "Carrie's bathroom" and never thought twice about it. I respected her privacy and only used it once, when I fell in an ice-covered pond down the street and Carrie put me in her bathroom and wrapped me in warm towels just out of the dryer. I remember she kept her purse and coat in there. I don't know that the bathroom was ever actually discussed; it's just that I knew and everyone else knew it was "Carrie's bathroom."

Recently, by coincidence, I ran into Carrie at a memorial service. She looked great and was still working. I spoke with Carrie and told her about my story in this book. She told me about the time she got locked in her bathroom, and no one could get her out. They had to get the locksmith, and the bathroom never had a lock again by her request! We had a good laugh.

Beth Walker, from northeast Arkansas (born 1951). "My story also has only one act, but every time I open the diversity text and begin to teach . . . that act is replayed in my mind."

A professor and dean of social work, Beth Walker has one striking memory that is forever imprinted in her mind, a comment her mother made about the maid. Because of this experience, she now is better able to impart an understanding to her students about the nature of prejudice.

I grew up in northeast Arkansas, about a two-hour drive from Memphis. An only child of two only children, I was the apple of each and every grandparent (for a total of three) in the family. I was born in 1951. My mother was the registered physical therapist at the local hospital, and my father an accountant for the power company.

My maid story has one main character—whose name escapes me. I would assume that the "escape" was racist if some days—when teaching and doing committee work and dean-ing—my own name doesn't escape me. But the maid came to our house probably three times a week, and did all the things my mother didn't have time to do. Both grandmothers were stay-at-home women, and during the days that I did not attend school, or during the summers, I shuttled back and forth spending one week at a time with each. So the maid came to our house and cleaned and did the laundry and made the beds. She wore a uniform—not expensive, and not a frilly apron, but my recollection is that it had "maid" written all over it. She didn't cook, but then neither did my mother; after my father's death when I was in junior high school, my mother and I ate TV dinners almost nightly on TV trays. My mother was a whiz at overbaking a roast (and to this day, I do not like roast) during church on Sundays, but that was about the extent of it.

My story also has only one act, but every time I open the diversity text and begin to teach, whether it is my BSW [bachelor of social work] or my MSW [master of social work] students, that act is replayed in my mind. It has a clarity that even the drug-induced delivery of my first child is lacking. As I crack the text open, I see my little child's hand reaching into the kitchen cabinet where the glasses were kept, and hearing my mother's voice in my ear, "Oh, Beth! Don't EVER touch the green glass. It's for HER to drink from, and we don't EVER use it." The glasses were those metal ones, in bright colors, with a matching pitcher. If you are of that vintage and of the South, you are probably seeing them in your head right now, sitting on a wire table outdoors and sweating—and dripping—condensation on their outsides.

I will conclude with this thought—I believe to this day that I am a better woman, and a better social worker, and a better social work educator, for that experience.

Walker's piece is supplemented with some follow-up questions posed by Katherine van Wormer.

Interviewer: How did this experience make you a better social worker?

I sometimes reflect on how what my clients experienced growing up made them the "clients" of today—that is, had I not had this experience, and many others in my segregated elementary school, I might not have become as sensitized to the effects of ethnicity on our world today.

Interviewer: When you were growing up, did you ever confront your mother about her beliefs?

No. I'm not sure why, but I think that I would just as likely have confronted her about the sky being blue, or fried chicken always arriving with potato salad. I didn't "outgrow" my sense that segregation was "right" until after I attended Ole Miss for undergrad, left there, and grew up. By then, my mother's opinions of how the world works were no longer . . . uh . . . relevant or had an impact on me. I married a very liberal young man of the 1960s, and we had a quite different life from Mother's.

Interviewer: Did you love your maid and see her as one of the family?

I cared for her—but not sure I'd categorize it as "loved." And yes, I saw her as one of the family, but in a quite concretely different category of family member.

Interviewer: Were you involved in the civil rights movement?

On the fringes. My husband joined the Reserves when he got a low lottery number, probably in 1970, although I don't remember exactly. He did a few sit-ins in college, but at the time, I was a married math major with too much homework!

Barbara Jentleson, from Panama City, Florida (born 1951). "It remains a difficult topic to discuss in polite company."

An assistant professor of education at Duke University, the following respondent describes her Louisiana-born mother as violating the norms of segregation that were strongly enforced through social sanctioning by other whites at that time. The norms for seating arrangements when riding in the car were especially pronounced.

My mother worked full-time from the time I was three years old, teaching high school in Panama City, Florida. We had a full-time housekeeper, who was a middle-aged African American woman named Julia. Julia was married, and her husband was self-employed with his own business; they had no children of their own. Julia did not wear a uniform, and she used the same doors and bathroom in our home as we did. She cooked lunch and snacks for us as well as took care of keeping the house and laundry. I do not remember her eating with us, so that seems to be one distinction. I remember the ironing being a particular chore, with starching procedures that seemed complicated.

My mother would sometimes take Julia home, and she sat in the front seat with my mother and we would sit in the back. The decision to have Julia ride in the front seat with her was a real statement; most maids of that time period rode in the backseat, even if there were only the two ladies in the car. Mom was definite: kids in the back, adults in the front.

She was adamant that when she wasn't home, Julia was in charge. Julia was the boss of our household for sure, and we definitely had to do whatever she asked us to do. When she told my mother of our misbehavior or problems, my mom backed her to the hilt, and she was given permission to discipline us when needed (which wasn't too often; she usually just threatened to punish us and that did the trick). We were also given chores to help her out—for example, I had the "job" of folding clothes and would find them on my bed when I came home from school. I can't remember if we gave her hand-me-downs or other gifts.

My younger brother had a serious medical condition that required serial casting of his legs (toe to hip) for the better part of a year and then follow-up care. Julia was very strong and helped my mother with some of the difficult tasks involved in bathing and caring for him. They became quite close over this experience. However, Julia and her husband were very proud folks, and he never liked her working as a housekeeper. Eventually, she left us at his urging, which led to much sadness on our part.

We moved to Auburn, Alabama, so that my mother could attend graduate school, and because we were older, we had another housekeeper, Hertis, who came twice a week to help out with household chores. Hertis was an older woman who only worked for grad students who needed the help and really was one of the nicest people ever. She and her husband had a farm and grown children of their own. They both took care of our family, providing us with firewood and food from the farm—they were just really giving people. My mother and Hertis became very close because we were in Alabama during the early 1960s when much of the civil rights unrest and legislation was happening. I can remember them crying together over Kennedy's assassination and also sharing tears of joy when the Civil Rights bill was passed.

When my mother finished graduate school, we moved to Atlanta. My mother and Hertis continued to exchange holiday cards for many years after this move. Like Julia, Hertis did not wear a uniform or use a separate bathroom or door to the house. She had her own transportation, and we were expected to treat her with respect at all times.

I think, in retrospect, that both of these experiences happened at a transitional time in the South, and that my mother grew and changed in her relationships with both women. I do remember that the pay was low, and surely this must have been an issue. We addressed both women by their first names, but were expected to be respectful, particularly since they were older women.

Yes, it was a remarkable time, and in many ways, when I read/saw *The Help,* I felt it was my mother's story about her relationships more than my own. I am only sharing the bits I remember, but for my mother the reality was much more intense. My mother came from a traditional south Louisiana family, but was the first in her family to be college educated, and her views significantly evolved over time from her personal and professional experiences. The car-driving norms were quite rigid as were many other norms that governed black/white behavior. I think those attitudes were typical of many folks, white and black, of that time period—but it remains a difficult topic to discuss in polite company.

Ann Levy (not her real name), from Detroit, Michigan, and Dallas, Texas (born 1952). "She remembered me as a small child."

This short interview with a professor of social work is unique among the white narratives in describing the situation of a southern white woman, Ann Levy's grandmother, who had an African American maid in the North. The grandmother treated her maid in the old southern tradition, which struck her grandchild as strange. Then her family moved to the South.

My father's mother grew up in Waco, Texas. She, my grandmother, would eat in the dining room, yelling to her maid, who was eating in the kitchen. I thought this was strange. She was Jewish; she kept kosher. This got really complicated for the maid, who had to learn which of the silver went into which drawer. One was for use with dairy, and one for use with meat. The African American had to learn all this.

When my father became sick, my mother needed help. So we got John Eva. We were very attached to her. This was in Detroit. Then a few years ago—my mother was now in a wheelchair—we found where John Eva lived and went to her house. "Oh, I want my baby, Ann (she called me that) to come into my house!" she called out. She was so excited to see me; we were very attached to each other. My mother couldn't get up the steps, but I went in and visited with her. We had not seen each other in years and years, and she remembered me as a small child.

When we moved to Dallas in 1961, to me it was shocking. A kid in class used the N word. The teacher never did anything. I remember in Dallas conditions were more oppressive than they had been up North. The cleaning people would all be waiting together at the bus stop in their uniforms. They had walked from all the houses to take the bus to their homes.

Mother hired Hannah. My father had some of the ideas [of separation of the races] that he learned from his mother. Still, he dutifully paid Hannah her Social Security every month during a time when most employers found a way around this. I did not realize until recently that the New Deal had exempted household work and farm labor from the Social Security Act. It was only later [in 1951] that domestic workers were included in the act.

Hannah was a single woman with no children. She was already old when she worked for us and had no family of her own. My father arranged to get her into a nursing home so she'd be taken care of. I feel that my parents did right in looking after her in that way.

Susan Burdon Hudgens, from New Orleans, Louisiana (born 1954). "These photos have been in every kitchen I have ever had."

Susan Hudgens and her sister Paula pose in their backyard with their devoted maid and cook, Elizabeth Griffin. Susan *(right)* has a sharp memory of Elizabeth's large hands and long, bony fingers. *From the family album of Susan Burdon Hudgens.*

This powerful tribute is written by a first cousin of Katherine van Wormer. If any maid really did become a part of the white people's family, it would have been Elizabeth Griffin. And if you don't believe that personal bonding can take place across racial lines within a social system built on white supremacy, read the following tribute to a woman who loved as she was loved. Two facts of significance that we can add to this memoir are, first, that the writer's older sister named her daughter Elizabeth after this maid, and, second, that this woman not only helped raise this generation but also the previous generation in the very same house.

Memories of Elizabeth Griffin (1911–1986)

My memories of Elizabeth are more sensory than specific events or conversations. I have a strong memory of her hands; large palms, long bony fingers, they seemed enormous to me and very capable. With those hands she cooked incredible meals for us, kept our silver sparkling, scrubbed us clean in the bathtub, and kept my brother and me in control. When we got too rambunctious, she would wind up the dishtowel that was always nearby and pop it hard in our direction. It would be an extension to her long powerful hands, and we would know Elizabeth means business and mind your P's and Q's. The dishtowel never touched us, but the popping sound I remember well. There was always a bit of a smile with it. She loved us dearly.

Elizabeth worked for my mother's family, so she had a strong hand in raising my mother and her sisters. When my grandfather retired and moved, my mother bought the family home and Elizabeth worked for her. I was six when we moved into the "big" house. Even as a young child, I was aware of an unusual relationship between Elizabeth and Mom: part employee and employer, particularly when company was around (she was Mrs. Burdon then); part coparent with us four kids; and part parenting adult to Mom. That was when she called my mother "Miss Jane." Usually Mother had done something Elizabeth did not approve of, or maybe it was just one of those tender moments. They were devoted to one another. The relationship with my Dad was very different; he was always Dr. Burdon. She would never dream to be casual around him.

Elizabeth was truly an integral part of our family, not only to us, but also to our friends and extended family. It was like she came with the house—she was PART of the house. I can see her mopping the front porch with an old mop, back and forth with care, doing it just right so there were no streaks. Then she would move on to the brass doorbell and house numbers. Mother wanted them polished every week, and I can never remember a day when they were not. I think she took as much pride in the house as my mother did.

She was a very quiet woman, not one for idle chatter. She was a great listener, though, and I would spend hours talking and jabbering to her. We had a lot in common, Elizabeth and I. She was skinny, no curves anywhere, and so was I. Mother described us both as string beans. We both wore glasses, and we were both asthmatics. Breathing was not a given for us, and I was aware of the days she seemed tired and was moving slow, and she was always comforting to me as I sat wheezing in the kitchen or den. It was an unspoken bond between us. She seemed to understand me. Because I was a sickly, rather delicate child, I spent many days at home from school in the kitchen with her. She wouldn't shoo me out because she had work to do; she would just go about her business and I would watch. She comforted me. Then she would make me something to eat, usually an egg salad sandwich, before I headed off to bed again.

I always felt special to Elizabeth. I think I was. So was my brother, John. He was the male, and we were buddies and playmates. We would run around together, and Elizabeth often brought us brownies and milk in the afternoon. If she were feeling particularly sweet, she would reach into her deep pocket and pull out a peppermint for you. I never really liked peppermints, but I realized even when I was young that it was a special offering.

I was fair and my face was often flush; it was a source of great embarrassment to me, but Elizabeth turned it into a loving unique quality when she called me "little Miss Pink Face." I always loved that. I can hear her voice now. She had a deep voice, at least it seemed that way to me. All the women in our family have high registers that seem to float to even higher octaves when we are excited. Elizabeth was calm, steady, and deliberate in her voice. I remember she loved gospel music and she would occasionally have it on the radio back in the ironing room. It would be barely audible, so no one else could hear it, but she could listen while she ironed.

Elizabeth and the ironing board seemed inseparable. She was a master, and with our big family there was always much to be done. I learned to iron from her. To start with the collar, then the shoulders, and how to fold the sheets so the monogram is centered. My girls think they learned how to fold a sheet from their grandmother, but she learned from Elizabeth.

Elizabeth was also a master cook; she never measured anything: just a little of this and a handful of that. I remember when I was older and wanted some cooking tips and recipes, it was almost impossible to get anything written down. Her knowledge was secure in her head—few secrets were given out. She was allergic to shellfish, so we did not have the usual New Orleans seafood recipes at home. On occasions, Mother would get crabs or crawfish on the weekends when Elizabeth was not there. I remember Mother would be fanatical about the cleanup; getting all remains bundled and out of the house so Elizabeth would not get sick when she returned to work. My mother was very protective of Elizabeth.

Mother and Dad loved to entertain, and all their friends looked forward to a meal made by Elizabeth. She would formally serve the guests and everyone would acknowledge her. This formality was not saved for the guests, as we were served dinner at 5:30 every night. Hard to imagine now, but for many years she would serve us each dish (serve from the left, pick up from the right!) in her white uniform. As she got older and Mother less formal, we often ate family style with the food on the table, but special events were always served. I don't recall ever seeing Elizabeth eat. She must have taken her food into the back and eaten when we were not around. She was very private and kept certain things separate. I can't imagine that was mother's choice; I think it was hers. I hope so.

Separate. Bathrooms were always separate. Hers was in the shed area. I know in later years, when Mother had other domestic help, they used the bathroom inside, but I doubt Elizabeth ever did. We never thought this was strange when we were young. It just was. Like coming in the back door. That also changed with time, but it was true when I was very young.

I know Mother knew about her personal life to some degree, but I never did. I believe she had once been married and had no children. As a young child I remember a tall black man that I saw a few times at the back door. She would speak softly to him for a few minutes and he would then disappear. I felt uncomfortable that he was there. After that I never remember anyone else or her speaking about anyone. She lived only a few blocks from us as the homes for domestic help were often built close by the "big houses." She walked to work, and sometimes if it was cold or dark, we would give her a lift home. Her home was small and had a little front porch with a folding chair on it. As an adult I went to visit her after she retired, and she would visit with us in her small living room. I remember feeling it was homey but dark, not enough light. I was in her space and it felt strange. She had many pictures of her extended family and was always proud to show off a photo. Most of her family lived far away and had educated themselves, but she did not talk much about them, at least not to me.

I remember strong feelings about the inequality of the education system and the realization of the magnitude of challenges Elizabeth faced because she was basically illiterate. She knew enough to write certain grocery lists, very simple reading and basic math, but not much more. Once there was a program given at the local school to teach adults reading and math. Elizabeth was thrilled, and she would bring her books to the house and occasionally show me her work. I felt embarrassed that I knew more than she, and I was just a young child. She was so excited and proud to be learning; she loved it. I remember how happy Mother was for her. One day the funding stopped for the program and it all stopped. Just like that. I recall feeling that an overwhelming sadness just permeated Elizabeth. It was palpable in the kitchen for a long time.

After I had married and moved away, I can remember coming to visit and Elizabeth just loving hugging on my babies. She was proud, like it was another extension, another generation. She was excited to see me as a mother, but I was still "little Miss Pink Face" to her. I felt like I wanted her approval and got it.

When she died in 1986 at the age of seventy-five, the family was heartsick. My mother was a wreck and extremely emotional. The funeral was nearby in the Baptist church, and we were the only white people there. We took up two pews with all my aunts and relatives. There was a full gospel choir and many women with paper fans helping to cool down those of us who were overwhelmed by the heat and emotion. Elizabeth used to say one was "falling out" when you fainted. Mother was so overwhelmed that I think she might have succumbed if it had not been for her embarrassment of women fanning her like crazy and telling her Elizabeth was with Jesus now. Our family was mentioned in the write-up as she worked for us for more than forty years. I was acutely aware that she had a life very separate from ours, with her own friends, church, music, and social community that we knew little about. We were separate yet inseparable. It was a glorious service, full of hope and celebration. Elizabeth had touched many lives.

The strange part of the relationship with Elizabeth is how one-sided it was. I never really thought about this until much later. She knew so much about me, so much about all of my family and our weaknesses and strengths. Who had a temper, how we fought, how we played, what made us laugh, if we were not doing well in school, if we were having a fight with a friend, what we got for Christmas, when we were having our periods, who we were dating, who we decided to marry, our parenting skills or lack thereof. She was the outsider, who was an insider, who observed and interacted with us on what I would guess was a combination of Mother's terms and her terms. She probably had a better understanding of the inner dynamics of our family than we did. How strange.

My brother became a doctor and her physician. He would pay her house calls. He spent time with her as physician and patient, adult to adult. He was her physician when she died. He got to know her on another level. I left New Orleans as an adult and never spent more than a few weeks visiting at a time. I wished I had spent more time getting to know her on a more personal level. She was a wonderful woman, full of love and understanding. She was wise. I have two pictures of Elizabeth: one holding two of my children, and in the other she is cooking in mother's kitchen. These photos have been in every kitchen I have ever had.

I loved her.

Penny Hanks (not her real name), from Jackson, Tennessee (born 1954). "I wonder if May ever thought of us being spoiled, and just lazy little white kids."

Although this participant did not want her name used, probably because of her comments about her family members, she openly discusses in her social work diversity classes what she learned in her childhood about white privilege and racism from her own cultural background. Looking back on all this, Hanks has a sense of guilt about her role as a white child living under the norms of segregation. The following story was told in a telephone interview; the interviewee talked freely and needed no questions.

I was the fourth of three older children. My mother always had a black maid to help her part-time. The town was very segregated; you could always get a maid. This was the 1950s, before civil rights. When I was about five, going through a few growing pains, Mazelle Sally Bell Suzanne came into our lives. Her mother had given all her children three or four of these rhyming names. We called her May. May worked for my mother two days a week, for my uncle three days, and for my grandmother one day. She always wore a uniform, and brought her own fruit jar to drink out of. At my cousin's house, she had her own bathroom. In the others, she used their bathrooms.

To get to work, May had to walk to the bus stop, take the bus, and then walk the rest of the way to our house. No matter how hot it was, she had to walk up the hill. All the maids were walking from where they worked to get the bus. My mother could have driven her. I always thought of her as living far away; I never had seen the black people's houses. Later my brother told me she lived in a place around two miles away; all the maids lived there. The old women who had been maids would have been very poor as Social Security had been exempted under the New Deal for household workers. The maids were always paid in cash.

I remember May working for us; she had to run up and down the steps all day. She was the first black person we had a conversation about race with. We could ask her anything. My brother asked her, "What color are you inside?" "I'm the same color as you," she said. I asked my mother if I could hug her, and my mother said yes, so I did. May died when she was in her fifties. I was in high school. I didn't feel heartbroken. But my cousin probably did. She was practically raised by May. May was always holding her.

My grandmother, who was born in 1898, told me things that were not true about black people. She was raised in that era when blacks were thought to be subhuman. My grandmother lived to be 101. My mother fortunately rebelled from my grandmother and did not teach me those views.

My grandmother liked May and also had a black man to work in the yard, but her sitter was not black, except for one time she did have a black sitter. It was her practice to pronounce "Negro" as "Nigra" a bunch of times. One maid said to her, "Don't use that word around me." My grandmother, as I found out later, lectured her about how happy the slaves had been and that

"Nigras" should be grateful for the life they have. The next day, the sitter arrived wearing a sweatshirt with the words BLACK POWER on it! She then quit at the end of the day.

May was not like the sitter, though. She "knew her place."

I want to tell about a town where I also lived. This was in Sikeston, Missouri. There is a book called *The Lynching of Cleo Wright.* A black man who was drunk had broken into a woman's home and cut her in the stomach and attacked the police who came to arrest him. Before the night was over, the men of the town got him and burned him alive, dragging his body through the black part of town. Blacks were so afraid they left town. The only people who weren't in fear were the maids who worked for prominent white people. They had the protection of their employers. "That's the Wilson maid; that's the Roberts maid," they would say, and their families were protected.

In my diversity class I have students do a paper on master statuses. This assignment has them tell their experiences related to their race, social class, gender, being able-bodied or disabled, and sexual orientation. To help them be willing to share, I tell them of my experiences, such as I have told here. Also I have them read a short story by Langston Hughes called "One Christmas Eve." In the story, the black maid is forced to work on Christmas Eve, but she counts on this to get money to buy presents for her children. But then her employer says, "I don't have any money. You don't mind if I pay you later?" The maid just says, "Fine."

I had one white student who grew up in Arkansas about thirty years ago. She would visit her grandfather on the farm. On the farm lived a black man and wife who worked as "yard boy" and maid. Their names were Big Tom and Washerwoman. The children would give Big Tom orders to do anything they wanted, and Big Tom would obey them. It was the same with Washerwoman, who they would have running back and forth. So here were the servants being ordered around by children, and they felt they had to obey.

Thinking of all these incidents, I remember May working so hard, while we as children just would lie around watching *Tarzan* on TV. I wonder if May ever thought of us being spoiled, and just lazy little white kids. Yet even in grade school May addressed me as Miss Penny. Looking back on all this, I feel bad—guilty.

Barbara Lehmann, from New Orleans, Louisiana (born 1955). "My parents were civil rights allies, and this was the perspective I came from."

Many members of the Jewish community supported the civil rights movement from the start. One would expect then that the maid-employer relationship might have taken on a different character in a Jewish as compared to a Protestant or Catholic household, and indeed, this difference is strongly apparent here.

My mother's mother was from Donaldsonville, Louisiana, and my mother's father, my grandfather, was from Poland. He was an attorney and scholar who did civil rights work. One of his cases was to represent an African American, and my grandfather was run off the road for representing his client. My father was a lawyer as well and also did civil rights work. He was autocratic, though, perhaps because of all the loss he suffered as a refugee from Germany during the Holocaust. He came to America during World War II. I do respect him and the civil rights work that he did. Our maid had the chutzpah to make fun of him, always behind his back. She gave our family some levity. Her name was Ida Mae Johnson.

My mother at age twenty-nine had four kids; I was the third of four. I was a painfully shy kid, a funny-looking kid and highly emotional. I was in a public school in New Orleans the first time they were integrated. I played with a black child on the playground and got on *NBC News*—the Huntley-Brinkley news show.

Our maid, Ida, made me feel special and loved in a way that I never felt with my parents. My father was autocratic, as I said, and my mother was severely depressed. Ida Mae was our sanity; her behavior was predictable. Our relationship was almost that of a grandmother and a grandchild. She didn't correct me in the same way that parents do; there was no narcissistic injury with her.

I knew Ida's kids and played with them. They were older than me. The kids in the neighborhood couldn't play with us when we were playing with black kids. They could play with us later, but this led to social difficulties with their parents. My next-door neighbor had a shotgun during these times.

This is really an early part of my life. My first consciousness of segregation signs was when I went to Danneel Park [near St. Charles Ave.] and there were signs above the bathroom. My mother said, when asked, that this is not the law anymore. This really got to me—I was a child of the Holocaust.

My dad didn't objectify maids the way others did. In fact, when a job opened up at the synagogue, my father arranged for her and her husband to go work there. The synagogue had a house nearby that used to go with the school and was a house for janitors. Ida, her husband, and her children moved there. This made for a better life for her, but it was hard on me. I did get to see a lot of her at the synagogue, and it was always good to see her. The last time I saw her was when the synagogue moved. My father, though, stayed in contact with her.

After Ida Mae left, my mother had a succession of other women to work for her. These women were more socialized into the roles, wore uniforms and used the downstairs bathroom. Ida had always come in the front door, didn't wear a uniform, and we all used the same bathroom. Other maids who came later used the one downstairs. They called me Miss, and I called them by their first names. One day one of the new maids slapped me. She offered me money to keep my mouth shut. I told my mother, and she never came back. I felt both relieved and ashamed. Another woman worked for us. She was from the Lower Ninth Ward and was flooded out by Hurricane Betsy. She and her kids moved in with us on our ground floor.

Today my father is eighty-six and has a black housekeeper who is always caring for him.

Lacey Sloan, from southern rural Mississippi (born 1957). "We had a secret in my family, and that is that we were not really white—my father was Native American."

So many of our childhood memories have to do with food, and Lacey Sloan, who now teaches social work in New York, is no exception. Her story takes us back in time to when her grandmother referred to her maid in her will as "my colored girl" and later to an early "integrated" classroom. The past meets the present in the following story as the narrator reconnects with the family cook in later years.

I was an elementary school–aged child when integration occurred. My mother (1935–1990) and maternal grandmother (1902–1993) were from Woodville, Mississippi, a town where integration created intense reactions. My grandmother had a maid working for her for as long as I can remember, a caramel-brown woman named Marylee. In fact, my grandparents had two people they called "coloreds" working for them in the 1960s—Henry and Marylee—and I know that before my grandparents, my ancestors were slave owners. Of course, I am embarrassed and feel shame about this, but it is my burden to bear.

Henry was my grandfather's driver, general yard man, and later, his personal care attendant when my grandfather became paralyzed in the early 1960s. We called him Uncle Henry. Marylee was my grandmother's maid. She worked for my grandmother from at least the 1950s until my grandmother died. All of my aunts and cousins had black maids: Aunt Edna had Lee working for her; Maude worked for Aunt Mattie; and although I don't remember all the maids' names, I remember their presence in each home I visited. Maude was tall and slender, and she lived in a shack in the woods behind my aunt's house. She scared me with stories of creatures in the woods. Lee practically raised my cousin Jimmy, for all eighteen years of his life. She was dark and stout and quiet and was the only maid I remember wearing the traditional uniform of black dress and white apron. I was uncomfortable with the deferential way the maids treated me and my family, as they did all whites. Perhaps it was because we had a secret in my family, and that is that we were not really white—my father was Native American. He told me it was a "shame to be colored" and therefore we would not talk about being Native, especially in Mississippi.

Marylee used the back door at my grandmother's house, which led to the kitchen, but so did most people. The front door led to the formal living room, and that door was only used on special occasions, as was that room. Marylee's domain was the kitchen, and that is where she ate. The children would eat in the breakfast room, and the adults would eat in the dining room. I can even remember, in the 1970s, inviting Marylee to eat with us kids in the breakfast room, but she said, "No ma'am, I eats in the kitchen." She always called everyone "Yes ma'am" and "no suh," even to us kids. I told her she didn't need to call me "ma'am" because I was younger than her, and she said, "yes ma'am." This, too, caused me discomfort because my paternal grandmother had taught me to respect my elders and to treat all people as equal. These interactions with Marylee could not be made into that which I thought it should be, primarily because she refused. I know now it was probably for her own safety that she dared not talk to me any other way but the same way she did to all white people, lest someone overhear her. I don't know what they would have done to her, as I never saw anyone hit her or yell at her or do anything that looked like punishment. But Marylee was very compliant to my relatives and other white people.

Food was the conduit for my main relationship with Marylee. She's the reason we had such fabulous Thanksgiving and Christmas dinners (the noon meal). Not that Grandma couldn't have pulled it off, and I think she did help some, but Marylee stayed with the food in the kitchen for the duration. They made homemade creamy corn by shucking the corn off the cobs, and I think they cooked it with milk and sugar before freezing it. I also loved the fig preserves that grandma would peel, but Marylee would cook, standing over the *hot* stove in *hot* Mississippi. I never felt comfortable watching Marylee under these conditions, but I never knew what to do. As a teenager, I remember bringing home a friend who was black, and my mother being very polite and liberal about the whole thing. Then one day, she came to me and announced she had sat down and eaten with our maid in the breakfast room. She was so proud of herself, and I was, too. Breaking patterns is never easy.

I was just a child in elementary school when integration came to the U.S. due to the Civil Rights Act of 1964. I remember this as a time of distress in my maternal family. There were bombings at a movie theater in Mississippi. Thirty-one thousand National Guard troops were at Ole Miss on the day James Meredith demanded his right to admission. People were refusing to send their white children to public schools. On my first day of integrated school in Mississippi, my teacher sent all of the black children out of the class and then moved us all around so that the only seats left for the black children were three chairs in the back of the room. At the time, I didn't understand why my teacher had done that to the black children, and so I asked her. She explained to me that "coloreds" had to know their place and if they were allowed to sit all over the class, they might not remember that. I later told my parents and knew this was wrong, but they offered no solutions to fifth-grade me. It wasn't long before we would leave Mississippi for about ten years, returning only for holidays and funerals.

When my grandmother died, my siblings and our children stayed in my grandmother's home for the funeral. Of course, Marylee was still there, taking care of us. For some reason, my child was fussing about not wanting to use a certain bathtub, and Marylee came to me and said, "I didn't use that bathtub, and I didn't sleep in any of the beds. I slept on the cot and used the bathroom at my own home." I was shocked and reassured her that we did not care if she had slept in the bed, or if she had used the bathroom. By this time, I was an activist doing anti-oppression work. I tried to think of what else I could say to her for her to know I thought that how she was treated all these years was wrong. But I couldn't think of what I could say to her that would make any sense. Could I say to a woman who had devoted her life to caring for my grandmother that she had been mistreated? No, I could not. Marylee came and went every night and was not a slave to my grandmother. She was paid and given hand-me-downs for her children and family. She was given extra food to take home, too. All of my progressive training had not prepared me for this encounter with my grandmother's black maid in 1993.

One of the saddest things happened as my grandmother's will was read. I knew of no close relationships that formed between Marylee and anyone in my family. There was some type of relationship, obviously, between Marylee and my grandmother, but it was not the closeness that proximity would suggest. My grandmother referred to Marylee as "my colored girl." Apparently my grandmother had told Marylee that she would pay off her home (only a few thousand dollars out of a multimillion-dollar estate). Unfortunately, she left her only one thousand dollars in the will, and my cousins, the executors who never reconciled with integration, refused to pay off her home. I regret that my siblings and I did not take it upon ourselves to honor my grandmother's last wishes, wishes that suggest there was some closeness in her relationship with Marylee as she was the only person in the will who was not a grandchild (my grandmother outlived all her children).

I saw Marylee the last time I was in Woodville. We invited her over to eat and she declined. We told her we would cook. She declined again but invited us to her home for dinner. We agreed. My sister and I discussed the fact that once again Marylee would be cooking for us. But, we wanted her to see us as human and try to establish a relationship we could not have had thirty-five years ago. We learned she had been spending time with a daughter in the Caribbean. During our visit, I don't recall her calling me "ma'am."

(7) The White Family Narrative Themes

The mother who taught me what I know of tenderness and love and compassion taught me also the bleak rituals of keeping Negroes in their place.
—LILLIAN SMITH, *Keepers of the Dream*

THE VERY SYSTEM that made for the cheap supply of labor in the form of domestic service was also injurious in some unexpected ways to the very people whom it seemed to benefit at the time. Today, a whole generation or two of southern white men and women who grew up with servants in their homes or who were their employers are looking back with mixed emotions, partly because they had black servants at all, but mostly because of the social conditions under which the servants worked. Many potential narrators from this older white generation who have a lot they could tell us have been reluctant to do so. Unlike those who were deprived of their childhoods and of their educations and who look back in anger and even acceptance, members of the class of oppressors are often less than forthcoming, even refusing to look back at all.

Guilt, as we know, is a highly destructive emotion. This is not to say that many of the white employers were not kind or that it was wrong for them to have cooks, maids, and other servants. And this is not to say that they were individually responsible for the customs of the day. From our perspective, the cruelty was in the system, and many of the white folks did their best to get around the worst of the restraints. Certainly this is true of our white narrators because they are the ones who stepped forward to tell their stories. This fact alone means that they are probably not representative of all whites who grew up with or who employed maids. We can surmise that there are many others who perhaps are not proud of their treatment of their servants and do not wish to remember, much less to share, those facts. That said, we still can learn much from the facts revealed by these storytellers, facts that are surprisingly consistent with much that we learned from the stories told by our African American narrators.

Common to the narratives of the twenty-seven white women and the two white men who were willing to share their memories is the expression of ambivalence. On the one hand, there is the sense of love and devotion to the women who helped raise them and/or members of their family. On the other hand, there is an indomitable sense of regret punctuated by grief, regret for words unspoken, stories unshared, and grief over the maid's death. As one interviewee responded when asked why there were so few photographs of these "members of the family," "Apparently, they didn't count for much." But even that is too simple an explanation. Certainly they did count, but they counted in a different way. The white people's feelings are complex, but they are also very real.

Elise Talmage, the oldest of our white narrators, had earlier expressed these mixed emotions in a poem that she shared. We should explain that the words refer to traditions in New Orleans of the 1920s, a time when black women could be heard singing a French-inspired song as they rocked white babies to sleep. Research shows that the "doe-doe" of the song is most likely a corruption of *dormir* (the French verb for to sleep). The reference to flushing will be clear to readers of the full transcripts. The poem is entitled "Were Our Sins So Scarlet?"

Were our sins so scarlet?
Were our virtues so few?
We remember, we remember
Yellow heads on warm black arms
"Doe doe lil baby
Doe doe lil baby"
Rocking and rocking to soothe little hurts
But did you hurt too and did we know?
Dark rich voices crooning low
Doe doe doe doe.
And did we fail to pay a living wage?
It was ever so; it was ever so.
And were black babies left without a breast?
No voice to sing them "doe doe doe"
And did you crawl beneath the house
while white folks flushed?
And did we sow the seeds of hate?
Jim Crow Jim Crow

I remember, I remember
"Can I tote your books, Miss Leeze
Miss Leeze?"
They tried so hard to please.
Who can now sing as once they sang,
Dark rich voices crooning low?
Violet, Nicey, Many gone so long ago
So long ago.
It hurts to know:
Our sins were scarlet;
Our virtues were few.

Such a forthright expression of regret is rare. In general, people do not like to remember their unkindnesses, nor do they like to talk about the privileges that were bestowed upon them at the expense of others. So the reluctance that we encountered, the denial of the harm and the defensiveness, we should have anticipated from the start. No, we should not have been surprised when respondents' friendly chatter on the telephone suddenly stilled when the topic turned to maids. Suddenly the interviewees remembered they had to rush off and do some chore, and no, they wouldn't have time for a call-back either. Their avoidance maneuvers even took the form of questioning of the value of the project—to discover facts about the past—as well as unconvincing assertions that they could no longer remember, nonresponse to multiple requests, and promises to write that remain unfulfilled.

THE CHALLENGE IN OBTAINING THE WHITE INTERVIEWS

The story of the attempt made primarily by Katherine van Wormer to convince people who grew up with black women in their homes to share their memories is perhaps as significant as the white women's stories themselves. Growing up in New Orleans in the 1950s, van Wormer had access through alumni networking to former classmates and teachers. One might have expected that twenty or thirty former classmates from two well-known private schools would have volunteered to participate in interviews or to write out their stories. Announcements in the alumni newsletters from the schools did produce a number of promises to write, but only a few brief replies and two

Elise Talmage, mother of Katherine van Wormer, reading from her poem at her eightieth birthday celebration. *Photo by Robert van Wormer.*

thorough essays sent through e-mail. Personal requests from more personal childhood friends led for the most part to prevarication and failed promises to deliver. Of two former teachers who were consulted for this project due to their progressive views during those conservative times, one did not answer, while the other, a native of Alabama, provided the following thoughtful but unexpected reply dated June 1, 2010. It was unexpected because this teacher as a young woman had introduced the class to the horrors of southern racism as revealed in the then recently released novel *To Kill a Mockingbird.*

> As far as your present project goes, I don't think I can be of any help. My mother had a "nurse" for me when I was very little because she, too, was a teacher and had to have somebody to take care of me until I started school myself. That was so long ago that I really don't remember anything about any of them. Once I was in school, they were no longer there. In my married life I had various part-time maids but never a cook and never anybody more than once or twice a week for a few hours at a time, so the kinds of bonds you are looking for never had a chance to develop. I think Kathryn Stockett wrote a remarkable book in *The Help* and she may possibly have pre-empted the kind of book you are working on. Of course, yours will be a scholarly presentation where hers is fiction, but I imagine they cover much of the same ground. To be perfectly honest, having lived in Alabama for nearly twenty-three years,

> I am somewhat weary of the litany of how whites treated blacks during that era. While I am sure that many bad things did, in fact, happen, my interest now is that we all get past the old grievances and move forward together. My teaching at the Y has been very rewarding in that regard. I have some wonderful black friends (as well as whites) in my classes and we treat each other with great respect and friendship. I often say that if the attitude at the Y could be transferred to the rest of the world, there would be no racial problems anymore. Having seen how it can work, my interest now is in promoting good relations going forward. I hope this makes sense to you, but that is just how I see it.

We do not challenge the validity of her viewpoint or her sincerity, and she has made a contribution in offering this response. And thanks to people like her, towns across the Deep South have done much to get beyond their notorious past. But there are truths we can learn from the past, and we choose to go there.

Sum total, thirty women and two men who were known to have grown up with and/or to have hired maids themselves were consulted personally, on average two times each, and of these, nineteen came through with responses. Only one respondent volunteered in answer to announcements on private-school alumni websites. Six of the interviews were conducted by telephone, and the rest were obtained through e-mail or standard mail correspondence. In sharp contrast to our African American interviewees, all but one of whom were proud to have their names used, around half of those whites who shared their reminiscences wished to remain anonymous. As expressed by one correspondent, "Best not to use my name out of an abundance of caution. I would not want to offend or embarrass anyone." For the purposes of this chapter, all the names of the white interviewees and narrators have been changed at the request of the participants with the following exceptions: Glen Houston, Elise Talmage, Tina O'Niell Stuart, Milner Smith, Flora Templeton Stuart, Lettice Binnings Stuart, Susan Burdon Hudgens, and Hal Chase.

BASIC THEMES OF THE NARRATIVES

In our analysis of these personal narratives by white women and two men, the following themes emerged: cognitive dissonance; perspectives on southern history; dependence on the household servants; adherence to the norms of southern racial etiquette; awareness of black life apart from white life; maternalism; bonding between mistress and maid; expressions of regret; and defiance of the norms to stand up against injustice. In comparison with our black contributors, whose backgrounds included sharecropping and offered little hope of escape from their wretched circumstances, these white narrators, whether they were living in times of prosperity or economic depression, had reason to believe the future was theirs for the taking.

Cognitive Dissonance

Cognitive dissonance is a term from social psychology that comes to mind as we review this collection of white southerners' narratives. Akin to ambivalence, it refers to a situation in which an individual perceives two pieces of information as contradictory, and a state of discomfort for the individual results. Cognitive dissonance is defined by the psychologists Carol Tavris and Elliot Aronson (2007) as "a state of tension that occurs whenever a person holds two cognitions (ideas, attitudes, beliefs, opinions) that are psychologically inconsistent" (13). And when an important element of a person's self-concept is threatened, as Tavris and Aronson further indicate, he or she will feel much greater dissonance, because in the final analysis, people want to believe that they are good, moral beings and that they treat others well. And they generally want to believe the same of their families and their communities. At the personal level, people also want to believe that if they see an instance of deliberate cruelty or injustice, they would take a stand against it. The dissonance is caused by a discrepancy between the way things seemed at the time, as perfectly natural, and the way they seem later when viewed from the perspective of contemporary values. One will usually strive to find a way to resolve the dissonance and therefore to reduce the state of tension.

The contradictions inherent in the southern social system between the democratic ideals of the larger society founded on Judeo-Christian teachings and the harsh reality of race relations under Jim Crow laws created a dissonance even at the time. Southern whites had a lot of explaining to do to visitors from the North and to their children who had not yet been socialized into the norms of the code of etiquette. "Separate but equal" was the traditional defense given by segregationists. Or "this is just the custom." The contradictions between modern belief systems and the values subscribed to in the segregation era are even more apparent today. No one, for instance, advocates segregation anymore, and few would accept that separate is equal. So as older whites look back on the way they followed and enforced norms that would be considered unconscionable today, we can predict they would feel a sense of discomfort, maybe even embarrassment.

In our review of the literature on cognitive dissonance and oppression, we came across an interesting piece of research that queried white South Africans who had lived as privileged whites under conditions of apartheid. The investigation was conducted to discover how white South Africans viewed their earlier compliance with a system that so segregated and mistreated black people. Typical defenses given to the researchers of what we might call their involvement in a situation of collective national guilt were, first, that they did not know what was really going on, and second, that Africans were often heard singing and beating drums so they seemed happy at the time (see Klandermans, Werner, and van Doorn 2008; and Gibson 2005). In their survey, Bert Klandermans et al. found that the liberal white South African students had strong feelings of guilt about the past. Conservatives, however, displayed no feelings of collective guilt or shame. The truth that was revealed to the whole country and the world through the lengthy testimonials given before the Truth and Reconciliation Commission brought forth a cognitive dissonance on the part of white listeners as they were brought face to face with the horrors of apartheid. Creating such dissonance, as James Gibson suggests, is a first step toward personal and social change.

We can consider these findings in our review of these tapes and transcripts of older white southern women (and two men). The following questions are the most relevant here: As they describe their relationships with the black women in their lives, how do they now explain their earlier attitudes and behaviors? How do they view their society, their community, their parents and grandparents who would be regarded as racial bigots today? How do they feel today about their compliance with the rituals and regulations of their time? In short, how do they reconcile the dissonance between the beliefs they have now and the way they behaved then? These are not the questions we asked of the subjects of our investigation; these are the questions we wish to answer now.

Tavris and Aronson provide a list of ways of reducing the tension caused by the dissonance. Their list includes openly acknowledging the guilt, or conversely denying, justifying, and blaming. Denial and defensiveness are the defense mechanisms we are considering in this section. But other discussion categories or themes such as maternalism, which includes gift giving and personal care, defiance, and regret, also relate to strategies that help the teller reconcile the dissonance and in some cases feel perfectly okay about the way things were done.

This resolution is made somewhat easier when the various defenses are taught within one's social reference group beginning in early childhood.

Denial

Denial was evidenced in the large number of white women, as discussed above, who grew up with maids and who failed to respond to repeated requests to share their recollections. Our hunch is that they planned to do so, but when it got down to it, they felt uncomfortable and backed off. Keep in mind also that Kathryn Stockett, author of *The Help* (2009), indicates in her autobiographical appendix to the book that she was taught not to talk about such uncomfortable things as race relations, and certainly not in the presence of black people. Generations of whites, in fact, were brought up to keep their mouths shut. Race, like sex, was a forbidden topic in white southern households because these topics caused embarrassment and tension. Silence is also a way to preserve the secrecy of facts that are troublesome in some way. This tendency toward silence on emotion-laden subjects is evidenced also in the testimonials of some of our black narrators that they learned from an early age not to talk about the lightness in skin color of some of their brothers and sisters.

Glen Houston, aged ninety, a prominent resident of Aberdeen, Mississippi, which is in the northern part of the state, spoke openly and was proud to use her name. She had moved to this area from Michigan as a young woman. She did not mince her words:

> When I came here this was a totally new way of life. I heard more prejudice in Michigan than in this little town. . . . The television presented such a positive picture of this town when integration came, the kids going to college and such things. But when my son was in

school he was assigned to write a paper on integration. He interviewed a black school principal, Mr. Bell. We called black people colored then. Mr. Bell told his true feelings, that he believed the town was not really ready for integration, and he was disturbed about this fact.

We were in the majority as whites then. Now I get very aggravated. I saw only one white face graduating from the high school. Our school is one of the lowest-achieving schools. The black community used to take care of their people; today they are having babies to get the check. I was called to the school to teach eighth grade. I tried to get them to write, What I Want to Be When I Grow Up. What I got was: "I don't ever have to work; I get the government check." . . . Now this [the state of Mississippi] is the fat capital of America.

Defensiveness

Related to denial of one's involvement in a social institution of oppression is a sense of defensiveness when one's country or region of the country is criticized. Residents of a particular area naturally resent being made fun of by outsiders and being derided for their ways of life.

Defensiveness regarding the South is a part of the theme of cognitive dissonance because it shifts the focus away from the mistreatment of a whole race of people and onto the critics of the injustice. This theme is especially evident among our older storytellers, probably because they endured the negative stereotyping of white southerners as ignorant and bigoted people. This was the general representation of the Deep South perpetrated by the northern-based media throughout the days of the civil rights struggle and beyond. Echoes of this defensiveness could be heard in the letter by the English teacher quoted at the beginning of this chapter. Although she grew up after the civil rights era, Kathryn Stockett, in the autobiographical appendix of *The Help,* reflects these sentiments concerning attacks on her home state of Mississippi: "The rash of negative accounts about Mississippi, in the movies, in the papers, on television, have made us natives a wary, defensive bunch. We are full of pride and shame, but mostly pride" (451).

Resentment against the media stereotyping is reflected in the interviews and is, to some extent, justified. As expressed by interviewee Glen Houston of

Aberdeen, Mississippi: "All just loved our little town; people say hello to each other as they pass down the street. There are a lot of gossips in the South. But I take up for Mississippi; you're going to have to come down to here to visit." Similarly, Kay Patterson (not her real name), aged fifty-four, spoke in glowing terms about her hometown in the Mississippi Delta:

> Greenwood is a wonderful town. The black people didn't own their land. We owned a farm, and they lived on our place. My father took care of them, paid their medical expenses. Their ancestors worked for my daddy's family. They lived on our place. The people were treated very well. *The Help* is being filmed in this town right now; people are coming down here from New York. Some say they have heard stories about Greenwood. But they love this town. The people they meet on the street are so friendly.

Blaming the Victim

On the whole, the interviewees spoke of their former maids with great affection and compassion. Negative comments were reserved for the servants' husbands and family members, and black people in the town today. Glen Houston's comment quoted above about women having babies to get a welfare check might qualify for this section; she had only kind words to say about her servants, however. One comment by Margaret Smith did stand out. She was explaining how tough black women had it in the 1950s. Despite her progressivism (which is apparent in other excerpts from her writing), she seems to lack appreciation for the fact that black women's powerlessness persisted well after the days of slavery:

> But their day-to-day understated humbling is what really kept blacks in the yoke of slavery for so many years after they were freed. Perhaps most in our African American community have been like the circus elephants who are chained when young and can be kept under control long after they are able to break their bonds because they are still held firm by the belief that they are not free, or like hostages who side with their captors. Whatever the cause, it was what it was, and now is no more. Thank God.

Perspectives on Southern History

The Nobel Prize–winning author William Faulkner from Oxford, Mississippi, perceived the world from a white male perspective, but also with a haunting sense of the wrongs of the past. Through his character portrayals he conveyed great passion over issues related to race and class. To Faulkner, slavery was the great sin of the South, a sin that was punished through the devastation of the Civil War and its cruel aftermath.

In the majority of his books, Faulkner's emphasis was on the fading etiquette in race relations during the Depression era. His groundbreaking portrait of the Compson family, *The Sound and the Fury,* is a story of moral decline and generational conflict that can be read as a metaphor for a decadent civilization. One of the underlying messages of the novel is that white people—whether they are of gentry stock or what Dilsey, the family's black servant, calls the "trash white folks" (362)—inhabit a region that suffers from historical trauma.

None of our white participants in this project brought up the subject of slavery, but their sense of the legacy of slavery in the form of white supremacy was pronounced. The impact of integration figured prominently in the interviews of two of our interviewees, both from Mississippi. Nostalgia for the past was the theme in both of these interviews. Glen Houston, as quoted above, referred to her aggravation in not seeing any white faces in the school system after whites fled the schools. Melba White, a retired kindergarten teacher, was matter-of-fact about the changes in her region, the Mississippi Delta:

> In the past, there was a lot of work for people on the farms, but agriculture is depressed today, and this affects the whole region. Many of the residents are on welfare. The killing of Emmett Till was one of the horrible events that "spurred things on" in civil rights history. Cross burnings occurred as late as 1966. Today, the educational system is very poor, even downright dangerous. Children whose families can afford it send them to a private academy that charges $3,500 a year. There are few jobs for young blacks, and there is a lot of black-on-black crime.

Kay Patterson, a retired teacher from Greenwood, was critical of the way integration was handled: "At first when the school was integrated it was 10 percent minority. Not enough thought went into how it was done. These upper-end whites were paired with the lowest class of blacks that could be found. There are different classes of blacks. So the whites left for a private school that opened up." Leslie Stocker happened to be visiting her great-aunt in Greensboro, North Carolina, shortly after the lunch counter sit-ins had gotten under way. As she describes the scene:

> My aunt and her maid, Vera, seemed really close. While we (my parents and I) were visiting, the two women were hugging each other and laughing. They had just been weighing themselves on some kitchen scales and giggling that they both weighed 99 pounds. Later as we were eating, my aunt brought up the forbidden topic of integration. She was furious about the sit-ins. Most of the local black people were happy with the way things were, she said, and didn't want integration; these protesters were just troublemakers. Then to prove the point, she called for her maid to come out from the kitchen. "Vera, you don't want your grandchildren to go to school with white children, do you?" she asked. "No ma'am," said her maid.

Leslie Stocker told of a later experience, this time when she was staying with another aunt in New Orleans.

> It was 1968, a few months after Martin Luther King had been assassinated. My aunt said her maid had a weak heart so she had hired another maid to do some of the heavy work. This woman was college educated, and she thought they got along well. But the day after the assassination she had come to work and started shrieking at her, calling her a racist, and storming out. I felt bad for my aunt because she was fairly liberal and had been working toward integration at her church.

Dependence on the Household Servants

In Faulkner's classic tale of sound and fury, strength is found in the black caretaker of the family, "the Negro cook, Dilsey" (416). The dependence of the dysfunctional white Compson family on their dutiful black servant is a theme that echoed out of Faulkner's own personal and cultural background.

The two kinds of dependence that whites described were work-related dependence and emotional dependence. The first description we have selected is from the writing of Elise Talmage of New Orleans. During World War II, women were in demand to work in the factories connected to the war industry. Servants were known to be hardworking and disciplined, so they were in special demand. This excerpt describes how the Talmages lost their maid, Gladys:

> Gladys, our cook, walked out, much to our mother's consternation. We were totally dependent on servants because we had not caught up with the times. We had no washing machines and no dryer and sported a drop kitchen behind the house. Mother thought it cute. This was to keep cooking odors out of the home. Now food had to be carried up through the butler's pantry, the breakfast room, the hall, and into the dining room.

Jeannie Falkner, in a private conversation with Katherine van Wormer, told the story of a woman named Patricia who worked as a maid in her town of Greenwood, Mississippi. Patricia occasionally would get into trouble with the law because of drinking. The woman she worked for, Viola, would rush over to bail her out. Was this some form of paternalism? No, Viola just felt she couldn't do without her, needed to have her maid back as soon as possible.

Emotional dependence is a theme that runs through the stories of one of the men and several of the women as their memories take them back to childhood. Well-known autobiographical accounts such as those by Lillian Smith, Sallie Bingham, and Kathryn Stockett express the deep emotional hold that one of their earliest bonding experiences had on them forever after. Bingham (1989), of the Louisville newspaper-publishing dynasty, explains the feelings most poignantly: "One of these facts was the passionate love white children often developed for their black nurses, who had raised and loved them from babyhood, an attachment that must be suppressed as the white child came into maturity, and finally replaced by humorous stories about devoted darkies" (67).

Little boys, too, developed strong attachment to their maids as mother figures. In her biography of William Faulkner, Judith Sensibar (2009) devotes much attention to the role that his maid, Mammy Callie, played in his early life. "Faulkner's daughter Jill sees Callie Barr as 'one of the more important people in his life, particularly when he was growing up because Granny (his mother) was hardly affectionate. She was a very austere lady'" (78).

Elsie Mae Jackson, childhood maid of Hal Chase. "We were buddies," he says of their relationship. *From the family album of Hal Chase.*

One of our two male storytellers, Hal Chase, speaking in understatement, describes in some detail the attachment he felt toward a woman who worked for his family when he was very small. Of Elsie Mae Jackson he says: "She was a spirited woman, for sure, and attractive. She was a medium build, not thin and not tall. What I can also tell you is that I followed her around a lot as my two older sisters were already in school. When my mother would go out to do some errands or have lunch or attend a meeting, Elsie and I were in the house together. That's how I remember it. She was my buddy; she was the kind of older person that you knew everything was safe and sound as long as she was around." When his mother remarried and the family moved to southern Kentucky, his stepfather found her "uppity"; she came in the front door, for example. In answer to the question whether he felt sad about her leaving the family, Chase replied, "There was a gap there."

Elise Talmage still feels her childhood grief as she recalls her loss of her beautiful childhood maid, Violet.

Violet was marrying a man from their hometown in the country. Aunt

Mamie was pleased with the match as he owned a barber shop and was better fixed than most in their parish.

However, we three were very upset about losing Violet to anyone.

The room was crowded, but we glimpsed the groom, and he wasn't handsome like Violet and had acne scars on his face. Violet didn't even look like herself in her wedding dress with white powder on her pretty brown face. (There wasn't yet makeup available for people with dark skin.)

By the time the services started, the three of us were crying pretty loud while Daddy struggled to get us quiet, but we just sobbed louder and louder, and Daddy was helpless. When it was over, we three cried all the way home.

We loved Violet.

Awareness of Black Life apart from White Life

The fact that black people had a life apart from their life within the white families was rarely acknowledged by the white people for whom they worked. The engraving that William Faulkner placed on his maid's tombstone says it all: "Callie Barr Clark, 1840–1940, 'Mammy,' her white children bless her." As Sensibar (2009) notes, even in death, whites assumed exclusive ownership of their maid. Faulkner did realize as a small child that his beloved caretaker, his second mother, had her white family and her black family. This revelation came to him abruptly in childhood as he watched Mammie Callie with her own people. The difference in body language and voice modulations and words were to him "a painful education into race" that would ultimately find its way into fictional accounts of white children's responses to a similar revelation (Sensibar 81).

Sallie Bingham (1989) noted as a child that when she was eating in the kitchen with the servants she was in the presence of a level of communication that existed apart from words, "the silent language of rebellion" (39), as she put it. And on occasion, she would get a glimpse of the "colorful fabric of their lives" that was only partly visible to her (12).

One of our white storytellers experienced the same phenomenon in childhood, perhaps because children's presence so often goes unnoticed. As Elise Talmage shared:

> When I was little, I'd climb up in a tree in the backyard. There, I would overhear the cooks talking across the fence to each other. Their voices had a whole different pitch than they used to talk to white people. I remember once three or four black women came over to kill the snapping turtle. This was to be served in our soup for dinner. They teased the turtle with a stick, and one chopped its head off. I heard them talking. Their conversation was entirely different than their conversation in our house. I was twelve years old at the time.

Katherine van Wormer, too, has a story to add here.

> One day I was riding in the streetcar sitting right in front of the wooden sign that said "Colored." I should explain that this piece of wood had metal pegs that fit into holes on the back of seats so the whites could move it as far back as they wanted. Anyway, on this day I was right at the dividing line, and I heard the black women in the next row talking. "We love them so much," she said, "when we help raise them. Then they grow up and forget all about us." "No," I wanted to say, "We don't forget; we don't; we don't." It just never had occurred to me that they felt this way.

Adherence to the Norms of Southern Racial Etiquette

There is a lot of consistency in blacks' and whites' recollections of the rules of the day. The Jim Crow laws were pretty well enforced everywhere, and the customs that had grown up from slavery were generally honored. White women could usually expect a recently hired servant to follow the norms of decorum, addressing her as "ma'am," entering by the back door, and so forth. Everyone knew what the rules were, yet they were enforced differentially and much more so in the 1930s than in the 1960s and more in rural Mississippi than in New Orleans.

As in chapter 5 with data from the interviews with our African American respondents, we have constructed a breakdown of the numbers of reports of instances in which the rules of racial etiquette were enforced against black people. Because all but seven of our white storytellers wrote out their narratives, they often did not address the specific norms that were designed to draw clear boundaries between the races. The following information is drawn from the responses of twenty of the twenty-seven whites involved in the project:

~ Entrance and exit by the back or kitchen door only: 12
~ Given separate toilet or no toilet to use: 10
~ Wore a maid's uniform: 14
~ Their space was in the kitchen: 19
~ Addressed by first name while required to use formal address for the employer: 20
~ Ate after the family in the kitchen or took food home: 19
~ Specifically mentioned as being a member of the family: 11

Most southern white children, like their black counterparts, were strictly socialized into the white norms of proper racial etiquette. Exactly how the norms were interpreted, however, varied by family traditions, neighborhood, and region of the South. Two of our respondents who were Jewish, for example, had parents with far more progressive attitudes than did many of the others. Some of the white women who grew up with maids had liberal parents but maids who were trained into traditional norms of domestic service and who seemed to want to follow them. Often to small children these norms seemed an anomaly because they sensed a disjunction between the values of equality and kindness they were taught (for example, in Sunday school) and the behavior they witnessed. There was just a lot about the rules of segregation that didn't seem quite right, and since children are naturally inquisitive, they often asked embarrassing questions. Yet satisfactory answers were rarely forthcoming. One rule was an absolute: these things were not to be talked about. Elise Talmage remembers that as a little girl in the 1920s, she would pester her mother with questions such as, "How come Violet can't come in the front door? How come she can't eat with us at the table?" Her mother invariably would hush her up with the same reply—"It just isn't done." We get a glimpse of the way things were done in Elise Talmage's description of dinner service (as provided to van Wormer, her daughter) in the days of the Great Depression:

> Our house was a bungalow with only two bedrooms. Still, we had formal dining. The cook would enter to bring in only one bowl of soup at a time and always serving from the left, which Mother directed over

and over. The maid wore a stiffly starched white apron and head band over her white uniform and struggled around the hanging clothes. These had been hurriedly taken off the clothesline during the summer afternoon showers.

In her reminiscences, shared recently in e-mail, Milner Smith, born in 1944, and from Birmingham, Alabama, touches on the etiquette for servant–white family relations that were prevalent at that time:

> Since my earliest memory, I always had a "colored" servant in my home, I had a nanny named Estelle from the time I was born until around age two or so. I really don't know what became of her nor do I remember her except from the pictures and what I have been told about her devotion to me.
>
> Annie is the first maid I remember from my childhood. She called my stepfather Mr. Henry, always. She always called me Miss Milner and my mother Miss Helen out of respect for our station in life. Sometimes on rainy days mother or grandmother would take Annie to catch the bus and make sure she had exact change for carfare (as it was called in the late forties and early fifties).
>
> Annie would always sit in the backseat whether or not the front seat was empty. Naturally, Annie boarded the bus and made her way to the far back, behind where the door opened with stairs to get off. She would pull the cord and a buzzer would signal the driver to make a stop.
>
> Annie was paid a paltry sum per week by today's standards, but we considered her a member of the "family," and contributed food, clothes, and her uniform towards her upkeep. She left her uniform at our house and changed into it when she got off the bus and walked up the very steep hill to our house. Her duties ranged from babysitting, cooking, and cleaning, to caring for us when we were sick, serving at our parties, listening to our problems, and generally helping with whatever else was happening at our house. In short, Annie's presence was indispensable to the smooth operation of our home and lives.
>
> Yes, Annie always called me Miss Milner, and anytime even up until recently any maid we ever had always rode in the backseat. They were not comfortable riding in the front with the lady of the house.

Milner Smith *(left)* and Katherine Stuart van Wormer *(right)*, both at age thirteen in the 1950s in New Orleans. *From the family collection of Katherine van Wormer.*

For a northern view of the local customs in the age of segregation, we include a portion of an interview with Thelma Wagner, an army wife who moved from Iowa down to Woodville, Mississippi, during the World War II. She was provided with a cleaning lady through the military. She provides an outsider's perspective on how blacks were treated at that time:

> When we came back to Iowa we would tell our friends the stories, and they just could not believe that's how it was, because we didn't do anything like that up here. My folks came down and visited and just couldn't believe it was like that. When you passed blacks on the streets they got off the sidewalks. You know up here they didn't jump off the sidewalks. If you had asked them to get off the sidewalk, there would have been a fight! . . . In restaurants, the white people went in the front. Blacks ate in the kitchen. . . . My husband was upset at this treatment. But then his view changed after living there because he thought they were different and should be treated differently. I don't think they are any different from us. Just now I have them in

> the family! (*proudly referring to family picture of her grandson, his African American wife, and their children*).

In the next two sections, we provide further details in another context. These relate to the caretaking functions and obligations assumed by many of the employers of black maids.

Maternalism

Scholars of domestic labor have used the term *maternalism* to describe the treatment accorded to the domestic servant, who was often declared to be like a member of the family but who, in fact, was always treated as a social inferior. Custom decreed that the maid would receive little money for her work but that when the mood struck her, the mistress of the house would reward the maid with gifts of various sorts. Like her slave ancestors, as was shown in previous chapters, she could tote food home left over from the meal she had prepared. Also, like her slave ancestors, she was not often encouraged to pursue an education or to act in any way that could be taken as "uppity." There was no sign, however, among our white participants in the study that they desired their maids to be ignorant; several, in fact, encouraged them to work on their reading skills.

Caretaking

And as we hear from Greenwood, Mississippi, resident Kay Patterson:

> I grew up with Nan, Baby Ruth, Roberta. The one I went full circle with was Naomi. I was her legal guardian when she was old—in her seventies and eighties. Her grandchildren were stealing her blind. At some point she asked if I would help. A friend she worked for was a lawyer and drew up the papers. My husband was a banker, so he helped her pay back the money to a loan shark. I was her legal guardian and handled her accounts. When she died, there was enough for her funeral and burial. One of her daughters still keeps in touch today.

And from Glen Houston:

> When Nellie's one son got drunk and went to the grocery store and rung up a huge bill, we would pay the bill. And when she [Nellie] got sick in the bed, we would check on her. Today my son always goes to see Esther. We took her to the doctor. Now we take care of each other. They have taken care of me. James, the yard boy, will be here soon. It's like the movie *Driving Miss Daisy.* He told me that a woman said to him, "Are you Mrs. Houston's James?" He was laughing about it.

Gift Giving

Most of the white women interviewed gave examples of gifts they or their mothers gave the women who worked for them. It was the custom that the cooks could "tote," or take what food they wanted home. Also furniture that was no longer needed was offered to the maid. Some had their whole houses furnished with fine pieces passed down from their employers; they also received toys and hand-me-down clothes for their children. Our interviews with the forty African American women confirmed these customs. As shared by Margaret Smith: "My mother always said that Evelyn [their maid] toted things home. . . . When Evelyn retired on Social Security, Mother continued to send her money weekly until she died."

A lifelong Greenwood resident, Annette White, aged fifty-nine, was busy the morning before we called her; coincidentally, she had been acting as an extra in the film *The Help,* which was filmed right there in her town of Greenwood.

This is how Mrs. White described her elderly mother's relationship with the family maid: "She was called a housekeeper, not a maid. Eva toted food from dinner, which was served formally at noon. Eva came in her own car, which Mom paid to be fixed; she gave her the money for that. When Eva got old and had Alzheimer's she went to a nursing home. We took things to her there. Then when she died—this is the custom here—you give money for the burial to the next of kin."

Perhaps the oddest and most revealing gift of all was the one proudly mentioned by Kay Patterson. This was the building of a special bathroom for the maid. Without such a bathroom, she explained, the maid would have no toilet she could use. She could not use the residents' bathroom because of the belief current at that time that black people had germs that whites did not have. And in answer to the question where could they go to the bathroom, this interviewee responded, "The maid would have to go across the levee and squat by the river." Interestingly, the controversy over maids' toilets was a major theme of *The Help*. The movie made fun of the white women for constructing a special toilet for the maid. The context, however, was not made clear.

Bonding between Mistress and Maid

Virtually all the southern white women interviewed, when they spoke of their maids and "nurses," declared them to be like members of their family. Interestingly, none of the African American women interviewed who worked in the South, however close they felt to their employers, stated that they felt like a member of the family. Who else in the family was scrubbing the bathtub or toilet? Who else in the family was getting paid at the end of the week? Who else was dressed in a uniform? What the white respondents probably meant was they couldn't think of their family without the presence of the black woman who cared for them and cooked for them. The maid was in the home much of the time and privy to all of the family goings-on. To the worker, however, she had her own family to whom she was anxious to return. And yet there were exceptions—children who strongly bonded with their caretakers and vice versa, and black women and white women who shared the same joys and sorrows.

Like no other period in history, segregation in the South brought women from these two racial castes into close physical contact. Working together in the house, sharing gossip about the neighbors, and fighting the elements such as storms and other natural disasters, some degree of bonding would have been inevitable. Thus you would hear stories of women cooking together, laughing together, and raising the children together. Grief was commonly shared. In one of the white family narratives, the two adult women wept together upon the assassination of John F. Kennedy and celebrated together over the passage of the Civil Rights Act. Still, these women who came from such diverse cultural backgrounds rarely ate together and never lounged in the living room together. When they visited, it was generally in the kitchen, while the cook busily engaged making dinner preparations, often chopping vegetables or shelling beans.

Matters of gender played a huge role in white-black relationships in the

Jim Crow era. Black males provided labor usually outdoors; any personal contact between black male and white females was strictly proscribed. The white men of the household were largely absent as well, home only for a formal and well-prepared meal after a long day at the office. So this left the women together, their relationship uncomplicated by any ties to a man. Thus, although this relationship had complications of its own related to power differentials and financial arrangements, the kind of sexual jealousy that may enter into relationships between women of the same race was largely absent (Greif and Sharpe 2010).

Lorraine Wood, who grew up in the 1950s in New Orleans, expresses her love in these words:

> I have read *The Help* and have to admit that I grew up with an upstairs maid, a downstairs maid, and a cook!! It seems unreal to me now—now that I am all three and have been for forty years. But I adore our Gloria (who was, after our mother died, the cook and upstairs maid) and take her to Walmart every month (and so does my sister, so at least one of us sees her every other week). My Katrina story about her is too long to type but, in short, I called her when we were evacuating to beg her to come with us. She declined, saying she was going with her sister. (She didn't want to tell me she was sick and didn't want to sit in our car for twelve hours). When I was watching the TV coverage of all the people sitting at the Convention Center, I saw the large hot-pink purse I had just given her before I realized I was seeing her!! It was my worst Katrina moment, and I didn't sleep after that. I spent three days on the phone calling every reporter, including Geraldo Rivera, the Red Cross, everybody I knew to still be in New Orleans. I found out a week later that she had been taken to Dallas. It was the only time I cried.

"How we loved the people!" These are the words of Tina O'Niell Stuart, who has fond memories of her grandparents' maid, Mariah, who "ruled the roost," and their chauffeur, Noah, who had his own living quarters, and whom she can still picture dressed in his white jacket and chauffeur's cap. From her growing up in 1930s, New Orleans, she remembers:

> Lena raised me through grade school. She was our cook. Her mother

> also worked for our family. Some member of that family worked for us all those generations. My grandmother took care of them when they were sick. When Mariah passed away, my grandmother was devastated.
>
> One memory I have is that when I was a child, black children would take care of us, and they weren't much older than we were. But I think it was assumed that they knew how to do these things, how to care for children.

The custom of maintaining these ties intergenerationally, with mother and daughter working for the same family, is also reflected in the following account by Lettice Binnings Stuart (no relation to the previous respondent):

> Viola was my second mother. My real mother was the gracious soul of our antebellum home that was filled with antiques, silverware, porcelain, and portraits dating back to her great-grandparents' plantation, which at one time had one hundred slaves or more. After the Civil War, two of the slave women, now free, were "passed down" through the family, helping to raise my grandmother and later my mother. Mother loved Mammy and Ella, and so it was that she passed down to us a respect for all people, regardless of their skin color or station in life.

Kay Patterson, who told above how she became her former maid's legal guardian, said, "Naomi called me her white daughter. . . . When she died, her family was very appreciative and asked me to speak at her funeral."

Annette White, also of Greenwood, similarly attended the funeral of the woman who had helped raise not only her but also her children, and who was considered "a part of the family." In her old age, when she had Alzheimer's, they would take things to her in the nursing home. When she died, "as is the custom here," they gave money to the next of kin to help with the costs of the funeral.

Having grown up in a close-knit New Orleans neighborhood, Leslie Stocker could provide an overview of relationships between the white families and their black servants that she had observed as a child:

> Among my neighbors and the kids I grew up with, some maids just came in for the cleaning and from what I could tell were sort of

just in the background. Some had close ties with the white people but pretended to be in the background when company came. But others more openly played active family-style roles and helped raise the children. Two small children who lived two doors down from us had parents who were known to party a lot and who slept in in the mornings. These children were practically raised by their "nurse," as she was called, who often could be seen chasing after the children down the sidewalk. She took care of them in the morning while the parents were in bed and rounded them up at bedtime from our house. Then I knew an older single woman, a teacher, who had become close friends with her maid, a Creole woman, who had worked for her for over forty years. Her plan was to leave her her house upon her death. But the maid's grown children insisted she quit her job; they did not want their mother to be a maid. So she didn't get the house in the end.

Our own maid, Lula, was not very intelligent so I didn't feel close to her. But the woman who worked next door, Rachel, I had great respect for. I'll never forget how, when my dog was run over and lying dead along the street and I became hysterical, Rachel rushed over to comfort me. She put water on my face with a damp cloth and said, "This child needs her mother." But I remember thinking, "No! I don't want my mother." All I wanted at that moment was her.

Expressions of Regret

In *Killers of the Dream* (1949), a book that was one of the most personal critiques of the pre-1960s South of its day, Lillian Smith looked back sarcastically to the contradictions of her childhood, to what she was taught then and what she later could see as an enlightened adult. Her book graphically describes the intricate system of taboos concerning sexuality, gender, race, and vocabulary that she learned at her mother's knee. The following passage, laden with feelings of bitterness and guilt, gives a taste of the tone of the work:

> I knew that my old nurse who had cared for me through long months of illness, who had given me refuge when a little sister took my place as the baby of the family, who soothed, fed me, delighted me with her stories and games, let me fall asleep on her deep warm breast, was not

> worthy of the passionate love I felt for her but must be given instead a half-smiled affection similar to that which one feels for a dog. . . . I learned to cheapen with tears and sentimental talk of "my old mammy" one of the profound relationships of my life. (28–29)

The courageous and controversial autobiography of Sallie Bingham, *Passion and Prejudice: A Family Memoir* (1989), echoes this same theme of the minimization of a white child's love for her black caretaker and her gaining only in adulthood "a sense of the oppressive conditions of these women's lives" (39).

Four of our interviewees expressed feelings that went beyond regret to the emotional level of guilt concerning the treatment of their maids. Margaret Smith, aged sixty-six, of New Orleans, provided this matter-of-fact account:

> My family was poor and undereducated. In order to be better than somebody else, my family, although kind in many ways, felt superior to black people, called Negroes back then, or worse. There was a lot of derogatory talk. . . . My mother [who moved up in the world through marriage] for the first time in her life had some power, and like people born into ignorance do, she abused it. [When she followed Rita, the maid home one day] she found that she was living in the French Quarter with only a cloth covering for a door. She, who had just escaped from poverty herself, would then add importantly, "I couldn't have someone who was dirty working in my home, so I fired her."

And with reference to another maid:

> I guess you could say we were spoiled. We were certainly thoughtless. It never occurred to me to consider Evelyn when I put my dirty clothes in the hamper or left my books or stuffed animals tossed about the room. It was her job to pick them up. . . . I never felt privileged, just accepted our lives as what they were. I never felt that it should be any different, and when I thought of the future and dreamed of being married myself, I assumed that I would have servants.

Leslie Stocker, who also grew up in the 1950s with maids, stated in an interview:

> I cringe as I remember how we teased Lula. We, my little sister and I, got a kick out of pretending we thought her name was Lulu like the girl in the comic strip.
>
> One day she was combing my long hair that was full of knots, and I was fussing at getting my knots untangled. "Suppose," she said, "you had nappy hair like Lula's." I had never heard that expression before. Lula hated cats, and would go around the house muttering, "Nasty! Nasty!" because we fed the cats off of our own plates. So Lula took to eating out of the pots. Then for devilment we secretly fed the cats out of the pots. But that's not all. The cat had a set of mirror-twin black kittens. We named the pair Lulu and Nappy Lu. And we would refer to the kittens by name even when she was around. Of course most of the time, we were good to her, and she loved working for my mother. But these were the thoughtless things that I can't believe we did.

One of our writers who wished to make this statement anonymously had a memory that bothered her: "I can't believe I did this—but when I was a kid I would say 'Eeny, meeny, miny, mo / Catch a nigger by his toe. Eeny, meeny, miny, mo.' We would chant this right in front of the cook. We just didn't think anything of it."

One deep regret that was mentioned by several of the white writers was that, as they ponder these relationships today, they realize how lopsided they were, how their maids knew everything about them, but they knew so little about the personal lives of these women. Penny Hanks simply said, "Looking back on all this, I feel bad, guilty." And another narrator pondered how she could as an adult convey her regrets to the maid who was still working for the family years later. But she never could figure out what to say or how to say it, so she just played the role that was expected of her. Some others expressed the fact that now, as older adults, they would like to get to know them better, as full people, but in most of the cases, too much time had passed.

Defiance of the Norms to Stand Up against Injustice

In this category we located examples from the narratives that involved instances of the interviewee engaging in behavior that was inconsistent with the norms of segregation. Elise Talmage of New Orleans, who was very young in the 1940s, relates this experience:

> A college student who attended Dillard worked for us temporarily as a maid. On the first day of work, she rang the doorbell right in the front door. We lived on a crowded street so the whole neighborhood could see. But I didn't say anything. When it got to be lunchtime, I arranged for her to make some sandwiches for myself and the company. Then she served us lunch and sat down and ate with us in the dining room. I didn't say anything. I really got a kick out of it, but my friends were absolutely aghast. This is the way things were the whole time she worked for me. But then we had Ethel, and she always came in the back door just like all the other maids in the neighborhood.

The following correspondent, a sixty-six-year-old man, writes the following of his brother's wedding that took place in New Orleans in the 1960s:

> The wedding ceremony itself was in a Catholic church in Harahan. We had really never met any of her family or friends, nor had they met any of us. The question came up as to what to do with Anna, our longtime maid, at the wedding. My father thought she could sit in the back pew of the church in a maid's uniform. I hit the ceiling and said that there would be no such thing—that Anna would sit next to my mother in the groom's family pew. The plan was that I would seat Anna just before seating my mother.
>
> All went well, and during the Air from Handel's "Water Music," I marched Anna up the aisle. She was decked out to the nines, including her mink stole. I seated Anna and turned around to go back to the rear to then walk my mother up the aisle. I cast my gaze upon our side of the church at family and friends who were smiling happily at seeing Anna.
>
> Then I turned and looked at the bride's side of the church. The entire side of that church was completely stricken. I then realized that they all thought that Anna was the groom's mother—and that therefore the groom was black.

Defiance of the southern white codes of etiquette of course could be political as well. The lead character, Skeeter, in *The Help*, similar to the author of the book, reconciled herself to the injustice of the past by publishing the stories of the women of fortitude who told the truth like it was about working for white folks.

Elise Talmage, in her role as real estate broker, signed a newspaper petition in favor of integration in the early 1960s, and later, in Kentucky, helped to integrate a white section of town. Twice she appeared on a panel for a local TV show to describe life for blacks under segregation for Black History Month. Leslie Stocker threw herself wholeheartedly into the civil rights movement and engaged in the picketing of segregated establishments, street demonstrations, and sit-ins to block street traffic along the streets of a southern town.

Flora Templeton Stuart also got involved in the civil rights movement. As she remembers of her move to Chapel Hill, North Carolina, in 1963: "My sister, Katherine, and I immersed ourselves in the civil rights movement, which was organized through the black churches. We would sing 'We Shall Overcome' while holding hands. We even protested in the streets blocking traffic."

Hal Chase got involved in the struggle for civil rights as well when he was in graduate school. He specialized in African American history and until his recent retirement was an instructor of history at the urban campus of the Des Moines Area Community College. He conducts workshops and has made major contributions to organizations devoted to African American history in Iowa. A number of the social workers interviewed stated that after some involvement in the civil rights movement, they chose to go into social work to continue the struggle for justice.

CONCLUDING THOUGHTS

This chapter highlights the paradoxes and contradictions in race relations as blacks and white related to one another under traditions that had evolved from a time when one race was enslaved and one race free. Yet attachments grew that transcended the barriers of race, and in some cases these attachments endured until death. Some of the apologists for segregation seemed every bit as attached to their housekeepers as did younger and more liberal-minded employers.

One very important question that we asked of most of the narrators of this chapter was, "Do you have a photograph of your maid?" Nine times out of ten, the answer, often very regretful, was, "No." Today, some of them would give anything for a photo of a woman who had played such a significant role in their lives.

So this is the question we must ask ourselves—if these women were so loved and cherished, and if they indeed were members of the family, why weren't they in the family pictures? Why weren't they photographed at all? We can only surmise the answer. Perhaps they were just taken for granted; the children would grow and the parents get old, but the maid would always be there, waiting on the table. And then maybe she was not really considered a part of the family at all, but loved on a different level. One interviewee did treasure the memory of her maid so much that she kept two photographs of her in the kitchen. Another made a special trip back to New Orleans as a mature adult to the maid's neighborhood uptown. Today, she treasures that picture as do members of her family. So, in the final analysis, we can conjecture that perhaps these black women who served the whites are more appreciated now in their absence than they were when they were present. If the thinking had been verbalized, it probably would have gone something like this: "Photograph your children now because they are changing, and Grandma won't be around much longer. But your maid is your maid forever." History would change all this, and the attitudes of many whites, especially those who were coming of age during the civil rights period, would be forever altered. The stories that we solicited and included in this and the preceding chapter are not representative of southern whites who grew up with black maids, but they are representative of whites who feel moved by their experiences and who seemed to feel compelled to share them.

Epilogue

Children, I come back today
To tell you a story of the long dark way.
—LANGSTON HUGHES, "The Negro Mother"

WE CONCEIVED OF this book as a tribute to the black women who have shared their stories of hardship and survival, women who, like participant Irene Williams, might want to say to their grandchildren, "Honey, you just don't understand. This was real," or who, like Mamie Johnson, seek to explain, "It was surviving, just the way you had to survive."

The white narrators, too, seemed to feel they had some explaining to do about their roles and their family's roles in the treatment of the black servants in their homes. Focusing on the childhood period, and with searching honesty, they shared their gratitude and regrets—regrets about not really getting to know these women whom they regarded as members of their family.

Our gratitude goes to all our participants, both the descendants of slaves and the descendants of slave owners, who willingly stepped forward to help us fill in the dots of this social history. Given our personal closeness to the topic, all three of us had the opportunity to interview our relatives for the book. Oral history is truly a people's history.

Ultimately, these are the stories of women who insisted on being more than what others thought they were born to be. And they are also the stories of white women who were blessed in one way yet subordinate in another. They could not have known it then, but the very forces that would ultimately bring about fuller racial equality in society would also help liberate women, socially, professionally, and politically. The Civil Rights Act of 1964 would outlaw discrimination on the grounds of sex as well as race.

Because of the very personal nature of this undertaking for the authors, we each offer, in conclusion, our reflections on what we learned from our gathering of these women's stories.

KATHERINE VAN WORMER

"The history of memory considers the interplay of the past and the present" (Boehm 2009). Recording the memories of the blacks and whites who came forward to share them, poring over old photographs of women who worked in our and other people's families, brought forth emotions that had long been repressed, emotions that were at their peak years ago when many of us were clapping and singing about freedom and resistance in boarded-off streets. There were other memories, too, which went further back and were more disturbing. These were brought to the surface in my discussions with the white storytellers who, like the black participants, talked a lot about their childhood experiences. As I read or heard their stories, their sadness became my sadness and their regrets became my regrets—why did we not do more for these women who served us and who asked for so little? Why did we not defy the system?

The negatives that came out in the narratives of the African American women did not surprise me; the positives in the memories that were shared and in the warmth of the feelings conveyed for many of the white people—those were what stood out for me. And when I use excerpts from the tapes in my classes, this is what resonates.

On second thought, there was one aspect of life under segregation that did surprise me because it seemed too ridiculous to believe. This was the business of adult maids calling little white children "Mr." and "Miss." The first time I heard of this, I was interviewing a friend. She said her maid called her "Miss Milner" when she was a small child. I discounted this as a false memory. And when I heard it from Mississippi blacks, I thought, "Well, maybe in Mississippi for the older kids." But then I heard it again and again in the white women's stories, the claim that maids addressed the white children as "Miss" and "Mr." It even came out in my mother's story of when she was visiting in the country. So I had to admit it was true. This, to me, is one aspect of the culture that I grew up in, one small ritual of humiliation, that can be seen as key to the larger pattern. And it had somehow escaped me before.

In hearing the tapes and doing the interviews, I learned that segregation itself was played out in so many ways. Because in uptown New Orleans, where I grew up, the servants always entered by the back door and often had their own special bathroom, I assumed this was standard. But the narratives told me something else. The picture of the black and white women quilting together in each other's houses in rural Mississippi will stay with me always. And some of the descriptions of very close, almost mother-daughter relationships that formed between the younger migrant women and their older northern employers—I will always remember these as well.

Overall, these stories have impressed on me the sense that unchecked power inevitably leads to abuse; it brings out the worst in people. Yet they have also shown me that even within a system as oppressive as the one these interviews describe, kindness will manifest itself in the most unexpected and mysterious of ways.

DAVID W. JACKSON

Generations of women in my family worked as domestics in Des Moines and the surrounding area in Iowa. Listening to the narratives of these women who worked in the homes of southern white families was therefore especially meaningful to me. Many of the experiences these women described strikingly resembled the accounts of such work my grandmother and great-aunts shared with me as I was growing up. And there were stories I hadn't heard, too.

Dorothy Weathers, who worked for a prominent white family in Des Moines, offered a unique story about how she was well cared for by the family she worked for, and she expressed contentment with that part of her life. Through this working relationship she gained a best friend, an extended family, and lifelong financial security that have sustained her until today. Mrs. Weather's story taught me about such rare cases where the domestics were well treated.

I listened to the intimate details of Irene Williams's experience as a domestic servant. She endured some of the most exploitative life situations imaginable, but she survived, showing great strength in sharing some of her personal trauma with me for the sake of our future generations. My experience in interviewing Mrs. Williams showed me that the greatest form of personal strength is truly the human spirit. I was emotionally moved by her life story, which, for me, lent personal meaning and perspective to our work on this book.

This study is a continuation of my commitment to conduct research on the African American experience in Iowa, an area whose rich cultural heritage has been overlooked by scholars. I hope this study inspires other African Americans to learn more about their culture and history.

CHARLETTA SUDDUTH

All the stories of the women of the Great Migration taught me the power of "staying the course," the value of endurance. These women migrated to Iowa in search of a better life. The determination, perseverance, and faith that these women demonstrated affected my life.

During the almost overwhelming task of completing my dissertation, the talks I had with these women were what propelled me forward. Hearing the countless stories of humility as these women shared their stories of cleaning for white folks; being called nigger, gal, or girl; going to the back door; being told to clean over and over again gave me the strength to endure. These women still had joy, as demonstrated by the laughter we shared as they recounted their tales of hardships working as maids. Their resilience was and is remarkable. What should have destroyed them somehow made them better, stronger, happier, and proud to be black women.

References

Angelou, Maya. *I Know Why the Caged Bird Sings.* New York: Random House, 1969.

Arnado, Janet M. "Maternalism in Mistress-Maid Relations: The Philippine Experience." *Journal of International Women's Studies* 4, no. 3 (2004): 154–77.

Barnes, Charline, and Floyd Bumpers. *Iowa's Black Legacy.* Chicago: Arcadia, 2000.

Berlin, Ira. *The Making of African America: The Four Great Migrations.* New York: Viking, 2010.

Bindas, Kenneth, J. "Re-Remembering a Segregated Past: Race in American Memory." *History and Meaning: Studies in Representation of the Past* 22, no. 1 (2010): 113–35.

Bingham, Sallie. *Passion and Prejudice: A Family Memoir.* New York: Applause, 1991.

Blassingame, John W. Using the Testimony of Ex-Slaves. In *The Slave's Narrative,* ed. Charles T. Davis and Henry Louis Gates Jr., 78–98. New York: Oxford University Press, 1985.

Boehm, Lisa Krissoff. *Making a Way Out of No Way: African American Women and the Second Great Migration.* Jackson: University Press of Mississippi, 2009.

Botkin, Ben A. *Lay My Burden Down: A Folk History of Slavery.* Chicago: University of Chicago Press, 1945.

Bunch-Lyons, Beverly A. *Contested Terrain: African American Women Migrated from the South to Cincinnati 1900–1950.* New York: Routledge, 2002.

Burns, Ken. "An Intimate View of *The War.*" Interview by Alex Kingsbury. *U.S. News and World Report,* September 24, 2007, 51.

Clark-Lewis, Elizabeth. *Living In, Living Out: African American Domestics and the Great Migration.* New York: Kodansha International, 1996.

Cock, Jacklyn. *Maids and Madams: Domestic Workers under Apartheid.* London: Women's Press, 1989.

Conroy, Pat. *My Reading Life.* New York: Doubleday, 2010.

Davis, Charles T., and Henry Louis Gates Jr., eds. *The Slave's Narrative.* New York: Oxford University Press, 1985.

DeMichele, Kimberly. "Memories of Suffering: Exploring the Life Story Narratives of Twice-Widowed Women." *Journal of Aging Studies* 23 (2009): 103–13.

Dollard, John. *Caste and Class in a Southern Town*. 1937. Garden City, NY: Doubleday, 1957.

Ehrenreich, Barbara, and Arlie Russell Hochschild, eds. *Global Woman: Nannies, Maids, and Sex Workers in the New Economy*. New York: Metropolitan, 2003.

English, Karen. *Francie*. New York: Square Fish, 1999.

Escott, Paul. "The Art of Reading WPA Slave Narratives." In *The Slave's Narrative*, ed. Charles T. Davis and Henry Louis Gates Jr., 40–47. New York: Oxford University Press, 1985.

Faulkner, William. *Requiem for a Nun*. New York: Random House, 1951.

———. *The Sound and the Fury*. 1929. New York: Random House, 1956.

Gathorne-Hardy, Jonathan. *The Unnatural History of the Nanny*. New York: Dial, 1973.

Gibson, James L. *Overcoming Apartheid: Can Truth Reconcile a Divided Nation?* New York: Russell Sage, 2005.

Golden, Karris. "Stories of Women Involved in 'Great Migration': Empowering." *Waterloo-Cedar Falls Courier*, March 12, 2010, B4.

Greene, Roberta. "Risk and Resilience Theory: A Social Work Perspective." In *Human Behavior Theory and Social Work Practice*, ed. Greene, 3rd ed. New Brunswick, NJ: Transaction, 2008.

Greene, Roberta, Harriet L. Cohen, John Gonzalez, and Youjung Lee. *Narratives of Social and Economic Justice*. Washington, DC: NASW Press, 2009.

Greif, Geoffrey L. and Tanya Sharpe. "The Friendships of Women: Are There Differences between African Americans and Whites?" *Journal of Human Behavior in the Social Environment* 20 (2010): 791–807.

Handley, Fiona. "Memorializing Race in the Deep South: The 'Good Darkie' Statue, Louisiana, USA." *Public Archaeology* 6, no. 2 (2007): 98–115.

Harley, Sharon, Francille Wilson, and Shirley Logan. "Introduction: Historical Overview." In *Sister Circle: Black Women and Work*, ed. Harley and the Black Women and Work Collective, 1–12. New Brunswick, NJ: Rutgers University Press, 2002.

Harris, Trudier. *From Mammies to Militants: Domestics in Black American Literature*. Philadelphia: Temple University Press, 1982.

———. *Summer Snow: Reflections from a Black Daughter of the South*. Boston: Beacon Press, 2003.

Hartley, Leslie. *The Go-Between*. London: Hamish Hamilton, 1953.

Holland, Endesha Ida Mae. *From the Mississippi Delta: A Memoir*. New York: Simon and Schuster, 1997.

Hondagneu-Sotelo, Pierrette. *Doméstica: Immigrant Workers Cleaning and Caring in the Shadows of Affluence*. Berkeley and Los Angeles: University of California Press, 2001.

hooks, bell. *Sisters of the Yam: Black Women and Self-Recovery*. Cambridge: South End Press, 1993.

———. *Belonging: A Culture of Place*. New York: Routledge, 2009.

Hughes, Langston. "The Negro Mother." 1931. In *The Collected Poems of Langston Hughes*, ed. Arnold Rampersad, 155–56. New York: Vintage Classics, 1994.

Hunter, Kristin. *God Bless the Child*. New York: Scribner, 1964.

Hunter, Tera W. *"Joy to My Freedom": Southern Black Women's Lives and Labors after the Civil War*. Cambridge: Harvard University Press, 1997.

Jabour, Anya. *Scarlett's Sisters: Young Women in the Old South*. Chapel Hill: University of North Carolina Press, 2007.

Jackman, Mary R. *The Velvet Glove: Paternalism and Conflict in Gender, Class, and Race Relations*. Berkeley and Los Angeles: University of California Press, 1994.

Jones, Jacqueline. *Labor of Love, Labor of Sorrow: Black Women, Work and the Family, from Slavery to the Present*. 2nd ed. New York: Basic, 2010.

Kinney, Pat. "Great Migration: Railroad Strike 100 Years Ago Brought an Influx of African-Americans to Waterloo." *Waterloo-Cedar Falls Courier*, February 1, 2011, A1.

Kingsbury, Alex. "Making History." *U.S. News & World Report*, September 24, 2007. 49–53.

Klandermans, Bert, Merel Werner, and Majorka van Doorn. "Redeeming Apartheid's Legacy: Collective Guilt, Political Ideology, and Compensation." *Political Psychology* 29, no. 3 (2008): 331–49.

Lee, Harper. *To Kill a Mockingbird*. New York: Penguin, 1960.

Lemann, Nicholas. *The Promised Land: The Great Black Migration and How It Changed America*. New York: Vintage, 1992.

Manning, Carol. "Belle." In *The Companion to Southern Literature: Themes,*

Genres, Places, People, Movements, and Motifs, ed. Joseph Flora and Lucinda MacKethan. Baton Rouge: Louisiana State University Press, 2002.

McElya, Micki. *Clinging to Mammy: The Faithful Slave in Twentieth-Century America*. Cambridge: Harvard University Press, 2007.

McMillen, Sally G. *Southern Women: Black and White in the Old South*. Wheeling, Ill.: Harlan Davidson, 1992.

Moody, Anne. *Coming of Age in Mississippi*. New York: Doubleday, 1968.

Morrison, Toni. *The Bluest Eye*. New York: Random House, 1970.

Nicholson, Jessie R. "Giving a Hand Up: Providing Leadership for Today's Generation." Speech quoted in *Women and the Criminal Justice System*, by Katherine van Wormer and Clemens Bartollas, 344. Boston: Pearson, 2010.

Petry, Ann. *The Street*. Boston: Houghton Mifflin, 1946.

Powdermaker, Hortense. *After Freedom: A Cultural Study in the Deep South*. New York: Viking, 1939.

Raines, Howell. "Grady's Gift." *New York Times*, December 1, 1991. www.nytimes.com.

Randall, William L., and Gary Kenyon. "Time, Story, and Wisdom: Emerging Themes in Narrative Gerontology." *Canadian Journal on Aging* 23, no. 4 (2004): 333–46.

Ritterhouse, Jennifer. *Growing up Jim Crow: How Black and White Southern Children Learned Race*. Chapel Hill: University of North Carolina Press, 2006.

Rogers, Kim L. *Life and Death in the Delta: African American Narratives of Violence, Resilience, and Social Change*. New York: Palgrave/Macmillan, 2006.

Rollins, Judith. *Between Women: Domestics and Their Employers*. Philadelphia: Temple University Press, 1985.

Romero, Mary. *Maid in the USA*. New York: Routledge, 1992.

Sensibar, Judith L. *Faulkner and Love: The Women Who Shaped His Art*. New Haven: Yale University Press, 2009.

Smångs, Mattias. "Whiteness from Violence: Lynching and White Identity in the U.S. South, 1882–1915." Ph.D. diss., Columbia University, 2010.

Smith, Lillian. *Killers of the Dream*. New York: Norton, 1949.

Snedeker, Rebecca. *By Invitation Only*. 2006. New Day Films. www.newday.com.

SouthAfrica.info. You and Your Domestic/Madam. 2011. www.southafrica.info/services/rights/domesticrights.htm.

Southern, Eileen. *The Music of Black Americans: A History.* 3rd ed. New York: Norton, 1997.

"St. Augustine's Civil Rights Movement." ACCORD Freedom Trail. 2010. www.accordfreedomtrail.org/movement.html.

Stepp, Laura S. "Modern Flirting: Girls Find Old Ways Did Have Their Charms." *Washington Post,* October 16, 2003, C1.

Stockett, Kathryn. *The Help.* New York: Putnam, 2009.

Stovel, Katherine. "Local Sequential Patterns: The Structure of Lynching in the Deep South, 1882–1930." *Social Forces* 79, no. 3 (2001): 843–80.

Tavris, Carol, and Elliot Aronson. *Mistakes Were Made (But Not by Me).* Orlando, FL.: Harvest, 2007.

Taulbert, Clifton. *Once upon a Time When We Were Colored.* New York: Penguin, 1995.

Thernstrom, Abigail, and Stephan Thernstrom. "Black Progress: How Far We've Come, and How Far We Have to Go." Brookings Institute. 1998. www.brookings.edu/articles/1998/spring_affirmativeaction_thernstrom.aspx.

Tucker, Susan. *Telling Memories among Southern Women: Domestic Workers and Their Employers in the Segregated South.* Baton Rouge: Louisiana State University Press, 1988.

Tully, Michele A. "Lifting Our Voices: African American Culture Responses to Trauma and Loss." In *Honoring Differences: Cultural Issues in the Treatment of Trauma and Loss,* ed. Kathleen Nader, Nancy Dubrow, and B. Hudnall Stamm, 23–48. New York: Routledge, 1999.

Twain, Mark. *Life on the Mississippi.* 1883. New York: Oxford University Press, 1996.

Tye, Larry. *Rising from the Rails: Pullman Porters and the Making of the Black Middle Class.* New York: Holt, 2004.

van Wormer, Katherine, and Fred H. Besthorn. *Human Behavior and the Social Environment, Macro Level.* 2nd ed. New York: Oxford University Press, 2011.

Walker, Alice. *The Color Purple.* New York: Doubleday, 1968.

Whitfield, Stephen J. *A Death in the Delta: The Story of Emmett Till.* New York: Free Press, 1988.

Wilkerson, Isabel. *The Warmth of Other Suns: The Epic Story of America's Great Migration.* New York: Random House, 2011.

Winfrey, Oprah. Commencement Convocation, May 15, 2007. Washington, DC: Howard University.

Wing, Adrien K., and Sylke Merchan. "Rape, Ethnicity, and Culture: Spirit Injury from Bosnia to Black America." *Columbia Human Rights Law Review* 25, no. 1 (1993): 1–46.

Wise, Tim. *Color-Blind: The Rise of Post-Racial Politics and the Retreat from Racial Equity*. San Francisco: City Lights, 2010.

Woodruff, Nan E. *American Congo: The African American Freedom Struggle in the Delta*. Cambridge: Harvard University Press, 2003.

Woodward, C. Vann. *The Strange Career of Jim Crow*. 2nd ed. New York: Oxford University Press, 1966.

———. History from Slave Sources. In *The Slave's Narrative*, ed. Charles T. Davis and Henry Louis Gates Jr., 48–59. New York: Oxford University Press, 1985.

Yetman, Norman. "An Introduction to the WPA Slave Narratives." In *Born in Slavery: Slave Narratives from the Federal Writers' Project, 1936–1939*. Washington, DC: Library of Congress, 2001. http://memory.loc.gov/ammem/snhtml/snintro00.html.

Zinn, Howard. *A People's History of the United States:1492–Present*. New York: HarperCollins, 2003.

Zinn, Howard, and Anthony Arnove. *Voices of a People's History of the United States*. New York: Seven Stories Press, 2009.

Index